Jesus, Paul, and the Gospels

Jesus, Paul, and the Gospels

James D. G. Dunn

WILLIAM B. EERDMANS PUBLISHING COMPANY
GRAND RAPIDS, MICHIGAN

Wm. B. Eerdmans Publishing Co.
2140 Oak Industrial Drive N.E., Grand Rapids, Michigan 49505
www.eerdmans.com

Library of Congress Cataloging-in-Publication Data

Dunn, James D. G., 1939-
Jesus, Paul, and the Gospels / James D.G. Dunn.
p.   cm.
Includes bibliographical references (p.   ) and index.
ISBN 978-0-8028-6645-5 (pbk.: alk. paper)
1. Bible. N.T. Gospels — Criticism, interpretation, etc.
2. Paul, the Apostle, Saint.   I. Title.

BS2555.52.D86   2011
226'.06 — dc22

2011004302

In memoriam

*for a dear friend, colleague
and fellow-scholar par excellence*

Graham Stanton

Contents

CONTENTS

Preface

In the course of just over three weeks in April and May 2009, I was privileged to give several lectures and series of lectures. This was partly the result of the decision of Pope Benedict XVI to celebrate the year 2008-9 as the bimillennial year of Paul. In my view, the celebration came a few years too late, since I think it more likely that Paul was born close to what we now regard as the turn from BCE to CE (or from BC to AD). Nonetheless, the interest in Paul which this bimillennial year of Paul aroused among Catholics has been entirely welcome, and I found myself recipient of a number of invitations to lecture on Paul to Catholic (and other) gatherings. The invitations were too inviting for me to turn them all down, and I was more than happy to accept several, though the quickening of the work pace was somewhat more than I had bargained for. But how could I refuse? It was such a thrill for a mere Protestant to know that his Catholic brothers and sisters wanted to rediscover Paul — or as a senior Catholic friend corrected me: 'Not *re*discover, but *discover* Paul'!

The first was a series of lectures to an International Seminar on Saint Paul organised by the Societa Sao Paolo at its centre at Ariccia on Lake Alban. The Society kindly invited my wife and me to spend a few days in Rome before and after my one day at the Seminar, an invitation not hard to accept. We are most grateful to Brother Walter Rodriguez for organising our whole visit, including special arrangements for various excursions in Rome. The invitation to the Seminar was for me to speak on the main themes of Paul's theology. But since I had already written at length on Paul's theology, in the event it seemed more appropriate for me to focus on why Paul remains such a crucial figure for Christianity, who he was, what he stood for, the gospel which he lived and died for, and the church(es) he established and sought to instruct and guide through his letters. These form chapters 6–9 of this book.

Another invitation was to an international symposium on 'Jesus and Paul' to be held at the Theological Faculty of Catalonia (Barcelona). This involved only one lecture, but gave me the opportunity to respond positively to my old friend Armand Puig and to revisit Barcelona, though sadly, this time on my own (the call of grandparental responsibility keeping my wife in the UK). This lecture forms chapter 5.

I had flown to Barcelona from Israel where I took part in yet another conference on Paul ('Paul in His Milieu: Land, Religion and Culture') at the Tantur Ecumenical Institute for Theological Studies. My lecture there ('In Search for the Historical Paul') overlapped too much with the above lectures for me to include it in what follows. But I wish here to express my gratitude to Fr. Michael McGarry and his staff for organising the conference and its very interesting programme.

Prior to the Tantur conference I had delivered the Deichmann lectures at the Ben Gurion University in Beer Sheva, at the invitation of Dr. Roland Deines on behalf of the Deichmann Program for Early Jewish and Christian Literature of the Hellenistic-Roman Era. These were not on Paul, but at Dr. Deines's request, on the Gospels. The concern was that Hebrew-speaking students interested in the New Testament writings and the beginnings of Christianity have too few textbooks in Hebrew with which to work. So lectures on basic and fundamental themes for understanding the New Testament and earliest Christianity are an essential part of the programme. There naturally was interest in the historical value of the Christian Gospels, and it seemed important to me to fill up the gap between Jesus and the Gospels, as well as to explain how the Gospels formed a new literary genre, and how the Fourth Gospel fitted with the others. For the invitation and visit I will always be grateful to Dr. Deichmann, Dr. Deines, and the other members of the Ben Gurion team, Prof. Zipi Talshir and Dr. Cana Werman; also for their memorable hospitality and to Dr. Deines for fulfilling so well the additional role of an accomplished tour guide.

As the three weeks rolled on I became aware that nine of the ten lectures would form a rather coherent and potentially interesting (even valuable) little book. In each case I had had to write out the lectures in full beforehand, since translated texts or simultaneous translation was desirable. So not much more was required to put the nine lectures into publishable form. It made most sense to put them in the sequence used for this publication. On reflection, it seemed best to begin with the four Beer-Sheva lectures on the Gospels (chs.

1–4), not least since it was probably Paul who gave the term 'gospel' its decisive Christian stamp. And the Barcelona lecture (ch. 5) neatly provides a bridge from Jesus to Paul. The Ariccia lectures on Paul could then provide the follow-through to Paul (chs. 6–9) and leave the reader with the challenge which the bimillennial Paul still makes to contemporary Christianity, as he did to Christianity's first generation.

In further discussion I have made some emendations to the lectures as originally delivered. This is principally because five of the nine lectures were delivered to almost exclusively Christian audiences, whereas the other four were delivered in a predominantly Jewish setting. To put them all together for publication in both settings called for only a slight moderation of the conclusions to the lectures on Paul — it being all the easier to do so, since the Jewishness of Paul was one of the main themes of the Paul lectures. There was also some small overlap between two or three of the lectures, but on balance it seemed best to let the lectures stand as delivered rather than abbreviating the lecture into what would then appear as a somewhat curtailed chapter.

As I prepared the lectures for publication, the other problem confronting me was the extent of the footnotes and cross-references to other bibliography. I had not set out to provide a review of literature on each of the subjects addressed. That would have required additional sections for individual lectures and perhaps a completely new chapter. In fact, I have added some bibliographical references where I could do so without getting into lengthy discussion with other views. But to do more, it seemed to me, would change the character of the lectures and the book itself. I comfort myself with the thought that I have interacted very fully with other literature in the volumes which precede this small offering — *The Theology of Paul the Apostle* (Eerdmans, 1998), *Christianity in the Making*, vol. 1, *Jesus Remembered* (Eerdmans, 2003), and vol. 2, *Beginning from Jerusalem* (Eerdmans, 2009) — and invite those who want further bibliography to follow up particular points or issues in these volumes.

Since I will be unknown to many of my readers, at Dr. Deines's suggestion I have added a brief 'Personal Introduction' after the preface.

My hope and prayer is that these lectures will help give a fuller appreciation of Jesus, Paul and the Gospels, of their relation to one another and of their continuing importance for Christian self-understanding and for the growth of mutual understanding and respect between Jew and Christian.

JAMES D. G. DUNN
August 2009

Personal Introduction

My interest in the New Testament and the beginnings of Christianity goes back to my teenage years when I followed a 'quiet time' spiritual discipline of reading my Bible and praying at the beginning of every day. Already then the fascination of Jesus' life and teaching, his death and (as Christians believe) his resurrection, gripped my attention and my curiosity. The story of Christianity's beginnings (the Acts of the Apostles) was intriguing and inspiring, and the theological acumen of Paul stimulated and tested my growing awareness of issues and problems. No less of interest were the historical writings of the Old Testament.

My fascination with the biblical writings grew during my university years, first in Glasgow and then in Cambridge. My first degree was an MA in Economics and Statistics (at that time Theology/Divinity could be taken only as a second degree), which 'plugged me in' to the world of finance and markets — an interest I have never lost. But it was the biblical subjects of my second degree, a BD, which really captured my interest, and I seemed to do well in them (my school education in Latin and Greek helped). These were quite conservative years (conservative theologically) as I began to grapple with theological giants like John Calvin, and to confront the challenges of historical study of the biblical writings.

The possibility of research at Cambridge, under the great New Testament scholar C. F. D. Moule, opened up a whole new window for me and my new wife (Meta). There for the first time I seriously grappled with the character of the New Testament writings and learned to follow where the evidence led me. I took seriously the task of historical criticism — not in the negative sense it often carries for some people (historical scepticism), but in the positive sense of seeking to know better what actually happened, what the various New Testament texts must have been heard to say by those who first read or heard them, what the first Christians actually believed. That was a liberating experience — a liberation from having to ensure that my findings on any question were properly in accord with the traditions I had inherited — a liberation to follow the truth in its own terms, to let the New Testament texts shape my views rather than the reverse.

I had always been interested in spiritual renewal or revival, and early in 1964 news of strange goings-on among Episcopalians in California made me wonder if 'the new Pentecostalism' in traditional churches (baptism in the Spirit, speaking in tongues) might be a new wave of revival. This suggested my thesis topic for Cambridge — how the Pentecostal claims for 'baptism in the Spirit' fitted with New Testament teaching — and this gave me three to four years of fascinating research. My first book, *Baptism in the Holy Spirit* (SCM, 1970), was my revised PhD thesis.

After three years, assisting in a Glasgow parish and then as chaplain to overseas students in Edinburgh, I was appointed to a lectureship in Nottingham, where I stayed for twelve years (1970-82). My head of department, A. R. C. Leaney, kindly gave me my head and encouraged me to devise a new syllabus for the New Testament side of the degree. So I began a two-year course 'Beginnings of Christianity', which, under different names, became a core of my principal teaching programme for the next thirty years and now provides the framework for my main current writing project — the trilogy *Christianity in the Making*.

The first years of a new lectureship are of necessity given principally to the preparation of new lectures and seminar materials. But with my first study leave I was able to pick up where I had left off, with an examination of spiritual and charismatic experience in the New Testament, entitled *Jesus and the Spirit* (SCM, 1975). The exercise reinforced my conviction both that recognition of a vital religious experience was an important way in to understanding how Christianity flourished and that one's own religious experience was a vital part of critical interaction with these ancient scriptures.

This was followed by the first spin-off from my larger 'Beginnings of Christianity' project. I had been intrigued by Walter Bauer's *Orthodoxy and Heresy in Earliest Christianity* (SCM, 1971), with its argument that the earliest forms of Christianity in several major Mediterranean centres may have been much more mixed, more factionally diverse than later perspective dictated, that 'orthodoxy' may have been the faction which won and 'heresy' the faction which lost. I determined to pursue the question back from the second century, on which Bauer had focused, to the first century. How diverse or how unified was first-century Christianity, was, indeed, the New Testament? The result was what I presented as a more demanding introduction to the New Testament for those who had already gone well beyond the *who, where* and *why* questions of most introductions — *Unity and Diversity in the New Testament* (SCM, 1977, ²1990, ³2006). The result was quite challenging for many: that the New Testament canonized diversity as much as unity; that the unifying factor was Jesus Christ, and that whenever one moved to a more elaborate 'unity', the 'diversity' immediately became evident and quickly built up as authors, circumstances and genres changed.

A sharp debate in the late 1970s on the Christian concept of the incarnation (of Jesus) gave me my next topic — *Christology in the Making* (SCM, 1980, ²1989), an inquiry into the origins of the doctrine of the incarnation. Here it became clear to me that responsible exegesis has to retain awareness of two important factors. One is that conceptuality (particularly of how God interacts with his creation and his people) has never been static, but is dynamic, with the earlier language posing questions which the earlier users had not considered and with the same language developing new meaning to successive readers. The other is that in consequence the exegete has to allow the writer to stay within the horizons of his time; his texts may come to mean more, but that 'more' should not be attributed to the original author. The tension between exegesis and hermeneutics at this point can become quite uncomfortable.

Early in the 1980s (I moved from Nottingham to Durham in 1982) two strands assumed dominant roles in my continuing research. One was the relations between earliest Christianity on the one hand and late Second Temple Judaism and earliest rabbinic Judaism on the other — within a context of Jewish/Christian dialogue. My early work on 'Beginnings of Christianity' had made clear to me that this was unavoidable; the issue, posed by F. C. Baur a century and a half earlier, remained — how was it that Christianity emerged from the matrix of Second Temple Judaism? And the rather delayed reaction of New Testament scholarship to the implications of the Holocaust made the issue all the more pertinent. Apart from various articles, my major contribution on the subject has been *The Partings* (note the plural) *of the Ways between Christianity and Judaism* (SCM, 1991, ²2006). Unfortunately some critics paid too little attention to the rest of the title: *and Their Significance for the Character of Christianity*. I leave the significance of the *Partings* for Judaism to others better qualified than I am, though interaction with Jewish scholars interested in the emergence of Christianity from Second Temple Judaism, particularly with Daniel Boyarin, should be stimulating for both sides; most notably and most recently his *Border Lines: The Partition of Judaeo-Christianity* (Philadelphia, 2004).

The other strand was my ever deepening fascination with Paul. This reached a climax in my two-volume commentary *Romans* (Word, 1988) — a task I at times wondered if I would ever complete. But it has continued in commentaries particularly on Galatians (Black, 1993) and on Colossians (Eerdmans, 1996), and reached a fresh climax in my *Theology of Paul the Apostle* (Eerdmans, 1998; Clark, 1998). In the last-named I have tried to provide as complete a sketch as possible of Paul's theology when he wrote his letter to Rome, as indicated mostly, of course, by the way he set out in that letter his understanding of the gospel which he had been commissioned to preach.

However, the main thrust of my work on the Paul strand has become known as 'the new perspective on Paul', a surprisingly controversial topic for many well schooled in the theological inheritance of the Protestant Reformation in Europe. For me it started with a lecture with that title which I gave in Manchester just after my move to Durham. The stimulus for it was E. P. Sanders's demonstration that Second Temple Judaism was not at all as legalistic as Christian scholarship had depicted it to be and that Judaism's 'pattern of religion' is better characterized as 'covenantal nomism' (*Paul and Palestinian Judaism* [SCM, 1977]). This undermined Lutheranism's oversharp antithesis between law and gospel and the assumption that when Paul set faith and 'works of the law' in antithesis, he meant good works by which one earned acceptance by God. The problem for me, however, was that Sanders failed to show how Paul dealt with that 'covenantal nomism' and what he meant by 'works of the law'. I tried to complete Sanders's new perspective on Judaism by showing that Paul was in fact addressing the kind of Judaism that Sanders had depicted. The clues for me were Paul's own repeated insistence that he was apostle to non-Jews/Gentiles, and the clear evidence that his teaching on 'justification by faith' came to clearest expression when he was defending his conviction that the gospel about Messiah Jesus was also for non-Jews, to be received by faith. The obvious inference, as I saw it, was that this insistence on justification by faith was over against the alternative that participation in the inheritance of Abraham required non-Jews to join Israel, to become proselytes. Here the Pauline antithesis between 'faith' and 'works of the law' amounts in the first place to Paul's refusal to require Gentile believers to take on the yoke of the Torah, all that the Torah laid down. As Paul's first statement on the issue makes clear, to require 'works of the law' of non-Jews (in addition to faith) was, in Paul's view, to 'compel them to Judaize' (Gal. 2.14-16).

As mentioned, this attempt to show that for Paul the horizontal dimension of breaking down the barrier between Jew and Gentile (Eph. 2.14-16) was as integral to his gospel as the vertical dimension of peace being made between God and individuals, has not gone down well in some Reformed circles. I have tried to address these and other concerns in *The New Perspective of Paul* (Mohr Siebeck, 2005; Eerdmans, [2]2008). But it is equally important to reflect further on Paul's relation to the Judaism of his day, and whether Paul's attempt to build community by playing down ethnic identity markers like circumcision, Sabbath, and laws of clean and unclean could ever hope to succeed among his fellow Jews. The two strands of my continuing research are intertwined. The challenge which Paul poses to his fellow Jews in particular remains: How else is the blessing of Abraham to come to all nations if not by those desirous of that blessing having to become proselytes? And his challenge to Christians in particular remains: What is Christianity if it is not defined and characterized by the blessing of Abraham?

In the most recent phase of my research I have returned to my 'Beginnings of Christianity', or now more precisely my *Christianity in the Making* project. The first volume was published in the year of my (early) retirement from Durham University — *Jesus Remembered* (Eerdmans, 2003). In the course of preparing for it I became more and more intrigued by the recognition that the early Jesus tradition must have circulated in oral forms for twenty to forty years. In contrast, most inquiries into the tradition-history of the material making up the Christian Gospels have focused almost exclusively on their literary interdependence, feeding the inference that the development from Jesus to the written Gospels not only could but should be understood in literary terms of copying and redacting written sources. Now it is true that the first three (Synoptic) Gospels show a significant proportion of their shared material to be in closely parallel or near identical terms. And the logical conclusion is that such a degree of similarity is best explained by literary interdependence. But more than half of the material shared by the Synoptic Gospels is quite different, and *not* well explained in terms of literary interdependence. I try to show in *Jesus Remembered* and the briefer *New Perspective on Jesus* (Baker, 2005) that an *oral* traditioning process makes better sense of that latter material. The consequences include that the differences between the Gospels should not be regarded as 'mistakes' or 'contradictions', but simply as the diverse forms which the oral forms of the same tradition take. Also that the living character of the Jesus tradition should warn us against becoming too bound and limited by particular formulations.

Volume 2, *Beginning from Jerusalem* (Eerdmans, 2009), takes the story from 30 CE to the failure of the first Jewish revolt against Rome and the destruction of the Jerusalem Temple in 70. It starts by describing the beginnings of the sect of the Nazarenes in Jerusalem, the expansion of the Hellenists, the

conversion of Paul and the mission of Peter. As both Acts and Paul's letters indicate, a major focus has to be on Paul. This enables me to complete my study
of Paul, by focusing now on his self-understanding, the strategy and
practicalities of his mission, his church-founding and pastoral dealings with
his churches, and his attempt to heal the breach with Jerusalem by making a
collection among his churches for the poor among the saints in Jerusalem. It
ends by recounting the deaths of the three leading figures of first-generation
Christianity — Peter, James and Paul — and by evaluating the importance of
the roles they played as indicated by the letters of 1 Peter, James and Ephesians. If Paul dominates the New Testament epistolary heritage, we should not
neglect or underestimate the significance of the roles played by Peter and
James.

Next step is volume 3, taking the story, *deo volente,* forward by another
one hundred years. In the meantime I have completed the little volume *New
Testament Theology: An Introduction* (Abingdon, 2009) as part of a Library of
Biblical Theology, which, *inter alia,* argues that one cannot do NT theology
except as biblical theology! As such, NT theology should also be regarded as
part of the ongoing dialogue between Judaism and Christianity. And then
there's the volume which follows. So, read on!

JAMES DUNN
August 2009

List of Abbreviations

AB	Anchor Bible
ABD	*Anchor Bible Dictionary* (ed. D. N. Freedman; 6 vols.; New York: Doubleday, 1992)
ANRW	*Aufstieg und Niedergang der römischen Welt* (ed. H. Temporini and W. Haase; Berlin: De Gruyter, 1972-)
b.	Babylonian Talmud
BAGD	W. Bauer, W. F. Arndt, F. W. Gingrich, and F. W. Danker, *A Greek-English Lexicon of the New Testament and Other Early Christian Literature* (Chicago: University of Chicago Press, 1979)
BDAG	F. W. Danker, W. Bauer, W. F. Arndt, and F. W. Gingrich, *Greek-English Lexicon of the New Testament and Other Early Christian Literature* (3rd ed.; Chicago: University of Chicago Press, 2000)
BibInt	*Biblical Interpretation*
BNTC	Black's New Testament Commentaries
BR	*Biblical Research*
BU	Biblische Untersuchungen
BZNW	Beihefte zur Zeitschrift für die neutestamentliche Wissenschaft
CBQ	*Catholic Biblical Quarterly*
ch(s).	chapter(s)
DPL	*Dictionary of Paul and His Letters* (ed. G. F. Hawthorne and R. P. Martin [Downers Grove, IL: InterVarsity, 1993])
EDNT	*Exegetical Dictionary of the New Testament* (ed. H. Balz and G. Schneider; ET Grand Rapids: Eerdmans, 1990-93)
EKK	Evangelisch-katholischer Kommentar zum Neuen Testament

ExpTim	*Expository Times*
GLAJJ	*Greek and Latin Authors on Jews and Judaism* (ed. M. Stern; 3 vols.; Jerusalem: Israel Academy of Sciences and Humanities, 1976-84)
Hatch & Redpath	E. Hatch and H. A. Redpath, *A Concordance to the Septuagint* (2 vols.; Oxford: Clarendon, 1897)
HTR	*Harvard Theological Review*
ICC	International Critical Commentary
JBL	*Journal of Biblical Literature*
JJS	*Journal of Jewish Studies*
JSJ	*Journal for the Study of Judaism*
JSNTS	Journal for the Study of the New Testament: Supplement Series
JSS	*Journal of Semitic Studies*
JTS	*Journal of Theological Studies*
KD	*Kerygma und Dogma*
LSJ	H. G. Liddell and R. Scott, revised by H. S. Jones, *A Greek-English Lexicon* (9th ed.; Oxford: Clarendon, 1940); with supplement (1968)
LXX	Septuagint
m.	Mishnah
NDIEC	*New Documents Illustrating Early Christianity* (9 vols.; Sydney: Macquarie University; Grand Rapids: Eerdmans, 1981-2002)
NIDB	*The New Interpreter's Dictionary of the Bible* (ed. K. D. Sakenfeld; 4 vols.; Nashville: Abingdon, 2006-9)
NIGTC	New International Greek Testament Commentary
NovTSup	Supplements to Novum Testamentum
NT	New Testament
NTS	*New Testament Studies*
OBO	Orbis biblicus et orientalis
OCD	*The Oxford Classical Dictionary* (ed. Simon Hornblower and Antony Spawforth; 3rd ed.; Oxford: Oxford University Press, 1996)
par(s).	parallel(s)
PGM	*Papyri graecae magicae: Die griechischen Zauberpapyri* (ed. K. Preisendanz; Berlin: Teubner, 1928)
SBLSymS	Society of Biblical Literature Symposium Series
SBS	Stuttgarter Bibelstudien
SNTSMS	Society for New Testament Studies Monograph Series
t.	Tosefta

TDNT	*Theological Dictionary of the New Testament* (ed. G. Kittel and G. Friedrich; Grand Rapids: Eerdmans, 1964-76)
TDOT	*Theological Dictionary of the Old Testament* (ed. G. J. Botterweck and H. Ringgren; Grand Rapids: Eerdmans, 1974-)
VTSup	Supplements to Vetus Testamentum
WBC	Word Biblical Commentary
WMANT	Wissenschaftliche Monographien zum Alten und Neuen Testament
WUNT	Wissenschaftliche Untersuchungen zum Neuen Testament
ZNW	*Zeitschrift für die neutestamentliche Wissenschaft und die Kunde der älteren Kirche*

PART ONE

WHAT ARE THE GOSPELS?

CHAPTER 1

Fact or Fiction? How Reliable Are the Gospels?

What do we know about Jesus of Nazareth? What are the sources of our knowledge of Jesus? Apart from the Christian Gospels, there are very few. Two early-second-century Roman historians refer to Jesus. Tacitus refers to those blamed for the great fire of Rome during Emperor Nero's reign as 'Christians', and adds the explanation: 'Their name comes from Christ, who, during the reign of Tiberius, had been executed by the procurator Pontius Pilate' (*Annals* 15.44). And writing about the same time, Suetonius makes a confused reference to Jesus when talking about the expulsion of the Jews from Rome in 49 CE: 'Since the Jews were constantly causing disturbances at the instigation of Chrestus, he [Claudius] expelled them from Rome' (*Claudius* 25.4). 'Chrestus' and 'Christus' are very similar sounding, and it is usually inferred that Suetonius was referring to 'Christus', the Christian reference to Jesus as Messiah, *Christus*. But that tells us next to nothing about Jesus as such.

The Jewish historian Josephus, writing in the 90s, probably refers to Jesus twice in his *Antiquities*. The main passage looks as though it was edited and enlarged in Christian versions of Josephus. But the probably original, briefer reference speaks of Jesus as 'a wise man . . . a doer of startling deeds, a teacher of the people', who gained a substantial following, before he was condemned to the cross by Pilate (18.63-64). And the second, less questioned reference is to the summary execution of James, described as 'the brother of Jesus who is called Messiah' (20.200), in 62 CE. The first reference tells us a little more about Jesus, but still very little indeed.

There are also possible references to Jesus in rabbinic tradition. The

3

most plausible reference is in *b. Sanhedrin* 43a, to Yeshu who was hanged on the eve of Passover and is described as a magician who beguiled Israel and led it astray. But again, that does not take us very far.

So, all the information we have about Jesus, apart from Christian writings, is that he was known and remembered as a teacher, 'a doer of startling deeds' or who exercised magical powers, who gathered a significant following, and who was executed by crucifixion at the order of the Roman governor of Judea. We could draw other inferences from these details: asking in particular why the Roman authorities crucified this Jesus, and why the rabbis regarded him as a magician. But still the information we have about Jesus from non-Christian sources remains minimal and hardly sufficient to give us an adequate picture of this Jesus.

In consequence, we are forced to depend on the Christian writings, and particularly the Christian Gospels, to fill out our picture of Jesus. But this immediately poses another problem for us. For if we have to rely so fully on the Christian Gospels, we can hardly proceed without noting that they are *Christian* Gospels. That is, it cannot be assumed that they are unbiased or objective in their portrayal of Jesus. The problem should not be exaggerated, of course. Few if any historical sources regarding figures or significant events of the past are unbiased or completely objective. Historians have long learned the danger of thinking of the past in straightforwardly 'objective' terms. So they are well aware that account has to be taken of such bias in their own handling of historical sources — including their own bias! This is simply integral to the skill and art of all history writing. The fact that our dependence on the Christian Gospels is almost entire makes the problem particularly acute in the case of writing the history of Jesus. But the problem as such is familiar to all historians.

Our first main issue, then, is to assess the reliability of the Christian Gospels to provide trustworthy information about Jesus.

Four Presuppositions

I start with four presuppositions — presuppositions which have proved to be much more controversial than most would have anticipated, but which I maintain have an *a priori* givenness.

The first is that there *was* a historical person called Jesus who functioned in the land of Israel, probably in the late 20s or early 30s of the common era. This starting point has to be made explicit, since about once in every generation someone reruns the thesis that Jesus never existed and that the

4

Christian traditions about him are a wholesale invention.[1] The basic argument reflects the broader claim often made that Paul was the real founder of Christianity, rather than Jesus. And the relation between Jesus and Paul is a major issue for Christian scholarship, which we have no time to address here. But in the 'Christ myth' or 'Jesus myth' thesis, the tension or gap between Jesus and Paul is pushed to the extreme. It is argued that Paul in effect invented Christianity; that the belief in Jesus' resurrection simply grew out of the widespread belief in the Mediterranean world in a dying and rising god — Attis, or Osiris. According to this thesis, for some reason, never adequately explained, this belief in a dying and rising god became attached to an otherwise unknown, and apparently not very significant, Jewish figure by the name of 'Jesus'. Each time the thesis is revived, however, its ignorance or ignoring of the most relevant evidence, its tendentious reading of other evidence and its overall implausibility are self-evident to the great majority of open-minded inquirers. And it can be safely concluded that the thesis soon falls apart under the weight of its own improbabilities, and is dismissed or simply ignored by the great body of serious students of the subject.

So, the first presupposition, that there was a man called Jesus to whom the Christian tradition and beliefs refer, is sound — though, of course, the question remains, how justified, in historical terms, are the traditions and beliefs about this Jesus?

The second presupposition I make is that this Jesus was a *Jew*, a Jew from the Galilee, who functioned mainly in the Galilee. This would seem to be as uncontroversial as the first presupposition. But here we immediately encounter the shameful Christian tradition of anti-Judaism. From the second century onwards, it is simply a historical fact, a rather stark historical fact, that Christianity tended to define itself over against Judaism, in distinction from Judaism. To understand itself, Christianity distanced itself from Judaism — even though two-thirds or three-quarters of the Christian Bible consists of the scriptures of Israel, the Tanak. In terms of Christian understanding of Jesus through the centuries, the result was a persistent and indeed a growing attempt to deny Jesus' Jewishness. In the second half of the nineteenth century some of the most prominent and popular treatments of Jesus could even affirm that 'fundamentally there was nothing Jewish about Jesus'; that after visiting Jerusalem, 'Jesus was no longer a Jew' (Ernest

---

1. The most persistent recent proponent of this thesis is G. A. Wells, *The Jesus of the Early Christians: A Study of Christian Origins* (London: Pemberton Books, 1971); also *The Historical Evidence for Jesus* (Buffalo: Prometheus Books, 1988).

Rénan);[2] that Jesus renounced Judaism and its law, creating 'a sharp dividing line between his teachings and those of the Jews' (Albrecht Ritschl).[3] In the Nazi period it was even argued that 'Galilee was Gentile' and that 'Jesus was no Jew' (Walter Grundmann).[4] The claim, of course, was partly based on Isaiah's reference to Galilee as 'Galilee of the nations' (Isa. 8.23/9.1). But the determining factor was the desire to distance Jesus as far as possible from the Jewish people. And one of the most distressing features of the so-called Jesus Seminar in California in the 1990s was the revival of the attempt to characterise first-century Galilee as pervaded by a Hellenistic ethos and largely pagan in character (Burton Mack, Robert Funk).[5] The instinct was still there: to give Jesus a universal significance, he had to be as much disentangled from his Jewish context as possible.

Thank God, this anti-Jewish Jesus has largely faded from the scene. The predominant feature of current attempts to get through to the historical Jesus is the recognition that Jesus was a Jew.[6] Consequently, the attempt to characterise Jesus solely by reference to his disputes with Pharisees, to find the most important features of his mission in points of distinctiveness from Second Temple Judaism, is now widely recognised to be wrongheaded. Jesus can be understood properly only as a Jew, within his context of Second Temple Judaism, not despite that context, or in disregard for that context. The reaction against the thesis of an anti-Jewish Jesus has been hugely reinforced by the recent archaeological findings in the Galilee. That the leading cities in Galilee in the Herodian period, Sepphoris and Tiberias, were not in fact Hellenistic cities, like Scythopolis (Bet Shean) and Caesarea, but minor provincial capitals with only a thin veneer of Hellenism. In late Second Temple Galilee generally, there are no indications of large numbers of non-Jews and plenty of evidence of stone vessels, *miqwaoth,* absence of pork remains, and *kochim* shafted tombs with ossuaries.[7] Second Temple Galilee was as Jewish/Judean as Judea itself. There are no grounds for affirming that a Galilean Jew like Je-

---

2. S. Heschel, *Abraham Geiger and the Jewish Jesus* (Chicago: University of Chicago Press, 1998) 156-57. On the anti-Jewishness of nineteenth-century NT scholarship, see particularly 66-75, 106-7, 117-18, 123, 153-57, 190-93, 212-13, 227.

3. Heschel, *Abraham Geiger* 156-57.

4. W. Grundmann, *Jesus der Galiläer und das Judentum* (Leipzig: George Wigand, 1941) 166-75.

5. B. L. Mack, *A Myth of Innocence: Mark and Christian Origins* (Philadelphia: Fortress, 1988) ch. 2; R. W. Funk, *Honest to Jesus* (San Francisco: HarperSanFrancisco, 1996).

6. See my *Christianity in the Making*, vol. 1, *Jesus Remembered* (Grand Rapids: Eerdmans, 2003), particularly 85-92, with further bibliography.

7. See particularly J. L. Reed, *Archaeology and the Galilean Jesus* (Harrisburg, PA: Trinity, 2000) 23-61.

sus was himself not Jewish. On the contrary, Jesus the Jew is as firm a starting point for any inquiry into the historical actuality of Jesus as can be desired. So, this is my second presupposition.

My third presupposition is that this Jesus was a figure of some influence, even if only among those who followed him. He made an *impact,* and, evidently, a lasting impact.

Like the second presupposition, this third presupposition is also, surprisingly, controversial. As most scholars attempting to write lives of Jesus were embarrassed by Jesus' Jewishness, so, even more, were they embarrassed by Christian faith. Understandably, they realised that the Jesus of Christian dogma, the God-man, the second person of the Trinity, must have been very different from the Galilean Jesus. The Christ of dogma obscured the historical reality of the first-century Jesus. The Christ of faith prevented us from seeing the Jesus of history. In consequence, however, they regarded all faith focused on Jesus as a negative factor which should be ignored or, better, stripped away to allow a clearer historical appreciation of Jesus. And since all the Christian writings from the first century, *not* excluding the Gospels, were written to express faith in Jesus, they could not be regarded as trustworthy witnesses to the historical Jesus. As soon as there is any sign in a Gospel of belief that Jesus had been resurrected from the dead and had been exalted to God's right hand, that Gospel's testimony could and should be discounted by historians of Jesus in Galilee.

However, such understandable attempts to uncover the historical Jesus below the layers of Christian faith should not ignore the *a priori* fact that *Jesus must have made an impact on those who followed him.*[8] To assume that there was a man called Jesus who lived a wholly insignificant life, but who, for some untold reason, became the central figure in traditions such as we find in the Christian Gospels, seems a ludicrous starting point for any inquiry into the historical reality of this Jesus. The very fact that such stories were being told about this Jesus, that such teaching as we find in the Gospels was being attributed to this Jesus, is most obviously to be explained by the fact that this Jesus was reckoned and remembered as a figure of some significance. Whether he said all that is attributed to him is a second, and important, question. But that what he did say resonated with his immediate followers and is the basis of what they subsequently claimed for his teaching is an obvious deduction hard to

8. This is one of the prime theses in my *Jesus Remembered.* I elaborate the point in *A New Perspective on Jesus: What the Quest for the Historical Jesus Missed* (Grand Rapids: Baker Academic, 2005) ch. 1.

deny. Again, whether he did all the actions that are attributed to him is a second and important question. But that what he did do evidently caught his disciples' attention, lived in their memory and is the basis for what they subsequently claimed for his mission is once again an obvious deduction hard to dispute. After all, it is the same Jesus who was, as is generally recognised, crucified by the Roman authorities. That the impact he made on his Jewish contemporaries is closely related to the impact which he made on Pilate and which presumably was the ground for his execution is another obvious deduction.

The problem this causes for a scholarship which wants to strip away all Christian faith from any evaluation of the historical significance of Jesus is obvious. The impact which Jesus had on his first disciples must be in some degree of continuity with the faith which they expressed in Jesus as risen from the dead and exalted to heaven. Whether we call the impression made by Jesus on his first disciples 'faith' or not, it can hardly be denied that the impact he made had the quality of faith. According to the Gospels, these first disciples dedicated themselves to following Jesus. They left their homes and their means of livelihood for his sake. They trusted this Jesus with their lives. He was the focus of their hopes. This can quite appropriately be described as 'faith'. And given that there is a high degree of continuity between Jesus' own leading followers and the leadership of the first churches — Peter and John in particular — there is bound also to be a similarly high degree of continuity between the early trust of Jesus' first disciples and the faith they went on to express regarding this Jesus. Indeed, they would presumably regard their subsequent faith in Jesus as a vindication of their initial trust in him, their subsequent faith in Jesus as in at least some degree rooted in and springing from the encounter with Jesus in Galilee which so transformed their lives.

So, I remain confident in my third presupposition: that Jesus made a significant impact during his mission and particularly on his own disciples. Just as we should not sideline all aspects of Jesus' Jewishness from any attempt to see Jesus in his historical actuality, so we should not sideline all indications that he made a lasting impression by what he said and did.

My fourth presupposition is that the Galilee of Jesus was an *oral* society. Once again this is a somewhat controversial claim. The Torah and the Prophets and some at least of the Writings had long been in written form, and were very familiar to Jews in the land of Israel and in the diaspora. First-century Israel could be described as a Torah-shaped society, and thus as a literary society. All that is entirely true. Yet it does not detract very much from the description of Second Temple Judaism as essentially an oral society. The most recent studies of literacy in the land of Israel during the Roman period are agreed that Jewish literacy in the first century was probably less than 10 percent (M. Bar-Ilan and C. Hezser).[9] And given that the small minority of literate Jews in Israel would have been almost exclusively royal officials, priests, Pharisees and scribes, the probability is that the great majority of Galileans, including the great majority of those who followed Jesus, were technically illiterate. The widespread knowledge of the Torah would have been gained by people *hearing* the Torah read to them, rather than by themselves reading it. For the great majority, the ability to read may not have extended beyond the recognition of the sense of inscriptions or of simple contracts, and the ability to write probably did not extend beyond a basic signature literacy.

To take seriously the reality of a historical society which functioned as an oral society is harder to do than most realise.[10] For five centuries we have been accustomed to the benefits of printing. Our minds are print-dominated. We have a literary mind-set. We think in terms of information typically conveyed in writing and by reading. We think more naturally of the reader reading as an individual than of the audience learning only by what it hears. We are comfortable with the knowledge that we have reference books and encyclopedias which we can consult for all sorts of vital information. To envisage a society without the facilities of the written word, without books to hand, is hard for us. Our memories are so generally unreliable, that we can scarcely appreciate a society where only the memory could be relied on to retain important information. And yet, that is what we must do when we try to access the information which gives us the clearest picture of what Jesus actually did and said. This means that we must reckon it overwhelmingly probable that the bulk of those impacted by Jesus were functionally illiterate. We must reckon equally with the probability that the earliest traditions about Jesus were transmitted by word of mouth; or, as I would say, that the impact made by Jesus on his first disciples was initially talked about by them, that is, in oral form.[11]

This is an aspect of our subject to which I must return in the second chapter. For the moment I simply draw attention to it as one of the presuppositions which I make when I approach the Gospel traditions about Jesus and attempt to use them to get closer to the historical figure of Jesus.

9. M. Bar-Ilan, 'Illiteracy in the Land of Israel in the First Centuries CE', in S. Fishbane and S. Schoenfeld, *Essays in the Social Scientific Study of Judaism and Jewish Society* (Hoboken, NJ: Ktav, 1992) 46-61; C. Hezser, *Jewish Literacy in Roman Palestine* (Tübingen: Mohr Siebeck, 2001).

10. See also my 'Altering the Default Setting: Re-envisaging the Early Transmission of the Jesus Tradition', *NTS* 49 (2003) 139-75; reprinted as an appendix in *A New Perspective on Jesus*.

11. This is another of the major theses of my *Jesus Remembered*; also *A New Perspective* ch. 2.

With these four presuppositions in mind, let me now take a first look at the Jesus traditions in the Gospels. For the time being I will focus only on the first three Gospels. The Fourth Gospel, the Gospel of John, is a special case which I will leave till the fourth chapter. The first three Gospels have a very striking feature: they have *a very high degree of material which is common to them*. Indeed, they are regularly referred to as the Synoptic Gospels. This is because they can be set out in parallel and looked at together, synoptically, that is, from the Greek, 'seen together'. We will go further into this in the second chapter. The point I want to make now is the degree of closeness between these first three Gospels. There are differences between these Gospels — which again we will return to later. But they are all clearly speaking about *the same person*. They are telling the same stories about him. They attribute the same teaching to him. This means that we can gain a clear picture of Jesus from them. As the doyen of British New Testament scholarship, C. H. Dodd, put it in his last significant book: 'The first three gospels offer a body of sayings on the whole so consistent, so coherent, and withal so distinctive in manner, style and content, that no reasonable critic should doubt, whatever reservations he may have about individual sayings, that we find here reflected the thought of a single, unique teacher'.[12] Permit me, then, in the second half of this chapter to fill out what Dodd's claim amounts to.

What Do We Know about Jesus?

In the past generation or two, scholars seeking historical information about Jesus from the New Testament Gospels tended to use a rather odd and questionable methodological principle. They looked for the *distinctive* features of Jesus' teaching. This makes apparent good sense — to ask what marked Jesus' teaching out from the views and teachings of the time. Unfortunately, the methodological principle was based on the same two flawed perspectives to which I have already referred. They wanted to find a Jesus who was distinct from subsequent Christian beliefs in Christ, different from the Christ believed in by the later Christians. This approach was flawed, precisely because it was unwilling to recognise that Jesus' own teaching may well have influenced and shaped, indeed probably did at least to some extent influence and shape, the memories and views of Jesus which his disciples held and proclaimed. The other flawed perspective was the desire to find a Jesus whose teaching was different from the teaching prevalent within Second Temple Ju-

12. C. H. Dodd, *The Founder of Christianity* (London: Collins, 1971) 21-22.

daism. This was another aspect of the unwillingness, conscious or unconscious, of so many Christian scholars to recognise Jesus' Jewishness. They assumed, wrongly, that for Jesus to have become regarded as someone who appealed within the wider Hellenistic world of the early centuries, he must already have transcended first-century Judaism. They were strangely unwilling to recognise that at many points it was the religion of Jesus' ancestors and his interpretation of the religion of his fathers which became integral and central to subsequent Christianity.

Consequently, I turn away from looking for the *distinctive* Jesus. Instead I look for the *characteristic* Jesus.[13] My logic is straightforward. If a feature within the Jesus tradition is characteristic within the Jesus tradition, then the most obvious explanation of its presence in the Jesus tradition is that it reflects the abiding impression which Jesus made on many of his first followers. Such a consistent feature across the diversity of the Jesus tradition, and across the different sources for that tradition, could technically be explained by the dominant influence of a single teacher within first-generation Christianity. But our other sources for the first generation indicate a degree of early diversity within this messianic sect. So it is doubtful whether any single teacher could have achieved such widespread influence and have remained unknown to Christian tradition. If there is such a dominant personality behind the Jesus tradition, determining its content and character, the only obvious conclusion is that the dominant personality was that of Jesus himself. This was precisely the sort of impact we should envisage Jesus as making, an impact like that of Israel's prophets of old, which left its clear mark on the tradition of his mission, of his teaching and activity. It was just such an impact, we may assume, which first drew his disciples into and constituted their community with other disciples. It was just such an impact, we may assume, which was celebrated (together with the beliefs in Jesus' death and resurrection) in the gatherings of the first churches through the first generation of Christianity. Some of these characteristic features will be relatively distinctive in comparison with other Jewish traditions of the time. But it is their *characteristic* features which attract our attention rather than their distinctive features. To say again, any feature which is *characteristic within the Jesus tradition even if only relatively distinctive of the Jesus tradition* is most likely to have been derived from Jesus, that is, to reflect the original impact made by Jesus' teaching and actions on several at least of his first disciples.

---

13. Again, the proposal that we should look for the characteristic rather than the distinctive Jesus is developed in *A New Perspective* ch. 3.

What, then, do we find when we look for the characteristic Jesus?

We can start with the beginning and end of his mission. All the Christian sources are agreed that Jesus is first remembered as having been baptised by John the Baptist — a baptising mission attested also by Josephus (*Antiquities* 18.116-119). It would not be an unfair evaluation of the evidence available to say that Jesus began as a disciple of John the Baptist. The testimony is all the more secure, since we can detect a clear sense of embarrassment in the Gospel accounts of this beginning. The first three Gospels begin their account of Jesus' mission *after* the Baptist had been imprisoned; they draw a veil over the period of overlap between John and Jesus which the Fourth Gospel briefly describes. Moreover, the fact that Jesus had undergone a 'baptism of repentance' (Mark 1.4) is a matter of some embarrassment in Matthew's account of the encounter between Jesus and John (Matt. 3.14-15). And the Fourth Gospel avoids mentioning the fact that Jesus was actually baptised by John. So, we can conclude that the memory of Jesus' emergence from the ranks of the Baptist's followers was too firmly rooted in history for it to be ignored or omitted. The Gospels also indicate that Jesus probably experienced something equivalent to a prophetic calling when he was baptised by John. So the Gospel writers could hardly fail to recount the beginning of Jesus' mission from his baptism by John.

Likewise, we can be sure of how Jesus' mission *ended*. It ended on a Roman cross. This is hardly to be doubted, since one can hardly envisage a sect which invented such an outcome for their leader. The earliest confessions of the first generation of Christians take the crucifixion of Jesus as a given. It is affirmed also by Josephus and Tacitus. And the *titulus* nailed to the cross on Pilate's order used a title for Jesus which the Christians subsequently never used by themselves — 'The King of the Jews' (Mark 15.26 pars.). It presumably provides the official reason why Pilate had Jesus condemned: whatever the justice or injustice of the execution, Pilate's excuse was that this man was a royal pretender — a more than sufficient reason for him to be crucified. It is regrettably true that the Christian accounts of the whole procedure tend to let Pilate off lightly from the responsibility for Jesus' death. And the degree of the high-priestly involvement in denouncing Jesus to Pilate is unclear. They almost certainly had some part in it, but the Christian sources tend to pile most of the responsibility on them. However, whether and how any blame for Jesus' crucifixion can and should be allocated, the central fact remains, that, in the words of the early Christian confession, Jesus was 'crucified under Pontius Pilate'.

Between this beginning and this ending to Jesus' mission we can begin to fill out quite a full picture.

First, consider again the *Jewishness* of Jesus. There is a consistent interest within the Jesus tradition for typically Jewish concerns — what obedience to the Torah involves, how to observe the Sabbath, what counts as clean and unclean, attendance at synagogue, the purity of the Temple.[14] It can scarcely be doubted that Jesus shared such concerns. What his attitude was on particular issues is open to debate, and evidently was a matter of some debate among those responsible for rehearsing and passing on the Jesus tradition;[15] but that he himself was engaged with such issues during his mission is clear beyond reasonable doubt. In the same connection, Jesus is consistently shown as engaged in dialogue and dispute with Pharisees. Here we can see how the tradition has been elaborated, with Matthew in particular extending the motif of debate with Pharisees quite substantially.[16] But that is obviously the way to express the point: Matthew *extended* a motif *already thoroughly integrated* within the Jesus tradition; Jesus was well remembered for his disagreements with various Pharisees. Despite the anti-Jewishness of previous phases of the quest, the Jewishness of Jesus' concerns is not in question.

Or again, it can hardly be doubted that Jesus spent much if not most of his mission in *Galilee.* The Synoptic tradition is so consistent on the point, and the Galilean provenance of the Synoptic accounts so clear, that it would be ludicrous to argue otherwise. It is not simply the fact that Jesus' mission is clearly remembered as being carried out predominantly round the Sea of Galilee (Kinnereth) and in its nearby villages. But Jesus' parables in particular are shot through with agricultural references and echoes of what we know to have been the social situation in the Galilee — wealthy estate owners, resentment over absentee landlords, exploitative stewards of estates, family feuds over inheritance, debt, day labourers, and so on.[17] To be sure, the Fourth Gospel's account indicates a much more Jerusalem-centred mission, though even so, three of the first four of the Fourth Gospel's 'signs' (miracles performed by Jesus) are located in Galilee. The resulting tensions between the Synoptics and the Fourth Gospel are unlikely ever to be satisfactorily resolved, but that does not

---

14. E.g. Matt. 5.17-48; Mark 2.23–3.5; 7.1-23; Luke 4.16; 19.45-48.

15. We need only compare the different ways in which Mark and Matthew portray Jesus' attitude to the law, as exemplified by the contrast between Mark 7.15, 19 and Matt. 15.11; see further my *Jesus Remembered* 563-83; and below, ch. 3.

16. Details in my 'The Question of Antisemitism in the New Testament Writings', in J. D. G. Dunn, ed., *Jews and Christians: The Parting of the Ways, AD 70 to 135* (Tübingen: Mohr Siebeck, 1992) 177-211 (here 205).

17. See e.g. S. Freyne, 'Jesus and the Urban Culture of Galilee', in *Galilee and Gospel* (WUNT 125; Tübingen: Mohr Siebeck, 2000) 183-207 (here 195-96, 205-6); and further Freyne, *Galilee, Jesus, and the Gospels* (Dublin: Gill and Macmillan, 1988).

change the overall impression that Jesus was a Galilean Jew whose mission was largely shaped by and focused on the circumstances of his Galilean homeland.

For the content and character of Jesus' mission we can be similarly confident on a number of features.

For one thing he was known as a *teacher* in the tradition of the sages of Israel. Most of the tradition of Jesus' teaching falls under this heading. The collections of material in what is usually referred to as 'the Sermon on the Mount' in Matthew's Gospel (Matt. 5–7), with its parallel in Luke's Gospel, usually known as 'the Sermon on the Plain' (Luke 6.17-49), contain the best examples of this wisdom teaching. We will see some examples in the second chapter. This fits with Josephus's reference to him as a 'teacher'. And later in the New Testament, the letter of James has a particular interest for us at this point. For this letter is attributed to James, the brother of Jesus, who became leader of the Christian community in Jerusalem till his execution in the buildup to the revolt against Rome in 62. And it is itself a wisdom document, in fact, the most characteristic wisdom writing in the New Testament. What is interesting for us is that the letter draws regularly on the Jewish wisdom tradition of Proverbs, ben Sira and Wisdom of Solomon, occasionally in direct quotation. But it equally draws on the Jesus tradition, as known to us in the Gospels of Matthew and Luke. What is interesting is that Jesus was evidently being remembered in the letter of James as part of Israel's wisdom teaching.[18] The fact that the letter of James was retained within the New Testament, despite its lack of distinctively Christian teaching, is salutary for us. It underlines the extent to which Jesus was remembered within early Christianity as a teacher of wisdom in the tradition of Solomon and Jesus ben Sira. And it reinforces the historical fact that Jesus operated for much or most of his teaching mission as a sage, a teacher of Jewish wisdom.

Much of this wisdom teaching was in aphorisms or epigrams. But it is even more striking that much of his wisdom was delivered in the form of stories, or parables, stories well reflecting the historical situation in the Galilee, and memorable for the surprising twist in many of the tales. The characteristic Jesus was a parabolist, a *moshel,* one who typically spoke in parables and pithy sayings *(meshalim).*[19] In this he should not necessarily be thought of as distinctive within Second Temple Judaism. The tradition of storytelling is

18. See particularly R. Bauckham, *James: Wisdom of James, Disciple of Jesus the Sage* (London: Routledge, 1999), which I largely follow in my *Christianity in the Making,* vol. 2, *Beginning from Jerusalem* (Grand Rapids: Eerdmans, 2009) #37.2c.

19. B. Gerhardsson, *The Origins of the Gospel Tradition* (Philadelphia: Fortress, 1979) 70.

long rooted within historic Judaism. But parables seem to have been particularly characteristic of Jesus' teaching. And once again, we can be confident that we are in firm contact with historical fact.

We also know what appears to have been the major theme of Jesus' teaching. He proclaimed 'the kingdom of God' or 'royal rule of God'. Here again no one who takes the Synoptic tradition seriously could even begin to doubt that the kingdom of God was at the centre and one of the most characteristic themes of Jesus' preaching. This too is one of the more distinctive features of Jesus' preaching in comparison both with the Judaism of his own time and with the Christianity which followed.[20] The thought of God as king was, of course, central in Israel's piety. But the theme of the kingdom of God is not very prominent, except in the postbiblical Jewish writings,[21] particularly the *Songs of the Sabbath Sacrifice* at Qumran.[22] And it is equally infrequent in the rest of the New Testament. Quite why Jesus' preaching on this theme stands out so distinctively is unclear. But the overwhelming testimony of the first three Gospels on the point cannot be gainsaid. Proclamation of God's royal rule was one of the most characteristic features of Jesus' mission. Consequently it hardly matters that we cannot be sure whether, for example, Mark's headline statement of Jesus' mission — 'The time is fulfilled, and the kingdom of God is at hand; repent and believe in the gospel' (Mark 1.15) — records accurately what Jesus actually said on entering Galilee or is Mark's own summary of Jesus' preaching. The point is that the motif is so well rooted in the Jesus tradition that a Markan summary is almost equally as effective in communicating the overall impression made by Jesus' kingdom preaching.

20. For details see *Jesus Remembered* 383-87.

21. 'The kingdom of God' (Wis. 10.10; *Pss. Sol.* 17.3). 'The kingdom *(malkut)* of Yahweh' (1 Chr. 28.5; 2 Chr. 13.8); 'my kingdom' (1 Chr. 17.14); 'his kingdom' (Ps. 103.19; Dan. 4.34; 6.26; Tob. 13.1; Wis. 6.4); 'your kingdom' (Ps. 145.11-13; *Pss. Sol.* 5.18). 'Kingship *(mamlaka, meluka)*' belongs to God (1 Chr. 29.11; Ps. 22.28; Obad. 21). Aramaic, *malkuta'* (Dan. 3.33; 4.34). Latin, *regnum* (*T. Mos.* 10.1). The fullest recent review is by O. Camponovo, *Königtum, Königsherrschaft und Reich Gottes in den frühjüdischen Schriften* (OBO 58; Freiburg: Universitätsverlag, 1984), concluding that the kingship of God is not a major theme in early Jewish literature, and that it functions 'as a symbol, not as a precisely defined concept' (437-38).

22. C. Newsom, *Songs of the Sabbath Sacrifice: A Critical Edition* (Atlanta: Scholars, 1985), lists over fifty references to God as 'king' *(mlk)* and twenty-five to God's 'kingdom' *(mlkuth),* typically 'his glorious kingdom' or 'the glory of his kingdom' (424-26). The Qumran songs can be properly described as 'the most important preChristian Jewish text on the theme of "God's kingship"' (A. M. Schwemer, 'Gott als König und seine Königsherrschaft in den Sabbatliedern aus Qurman', in M. Hengel and A. M. Schwemer, eds., *Königsherrschaft Gottes und himmlischer Kult im Judentum, Urchristentum und in der hellenistischen Welt* [WUNT 55; Tübingen: Mohr Siebeck, 1991] 45-118 [here 115]).

At this point we stumble once again into a peculiarly Christian controversy on Jesus' proclamation of God's kingdom. For in the Jesus tradition in the first three Gospels there are *two* somewhat different strands in the Synoptic kingdom motif: the kingdom as future though imminent, and the kingdom as already present and active through Jesus' ministry. Jesus, for example, in the spirit of an early form of the Kaddish prayer, encourages his disciples to pray, 'May your kingdom come' (Matt. 6.10/Luke 11.2). But he is also remembered as saying, 'If it is by the Spirit/finger of God that I cast out demons, then has the kingdom of God come upon you' (Matt. 12.28/Luke 11.20). A strong tradition in Christian scholarship has found it difficult to recognise that Jesus could have maintained both emphases, could have spoken of God's kingdom as both future and present.[23] In New Testament scholarship there has been a huge and long-lasting debate as to which of these two strands is the more 'original', although it has been a good deal quietened by the realisation that some of the Dead Sea Scrolls reflect a similar tension between an eschatological hope already fulfilled and a hope still maintained for imminent consummation. The debate within New Testament scholarship demonstrates more clearly than most others the futility of making conclusions regarding 'the historical Jesus' depend on individual verses and the conclusions that can be inferred from them. The fact is that *both* strands are well rooted in and run through the Synoptic tradition.[24] Both are characteristic of the Synoptic Jesus. How dare we exegetes and expositors insist on squeezing such diverse traditions into a *single* mould and on squeezing *out* what does not fit our own ideas of consistency and good sense. It is much more responsible for historians and exegetes to recognise that this double characteristic of the Jesus tradition is best explained as a double characteristic of Jesus' own teaching and mission. The overall two-sided impact of Jesus remains clear, even if it remains unclear how the two sides were held together by Jesus and his first disciples.

Beside or within these broad features of Jesus' mission and teaching we can even pick out a number of more specific details. One is that Jesus used the phrase 'the son of man', *bar ˤnasha (ben adam)*, and that he used it probably in self-reference. Here again the picture is clear, though, once again, New Testament scholarship has entangled itself in knots on the subject throughout the twentieth century.[25] The basic facts are these. The tradition of Jesus using the phrase 'son of man' is thoroughly rooted in the Gospel tradition. This is all the more conspicuous in view of the relative disuse of the phrase in the Judaism of

23. See e.g. below, ch. 5 n. 42.
24. Full documentation can be found in my *Jesus Remembered* ch. 12.
25. I deal with the issues in considerable detail in *Jesus Remembered* ##16.3–16.5.

Jesus' day (so far as we can tell), and in view of its almost total absence from early Christian tradition elsewhere. On any sensible reckoning, therefore, it can have *originated only within the Jesus tradition.* What is also striking is that the phrase appears so consistently on Jesus' own lips. It is not an identifying label used by others: Is Jesus the Son of Man? It is not a confession used by his disciples: Jesus *is* the Son of Man. All that the tradition requires us to say — but it does require us to say it — is that Jesus himself used the phrase. Here again, this compelling deduction does not require us to argue that every son of man/ Son of Man saying derived directly from Jesus. But the fact that any working over of the tradition worked within the tradition of a phrase used only by Jesus assuredly confirms that *the original form of the tradition derived directly from and directly reflects Jesus' own characteristic usage.*

It is also possible on the basis of the data to argue that the titular usage, 'the Son of Man', is in some/many cases at least a firming up of the Aramaic idiom, 'the son of man', that is, 'someone', 'a man like me'. What is *not* credible as an explanation for the data is that the complete motif was initially inserted into the Jesus tradition at a post-Easter or later stage. That some scholars should continue to argue to that effect, despite the overwhelming testimony of the data, is in my view an example of methodological perversity. To be sure, there is scope for debating how a philological idiom ('son of man' = 'man', 'one') could cohere with reference to the vision of Dan. 7 ('one like a son of man' coming on clouds to the Ancient of Days). The point here, however, is that both usages, both the philological usage and the Daniel allusion, are well rooted in and quite well spread across the Jesus tradition. A search for the characteristic rather than the idiosyncratic Jesus suggests that we should try to make sense of *both* emphases within the son of man/Son of Man material before assigning one or the other to the subsequent editing of Christian faith.

Still more striking for its characteristic distinctiveness is Jesus' use of the term 'Amen'. The term is familiar in both Hebrew and Aramaic *(amen)* as marking a strong, solemn affirmation of what has been said, most typically in a formal liturgical context. And the Jesus tradition gives clear testimony that Jesus used the term consistently in his own teaching.[26] But he did so in a quite distinctive way. For whereas in regular usage 'Amen' affirmed or endorsed the words of someone else, in the Jesus tradition the term is used without exception to introduce and endorse Jesus' *own* words, 'Amen, I say to you'.[27] This

---

26. Details in *Jesus Remembered* 700-701.

27. J. Jeremias, *The Prayers of Jesus* (ET London: SCM, 1967) 112-15: 'It has been pointed out almost *ad nauseam* that a new use of the word *amen* emerged in the four gospels *which is without analogy in the whole of Jewish literature and in the rest of the New Testament*' (112).

quite unique usage can hardly be attributed to the early Christians; their own use of 'Amen' was in accord with the traditional pattern.[28] Of course, once again, we can hardly exclude the likelihood that in performing the tradition the tradents/teachers extended the motif within the tradition. But neither can it be seriously doubted that the usage began with Jesus and was a characteristically distinctive feature of his own teaching style. Why else would the term have been retained throughout the Jesus tradition and in transliterated form? That must be one of the most secure conclusions capable of being derived from a serious engagement with the tradition-history of Jesus' teaching. And an obvious corollary lies close to hand: that Jesus used this formula to call attention to what he was about to say and to give it added weight.

So we can say quite a lot about Jesus' teaching and preaching, and more could probably be said if time permitted. But what can we say about Jesus' *activities* during his mission? What other characteristics are recalled through the Jesus tradition?

One is that he gathered *a group of disciples* round him. This is the group on which he made his greatest impact. This is the group, we can be quietly confident, who carried their memories of Jesus into the congregations of believers in Jesus as Messiah which sprang up soon after his death. This is the group, in other words, who began the Jesus tradition, that is, the process of recalling Jesus' mission and teaching in words they remembered and framed, taught and passed on, which became in due course the Christian Gospels. The most significant feature of this group was that it was *twelve* in number.[29] No one doubts the obvious significance of this number: that it reflects the historic character of the twelve tribes of Israel. But this must mean that Jesus intended the group around him to somehow represent Israel, the twelve tribes of Israel. This in turn strongly suggests what many recent studies of the life and mission of Jesus have argued: that Jesus saw his mission in terms of *the restoration of Israel*.[30] The twelve symbolised eschatological Israel, the renewed Israel of the end-time.

A second characteristic of Jesus' mission is that he was known as a

28. Of some thirty other examples in the NT, 1 Cor. 14.16 is the most interesting; otherwise it is characteristically attached to the end of a doxology.

29. A few scholars argue that 'the Twelve' only emerged as a group in the earliest days of Christianity. But most recognise the great unlikelihood that such a group would have included Judas, the disciple who is remembered as betraying Jesus. That it was Jesus who chose Judas as one of the Twelve, rather than some unknown storyteller in the early Christian churches, seems pretty obvious. See further *Jesus Remembered* 507-11.

30. See ch. 5 n. 2 below.

highly successful *exorcist.* His success as an exorcist and his reputation as an exorcist are both clearly attested in the Jesus tradition. Healing stories are frequently told about Jesus in the Synoptic Gospels, with exorcisms the largest single category. And his name was evidently prized as one that other would-be exorcists could call upon (Luke 10.17; Acts 16.18), no doubt precisely because he himself had been so successful in casting out demons. There are several stories within the New Testament of individuals trying to call on Jesus' name for their own attempts to heal or exorcise (Mark 9.38; Acts 19.13), and his lasting fame as an exorcist is probably indicated by the use of his name in some incantations preserved among the magical papyri[31] and in several references in the *Testament of Solomon.*[32] Here again we should recall Josephus's reference to Jesus as 'a doer of extraordinary deeds'. And the accusation of sorcery in rabbinic tradition is paralleled by the great opponent of Christianity in the second century who likewise attributed to Jesus 'certain magical powers'.[33] Moreover, more than one collection of Jesus' teaching on the subject has been preserved within the Synoptic tradition.[34] Whatever might be made of particular instances of exorcism in Jesus' mission, it can hardly be denied that he acted as an exorcist and healed people who were possessed. It would be odd indeed if a scholar accepted that Jesus acted as an exorcist but refused to accept that any of the actual accounts of Jesus' exorcism were based on sound memories of events in Jesus' mission.

The only other feature of Jesus' mission to which I wish to draw attention as firmly rooted in history is his *notoriety.* One of the main criticisms evidently made against him by some Pharisees of his time was that 'he ate with toll collectors and sinners' (particularly Mark 2.16 pars.), that he was 'a friend of toll collectors and sinners' (Matt. 11.19/Luke 7.34). What is particularly interesting about this criticism is that it reflects a feature of Second Temple Judaism which we know of from the literature of the period. As part of a dispute between groups, of factionalist disagreement, it became common to dismiss the others as 'sinners' *(r^{e}sha'im).* Already in Dan. 12.10 'the sinners' who fail to understand Daniel's revelation are contrasted with 'the wise' *(maskilim)* who do understand. In 1 Maccabees, 'the sinners and lawless men' certainly include other Jews/Judeans whom the Maccabees regarded as apostates (1 Macc. 1.34; 2.44, 48). Similarly the 'sinners' in various early Enochic writings are opponents of the self-styled 'righteous, who sin like the sinners' in

---

31. *PGM* 4.1233, 3020; 12.190, 390.
32. *T. Sol.* 6.8; 11.6; 17.4; 22.20.
33. Origen, *Contra Celsum* 1.28, 68.
34. Particularly Mark 3.22-29 and Matt. 12.24-32, 43-45/Luke 11.15-26.

following the wrong calendar (*1 En.* 82.4-7). In the same way, in the Dead Sea Scrolls *rsh'm* refers to the sect's opponents.[35] And the *Psalms of Solomon* are largely dominated by the 'righteous' denouncing the 'sinners', who appear to be the Hasmonean Sadducees who controlled the Temple cult.[36] Here is a case where Jesus belongs precisely within the disputes and arguments which characterised so much of Second Temple Judaism. His mission apparently reacted against the habit of 'bad-mouthing' opponents by referring to them as 'sinners'. He evidently saw his calling as taking his message of God's kingdom not least to those dismissed, effectively, as apostates, outlaws from the Torah-centred community.[37] Here we see both Jesus the Jew and Jesus taking a distinctive stand within the Judaism of his time, a stand his subsequent followers were to echo when they took what they regarded as their good news to 'Gentile sinners'.

To sum up, it is not difficult to build up a picture of the characteristic Jesus:

- a Jesus who began his mission from his encounter with John the Baptist
- a Jew who operated within Galilee, within the framework of the Judaism of the period and in debate with others influential in shaping the Judaism of the period
- a Jesus who characteristically proclaimed the royal rule of God both as coming to full effect soon and as already active through his ministry
- a Jesus who regularly used the phrase 'the son of man', probably as a way of speaking of his own mission and of his expectations regarding its outcome
- a Jesus who was a successful exorcist and knew it
- a Jesus whose characteristic mode of teaching was in aphorisms and parables
- a Jesus whose 'Amen' idiom expressed a high evaluation of the importance of what he said
- a Jesus who reacted strongly against the tendency to dismiss fellow Jews too lightly as 'sinners'

I could amass further characteristics of the characteristic Jesus, but hopefully these are enough to indicate how substantial a portrayal can readily

---

35. E.g. 1QS 5.7-13; 1QH 15.12; CD 4.6-8; 4Q174 2.3-4a cites Dan. 12.10, the sect presumably identifying themselves with the *maskilim* of Daniel.

36. E.g. *Pss. Sol.* 1.8; 2.3; 7.2; 8.12-13; 17.5-8, 23.

37. I deal with the point more fully below — #5.1.1b.

be achieved by simply directing our quest to the characteristic Jesus, to the Jewish Jesus. I repeat, such a reconstruction does not guarantee the historical accuracy of recall of any particular saying or episode. But the method must certainly provide a much sounder basis for a historical reconstruction than one which depends on the evaluation of particular sayings and episodes. I conclude that the Jesus traditions within the first three Christian Gospels give us a good deal of historical information about Jesus, historical information on which we can rely to give us a reliable portrait of Jesus. They seem to reflect the impact of a very strong and rather distinctive character. From the impression that they bear we can detect, and detect with remarkable clarity, the one who made that impression; from the stamp on the paper we can discern the stamp which made it. While the Gospels of course reflect in one degree or another the estimate of Jesus which became characteristically Christian over the next four or five decades, the Jesus they remembered by means of the Jesus tradition of the first three Gospels was much more fact than fiction.

CHAPTER 2

Between Jesus and the Gospels

As already indicated, Second Temple Judaism was predominantly an oral so-ciety. That is to say, the great majority of the people were technically illiterate. Reading and writing were predominantly the preserve of the nobility, of priests and scribes. This is why, for example, 'scribes' are such a prominent group within the Gospel narratives: the great majority of people depended on someone who was technically literate to write contracts and letters on their behalf. The society was, of course, also a Torah-centred society. People gener-ally knew the Torah and lived their lives in accord with its precepts. But their knowledge of the Torah did not come from personal copies which each had, as would be the case today. Nor did their knowledge come from their own personal reading of the Torah. For the great majority, Torah knowledge came from hearing it read to them by the minority who could read, Sabbath by Sab-bath in the synagogue.

All this would be true also of the group round Jesus, his disciples. It is certainly quite likely that a disciple such as Matthew, the toll collector, could read and write. But the only other profession or trade that we hear of in con-nection with the other close disciples of Jesus was fishing. And if Jesus' disci-ples were typical of the peasants, tradesmen and fishermen of Galilee, we can safely assume that the great majority of the disciples were functionally illiter-ate. We cannot exclude the possibility that Jesus himself was illiterate, or only semiliterate, though the very little evidence we have on the subject probably points to a more positive answer. On the other hand, no one has ever argued seriously that Jesus himself wrote anything or that Christian traditions about Jesus stem from his own pen.

The main points which immediately follow are twofold. First, Jesus' teaching was given *orally;* it began orally. And second, we can safely assume that the news about Jesus was initially passed around *orally.* The stories about Jesus would no doubt have been the subject of many a conversation in bazaars and around campfires. The disciples of Jesus no doubt spoke about what they had seen Jesus do, and about his teaching. This would have been the beginning of the Jesus tradition. It would be celebrated and meditated on in groups of his followers in oral terms. It would be passed on to the curious, to inquirers and to new disciples, in oral terms. We can certainly assume that the period between Jesus and the Gospels was filled with such tradition. The alternative is too improbable even to contemplate: that those who followed Jesus during his mission kept all that they had seen and heard to themselves. Or that it was only when the Gospel writers began to look for stories about the past that all this material was dug out, from the fading memories of older first disciples. The probability is much the other way: that much at least, if not the bulk, of the Jesus tradition, of the stories about Jesus and the main themes of his preaching and teaching, was being spoken about and celebrated, was the subject of much instruction, discussion and occasion for worship through the early years of the messianic sect of the Nazarene. This is not to deny that some of the Jesus tradition would have been put into writing quite early. But the probability is that in an oral society, the bulk of the Jesus tradition would have been oral tradition. If the period between Jesus and the Gospels is filled with material which was subsequently to go into the Gospels, that material would have been predominantly in oral form.

How does this insight help us to understand the period between Jesus and the Gospels? How does it help us to understand the character of the Gospels? Here we need to look more closely at the Gospels themselves — and particularly at the first three Gospels within the New Testament — Matthew, Mark and Luke. These, we recall, are regularly referred to as the Synoptic Gospels — from the Greek, *synopsis,* indicating that they can be read together. This is because the Gospels have a considerable amount of material in parallel. When these three Gospels are set down side by side, they are telling the same stories and recording the same teaching. The table on page 24 illustrates with a sequence of passages in the three Synoptic Gospels, where the parallels are clear.

So it is evident why the first three New Testament Gospels are called the Synoptic Gospels — because they run in parallel for so much of their content. And yet — and this is the fascinating bit — they regularly have the same subjects, but treat them differently. This feature poses a question which has troubled or held the attention of Gospel specialists for centuries. Why are the Syn-

EPISODE	Matthew	Mark	Luke
Jesus rejected at Nazareth	13.54-58	6.1-6a	
The sending of the Twelve		6.6b-13	9.1-6
Herod thinks Jesus is John raised	14.1-2	6.14-16	9.7-9
The death of John the Baptist	14.3-12	6.17-29	
The return of the Twelve and the feeding of the 5,000	14.13-21	6.30-44	9.10-17
The walking on the water	14.22-33	6.45-52	
Healings at Gennesaret	14.34-36	6.53-56	
What defiles a person	15.1-20	7.1-23	
The Syrophoenician woman	15.21-28	7.24-30	
Healing many sick people	15.29-31	7.31-37	
The feeding of the 4,000	15.32-39	8.1-10	
Pharisees seek a sign	16.1-4	8.11-13	
The yeast of Pharisees and Herod	16.5-12	8.14-21	
The blind man of Bethsaida		8.22-26	
The confession at Caesarea Philippi and first passion prediction	16.13-23	8.27-33	9.18-22
The conditions of discipleship	16.24-28	8.34–9.1	9.23-27
The transfiguration	17.1-8	9.2-8	9.28-36
The coming of Elijah	17.9-13	9.9-13	
The healing of the epileptic boy	17.14-21	9.14-29	9.37-43a
The second passion prediction	17.22-23	9.30-32	9.43b-45
The Temple tax	17.24-27		
The dispute about greatness	18.1-5	9.33-37	9.46-48

optic Gospels as they are? Why are they so *similar* and yet so *different*? Why are the *same* events narrated so *diversely*? Why are Jesus' teachings so differently formulated and grouped, often or usually the same message but presented with *different words* and in *different contexts*? The Synoptic Gospels are obviously interrelated; there is a manifest interdependence between the traditions which they variously reproduce. How best to explain this, and the differences between them?

The dominant answer to this question regarding the relationship of the Synoptic Gospels has been determined by the fact that there are many passages which are more or less word for word the same in two or all three of the Synoptics. These passages most obviously demonstrate a close *literary* interdependence — one Evangelist copying a written source available to him. The large consensus among New Testament scholars is, first, that of the three Gospels,

Mark is the earliest, and was used by both Matthew and Luke. And secondly that Matthew and Luke were also able to draw on a second source, mainly of Jesus' teaching, conveniently known as Q (from the German, *Quelle* = source).

However, there are an *equal* number of passages where the subject is more or less the same yet the wording or structure is noticeably *different*. This feature has not been given so much attention. The tendency has been to work from the identical and near-identical passages to deduce an *overall* literary interdependence, and then to adjust the thesis of literary interdependence to accommodate the other evidence, or to leave aside the very differing passages as problems to be solved some time in the future. In no case have the divergent passages been allowed to put a question mark against the primary thesis of literary interdependence. That thesis is too well rooted in the phenomenon of identical or near-identical passages for it to be called in question by the differing passages.

This way of treating the Synoptic problem, however, became increasingly unsatisfactory for me. Should not our understanding of the relationship between the Synoptic Gospels be determined by the *divergences* as well as the *similarities* between them? Are not the *differences* between the Synoptic Gospels as important as the *similarities*? Why should we base our theses concerning the interrelationships of the Synoptics only on *one* set of characteristic features? If we do not give the differences as prominent attention as we do the similarities, are we not in danger of failing to appreciate the full or real character of the Jesus tradition and the way the Evangelists handled it? Such questions as these have led me to give more attention to the oral character of the early Jesus tradition and to question whether the hypothesis of literary interdependence tells the whole story.[1]

I

I begin, then, by drawing attention to the character of the interrelationships between the Synoptics, and the diversity of these relationships.

First, **the cases of identical or near-identical wording**. I give two examples from the triple tradition — on the cost of discipleship (Mark 8.34-37 pars.) and on the parable of the fig tree (Mark 13.28-32 pars.); and two from the non-Markan parallel material in Luke and Matthew, usually designated as

---

1. In what follows I draw on my *Christianity in the Making*, vol. 1, *Jesus Remembered* (Grand Rapids: Eerdmans, 2003), particularly #8; also *A New Perspective on Jesus: What the Quest for the Historical Jesus Missed* (Grand Rapids: Baker Academic, 2005) 79-125.

Q — the preaching of John the Baptist (Matt. 3.7-10/Luke 3.7-9) and the parable of the returning evil spirits (Matt. 12.43-45/Luke 11.24-26). In each case I have highlighted and underlined the verbal agreement.

(1) The cost of discipleship (Mark 8.34-37 pars.)

Matt. 16.24-26	Mark 8.34-37	Luke 9.23-25
[24] Then Jesus told his disciples, 'If any man would come after me, let him deny himself and take up his cross and follow me. [25] For whoever would save his life will lose it, and whoever loses his life for my sake will find it. [26] For what will it profit a man, if he gains the whole world and forfeits his life? Or what shall a man give in return for his life?	[34] And he called to him the multitude with his disciples, and said to them, 'If any man would come after me, let him deny himself and take up his cross and follow me. [35] For whoever would save his life will lose it; and whoever loses his life for my sake and the gospel's will save it. [36] For what does it profit a man, to gain the whole world and forfeit his life? [37] For what can a man give in return for his life?	[23] And he said to all, 'If any man would come after me, let him deny himself and take up his cross daily and follow me. [24] For whoever would save his life will lose it; and whoever loses his life for my sake, he will save it. [25] For what does it profit a man if he gains the whole world and loses or forfeits himself?

(2) The parable of the fig tree (Mark 13.28-32 pars.)

Matt. 24.32-36	Mark 13.28-32	Luke 21.29-33
[32] 'From the fig tree learn its lesson: as soon as its branch becomes tender and puts forth its leaves, you know that summer is near. [33] So also, when you see all these things, you know that he is near, at the very gates. [34] Truly, I say to you, this generation will not pass away till all these things take place. [35] Heaven and earth will pass away, but my words will not pass away. [36] But of that day and hour no one knows, not even the angels of heaven, nor the Son, but the Father only.	[28] 'From the fig tree learn its lesson: as soon as its branch becomes tender and puts forth its leaves, you know that summer is near. [29] So also, when you see these things taking place, you know that he is near, at the very gates. [30] Truly, I say to you, this generation will not pass away before all these things take place. [31] Heaven and earth will pass away, but my words will not pass away. [32] But of that day or that hour no one knows, not even the angels in heaven, nor the Son, but only the Father.	[29] And he told them a parable: 'Look at the fig tree, and all the trees; [30] as soon as they come out in leaf, you see for yourselves and know that the summer is already near. [31] So also, when you see these things taking place, you know that the kingdom of God is near. [32] Truly, I say to you, this generation will not pass away till all has taken place. [33] Heaven and earth will pass away, but my words will not pass away.

(3) The preaching of John the Baptist (Matt. 3.7-10/Luke 3.7-9)

Matt. 3.7-10	Luke 3.7-9
[7] But when he saw many of the Pharisees and Sadducees coming for baptism, he said to them, 'You brood of vipers! Who warned you to flee from the wrath to come? [8] Bear fruit that befits repentance. [9] and do not presume to say to yourselves, "We have Abraham as our father"; for I tell you, God is able from these stones to raise up children to Abraham. [10] Even now the axe is laid to the root of the trees; every tree therefore that does not bear good fruit is cut down and thrown into the fire'.	[7] He said therefore to the multitudes that came out to be baptised by him, 'You brood of vipers! Who warned you to flee from the wrath to come? [8] Bear fruits that befit repentance, and do not begin to say to yourselves, "We have Abraham as our father"; for I tell you, God is able from these stones to raise up children to Abraham. [9] Even now the axe is laid to the root of the trees; every tree therefore that does not bear good fruit is cut down and thrown into the fire'.

(4) The parable of the returning evil spirits (Matt. 12.43-45/Luke 11.24-26)

Matt. 12.43-45	Luke 11.24-26
[43] When the unclean spirit has gone out of a man, he passes through waterless places seeking rest, but he finds none. [44] Then he says, 'I will return to my house from which I came'. And when he comes he finds it empty, swept, and put in order. [45] Then he goes and brings with him seven other spirits more evil than himself, and they enter and dwell there; and the last state of that man becomes worse than the first. So shall it be also with this evil generation.	[24] When the unclean spirit has gone out of a man, he passes through waterless places seeking rest; and finding none he says, 'I will return to my house from which I came'. [25] And when he comes he finds it swept and put in order. [26] Then he goes and brings seven other spirits more evil than himself, and they enter and dwell there; and the last state of that man becomes worse than the first.

In these cases we can see the force of the standard two-source theory for the origin of the Synoptic Gospels. Much the most obvious explanation for that degree of agreement between different documents is that one is copying from another, or both are copying from the same source. It will not do, for example, to argue that Matthew and Luke drew their non-Markan material from an Aramaic source, each making *his own* translation into Greek. That in such a case they would have ended up with more or less identical Greek for their independent translations is almost impossible to envisage. Much the more obvious solution is either that Matthew copied Luke, or Luke copied Matthew, or the source they drew on was already in Greek. Here the case for a Q document already in Greek becomes very strong.[2] Equally clear is the basic

---

2. See particularly J. Kloppenborg Verbin, *Excavating Q: The History and Setting of the Sayings Gospel* (Minneapolis: Fortress, 2000).

case for Matthew's and Luke's dependence on Mark (or alternatively for some other literary dependence of one Synoptic Evangelist on the written Gospel of another Evangelist).

Here I have given only four examples. But I could have given many more, for example, of the close agreement between Mark and Matthew in particular which can hardly be explained by other than literary dependence.[3] B. H. Streeter, for example, in the classic English language presentation of the two-document hypothesis, made much of the claim that 90 percent of Mark's subject matter reappears in Matthew 'in language very largely identical with that of Mark'.[4] Similarly, the support for the Q hypothesis from Matthew and Luke is clear from a good many more examples than the two given above.[5] So *the case for literary interdependence has a strong foundation.* For my own part, I am strongly convinced of Markan priority, and have no problem with asserting some form of the Q written document hypothesis. My question, however, is whether *all* the evidence has been taken into account, and whether the *other* data should be sidelined either in making the case for literary interdependence or in regarding the case for literary interdependence as the whole story or the sole story, the only story.

II

Second, then, I draw your attention to the Synoptic material where there is *not* close verbal agreement, and in **a number of cases hardly any verbal agreement although the subject matter is evidently the same.** Once again I give only a few examples, three from passages where Markan priority is usually inferred — the Syrophoenician woman (Mark 7.24-30/Matt. 15.21-28), the epileptic boy (Mark 9.14-27 pars.) and the dispute about greatness (Mark 9.33-37 pars.); and five from passages usually identified as Q tradition — Jesus'

---

3. Mark 1.16-20/Matt. 4.18-22; Mark 2.18-22/Matt. 9.14-17/Luke 5.33-39; Mark 8.1-10/Matt. 15.32-39; Mark 8.31–9.1/Matt. 16.21-28/Luke 9.22-27; Mark 10.13-16/Matt. 19.13-15/Luke 18.15-17; Mark 10.32-34/Matt. 20.17-19/Luke 18.31-34; Mark 11.27-33/Matt. 21.23-27/Luke 20.1-8; Mark 13.3-32/Matt. 24.3-36/Luke 21.7-33. A similar degree of literary interdependence, but arguably with significant Matthean editing, is evident in Mark 2.23–3.6/Matt. 12.1-14; Mark 6.45-52/Matt. 14.22-33; and Mark 8.27-30/Matt. 16.13-20.

4. B. H. Streeter, *The Four Gospels: A Study of Origins* (London: Macmillan, 1924) 151, 159.

5. Matt. 3.7-10, 12/Luke 3.7-9, 17; Matt. 6.24/Luke 16.13; Matt. 6.25-33/Luke 12.22-31; Matt. 7.1-5/Luke 6.37-42; Matt. 7.7-11/Luke 11.9-13; Matt. 8.19-22/Luke 9.57b-60a; Matt. 11.2-11, 16-19/Luke 7.18-19, 22-28, 31-35; Matt. 11.21-27/Luke 10.12-15, 21-22; Matt. 12.39-45/Luke 11.29-32, 24-26; Matt. 13.33/Luke 13.20-21; Matt. 24.45-51/Luke 12.42-46.

teachings on turning the other cheek (Matt. 5.39b-42/Luke 6.29-30), on the narrow way (Matt. 7.13-14/Luke 13.24), on dividing families (Matt. 10.34-38/ Luke 12.51-53 and 14.26-27), on forgiving sins seven times (Matt. 18.15, 21-22/ Luke 17.3-4), and the parable of the wedding feast/great banquet (Matt. 22.1-14/Luke 14.15-24). Once again the underlining indicates the extent of the verbal agreement.

(5) The Syrophoenician woman (Mark 7.24-30 par.)

Matt. 15.21-28	Mark 7.24-30
[21] Jesus left that place and went off to the district of Tyre and Sidon. [22] Just then a Canaanite woman from that region came out and started shouting, 'Have mercy on me, lord, son of David; my daughter is tormented by a demon'. [23] But he did not answer her at all. And his disciples came and urged him, saying, 'Send her away, for she keeps shouting after us'. [24] He answered, 'I was sent only to the lost sheep of the house of Israel'. [25] But she came and knelt before him, saying, 'Lord, help me'. [26] He answered, 'It is not fair to take the children's food and throw it to the dogs'. [27] She said, 'Certainly, lord, for also the dogs eat from the crumbs that fall from their masters' table'. [28] Then Jesus answered her, 'Woman, great is your faith! Let it be done for you as you wish'. And her daughter was healed from that hour.	[24] From there he set out and went away to the region of Tyre. He entered a house and did not want anyone to know he was there. Yet he could not escape notice, [25] but a woman whose little daughter had an unclean spirit immediately heard about him, and she came and bowed down at his feet. [26] Now the woman was a Gentile, of Syrophoenician origin. She begged him to cast the demon out of her daughter. [27] He said to her, 'Let the children be fed first, for it is not fair to take the children's food and throw it to the dogs'. [28] But she answered him, 'Certainly, lord, and the dogs under the table eat from the crumbs of the children'. [29] So he said to her, 'For saying that, you may go, the demon has left your daughter'. [30] So she went to her home, and found the child lying on the bed, and the demon gone.

(6) The epileptic boy (Mark 9.14-27 pars.)

Matt. 17.14-18	Mark 9.14-27	Luke 9.37-43
[14] And when they came to the crowd,	[14] And when they came to the disciples, they saw a great crowd about them, and scribes arguing with them. [15] And immediately all the crowd, when they saw him, were greatly amazed, and ran up to him and greeted him. [16] And he asked them, 'What are you discussing with them?' [17] And one of the crowd answered him, 'Teacher, I brought my son to you, for he has a dumb spirit; [18] and wherever it grabs him, it dashes him down; and he foams and grinds his teeth and becomes rigid;	[37] On the next day, when they had come down from the mountain, a great crowd met him.
a man came up to him and kneeling before him said, [15] 'Lord, have mercy on my son, for he is an epileptic and he suffers terribly; for often he falls into the fire, and often into the water. [16] And I brought him to your disciples, and they could not heal him'. [17] And Jesus answered, 'O faithless and perverse generation, how long am I to be with you? How long am I to put up with you? Bring him here to me'.	and I asked your disciples to cast it out, and they were not able'. [19] And he answered them, 'O faithless generation, how long am I to be with you? How long am I to put up with you? Bring him to me'. [20] And they brought the boy to him; and when the spirit saw him, immediately it convulsed the boy, and he fell on the ground and rolled about, foaming at the mouth. . . . [25] And when Jesus saw that a crowd came running together,	[38] And behold, a man from the crowd cried, 'Teacher, I beg you to look upon my son, for he is my only child; [39] and behold, a spirit seizes him, and he suddenly cries out; it convulses him till he foams, and shatters him, and will hardly leave him. [40] And I begged your disciples to cast it out, and they could not'. [41] Jesus answered, 'O faithless and perverse generation, how long am I to be with you and to put up with you? Lead your son here'. [42] While he was coming, the demon tore him and
[18] And Jesus rebuked him,	he rebuked the unclean spirit, saying to it, 'You dumb and deaf spirit, I command you, come out of him, and never enter him again'. [26] And after crying out and convulsing	But Jesus rebuked the unclean spirit,
and the demon came out of him,	him terribly, it came out, and the boy was like a corpse; so that most of them said, 'He is	convulsed him.
and the boy was cured from that hour.	dead'. [27] But Jesus took him by the hand and lifted him up, and he arose.	and healed the boy, and gave him back to his father. [43] And all were astonished at the majesty of God.

(7) The dispute about greatness (Mark 9.33-37 pars.)

Matt. 18.1-5	Mark 9.33-37	Luke 9.46-48
	33 Then they came to Capernaum; and when he was in the house he asked them, 'What were you arguing about on the way?' 34 But they were	
1 At that time the disciples came to Jesus and asked, 'Who is greater in the kingdom of heaven?'	silent, for on the way they had argued with one another about who was greater. 35 He sat down, called the Twelve, and said to them, 'Whoever wants to be first must be last of all and servant of all'. 36	46 An argument arose among them as to who of them was greater.
2 He called a little child, and put it among them, 3 and said, 'Truly I tell you, unless you turn and become like little children, you will never enter the kingdom of heaven. 4 Whoever humbles himself like this little child is greater in the kingdom of heaven. 5 And whoever welcomes one such little child in my name welcomes me'.	Then he took a little child and put it among them; and taking it in his arms, he said to them,	47 But Jesus, aware of their inner thoughts, took a little child and put it by his side, 48 and said to them,
	37 'Whoever welcomes one of such little children in my name welcomes me, and whoever welcomes me welcomes not me but the one who sent me'.	'Whoever welcomes this little child in my name welcomes me, and whoever welcomes me welcomes the one who sent me; for he who is lesser among all of you, that one is great'.

(8) Turning the other cheek (Matt. 5.39b-42/Luke 6.29-30)

Matt. 5.39b-42	Luke 6.29-30
39b But whoever hits you on your right cheek, turn to him the other also; 40 and to the one who wants to sue you and take your tunic, let him have your cloak also; 41 and whoever forces you to go one mile, go with him a second. 42 Give to the one who asks you, and do not turn away the one who wants to borrow from you.	29 To the one who strikes you on the cheek, offer the other also; and from the one who takes away your cloak do not withhold your tunic also. 30 Give to everyone who asks you; and from the one who takes what is yours, do not ask for them back.

(9) The narrow way (Matt. 7.13-14/Luke 13.24)

Matt. 7.13-14	Luke 13.24
[13] Enter through the narrow gate; for the gate is wide and the road is easy that leads to destruction, and there are many who enter through it. [14] For the gate is narrow and the road is hard that leads to life, and there are few who find it.	[24] Strive to enter through the narrow door; for many, I tell you, will try to enter and will not be able.

(10) Dividing families (Matt. 10.34-38/Luke 12.51-53 and 14.26-27)

Matt. 10.34-38	Luke 12.51-53; 14.26-27
[34] Do not think that I came to bring peace to the earth; I came not to bring peace, but a sword. [35] For I came to set a man against his father, and a daughter against her mother, and a daughter-in-law against her mother-in-law; [36] and a man's foes will be members of his own household. [37] Whoever loves father or mother more than me is not worthy of me; and whoever loves son or daughter more than me is not worthy of me; [38] and he who does not take up his cross and follow after me is not worthy of me.	[12.51] Do you consider that I am here to give peace on the earth? No, I tell you, but rather division! [52] From now on five in one household will be divided; three against two and two against three; [53] they will be divided, father against son and son against father, mother against daughter and daughter against mother, mother-in-law against her daughter-in-law and daughter-in-law against mother-in-law. [14.26] Whoever comes to me and does not hate his father and mother, and wife and children, and brothers and sisters, yes, and even his own life, cannot be my disciple. [27] Whoever does not carry his own cross and come after me cannot be my disciple.

(11) Forgiving sins seven times (Matt. 18.15, 21-22/Luke 17.3-4)

Matt. 18.15, 21-22	Luke 17.3-4
[15] 'If your brother sins against you, go and point out the fault when you and he are alone. If he listens to you, you have regained your brother'. . . . [21] Then Peter came and said to him, 'Lord, if my brother sins against me, how often should I forgive him? As many as seven times?' [22] Jesus said to him, 'I tell you, not seven times, but seventy-seven times'.	[3] Be on your guard! If your brother sins, rebuke him, and if he repents, forgive him. [4] And if someone sins against you seven times a day, and turns back to you seven times and says, 'I repent', you must forgive him.

(12) The parable of the wedding feast/great banquet
(Matt. 22.1-14/Luke 14.15-24)

Matt. 22.1-14	Luke 14.15-24
[1] Once more Jesus spoke to them in parables, saying: [2] 'The kingdom of heaven may be compared to a king who gave a wedding banquet for his son. [3] He sent his slaves to call those who had been invited to the wedding banquet, but they would not come. [4] Again he sent other slaves, saying, "Tell those who have been invited: Look, I have prepared my dinner, my oxen and my fat calves have been slaughtered, and everything is ready; come to the wedding banquet". [5] But they made light of it and went away, one to his farm, another to his business, [6] while the rest seized his slaves, mistreated them, and killed them." [7] The king was angered. He sent his troops, destroyed those murderers, and burned their city. [8] Then he said to his slaves, "The wedding is ready, but those invited were not worthy. [9] Go therefore into the streets, and invite everyone you find to the wedding banquet". [10] Those slaves went out into the streets and gathered all whom they found, both good and bad; so the wedding hall was filled with guests. [11] But when the king came in to see the guests, he noticed a man there who was not wearing a wedding robe, [12] and he said to him, "Friend, how did you get in here without a wedding robe?" And he was speechless. [13] Then the king said to the attendants, "Bind him hand and foot, and throw him into the outer darkness, where there will be weeping and gnashing of teeth". [14] For many are called, but few are chosen.'	[15] One of the dinner guests, on hearing this, said to him, 'Blessed is anyone who will eat bread in the kingdom of God!' [16] Then Jesus said to him, 'A certain person gave a great dinner and invited many. [17] At the time for the dinner he sent his slave to say to those who had been invited, "Come; for it is now ready". [18] But they all alike began to make excuses. The first said to him, "I have bought a farm, and I must go out and see it; please accept my regrets". [19] Another said, "I have bought five yoke of oxen, and I am going to try them out; please accept my regrets". [20] Another said, "I have married a wife, and therefore I cannot come". [21] So the slave returned and reported this to his master. Then the owner of the house became angry and said to his slave, "Go out at once into the roads and lanes of the town and bring in the poor, the crippled, the blind, and the lame". [22] And the slave said, "Sir, what you ordered has been done, and there is still room". [23] Then the master said to the slave, "Go out into the roads and lanes, and compel them to come in, so that my house may be full. [24] For I tell you, none of those who were invited will taste my dinner".'

What is striking about all these examples is *the lack of verbal agreement* — typically less than 40 percent, and more like 20 percent or less in some cases.[6] And yet in each case the story being told or the teaching passed on is clearly *the same;* the parables have *the same* image, structure and message. Why the divergence? Why the variation? Here the argument for literary interdependence is hard to make. If Mark was the only source for Matthew's and Luke's Gospels, why did they alter Mark in what seems to be often a rather cavalier or casual manner? In some instances a case can be made for Matthean or Lukan redaction of Mark. But overall many if not most of the variations are inconsequential; *there are no obvious reasons why Matthew or Luke should have departed from their sole source text,* presumably, on the literary hypothesis, their sole authoritative text. Similarly with the non-Markan agreements in Matthew and Luke, the Q material. While it is true that more than 13 percent of the pericopes common to them are more than 80 percent in verbal agreement, it is also true that the verbal agreement in over a third of the common material is less than 40 percent. The latter evidence covers *nearly three times as much material* as the former, and yet it is passed over and largely ignored when the thesis of literary interdependence is developed into the two-source theory. But why would Matthew or Luke make such arbitrary alterations to their Q source if they were so dependent on the hypothesized Q document for the textual tradition in the first place? If the close verbal interdependence of many Synoptic parallel passages counts as strong evidence *for* literary interdependence, then should not the more extensive *dis*agreements between parallel Synoptic texts be counted *against* the thesis or assumption of literary interdependence?

I repeat, I am very open to the possibility of a later Evangelist redacting his source — for example, with the majority I would consider it more likely that Matthew has modified Mark in each of the two following cases, rather than vice versa.[7]

Matt. 13.58	Mark 6.5-6
And he *did not do many* deeds of power there,	And he *could do no* deed of power there, except that he laid his hands on a few sick people and cured them. And he was amazed at
because of their unbelief.	their unbelief.

6. See also the summary of R. Morgenthaler, *Statistische Synopse* (Zurich and Stuttgart: Gotthelf, 1971), in Kloppenborg Verbin's *Excavating Q* 63.

7. See the full data collected by J. C. Hawkins, *Horae Synopticae: Contributions to the Study of the Synoptic Problem* (Oxford: Clarendon, 1898, [2]1909) 117-25.

Matt. 19.16-17	Mark 10.17-18
Then someone came to him and said, 'Teacher, what *good deed* must I do to have eternal life?' And he said to him, '*Why do you ask me about what is good*? There is only one who is good'.	A man ran up and knelt before him, and asked him, '*Good* Teacher, what must I do to inherit eternal life?' Jesus said to him, '*Why do you call me good*? No one is good but God alone'.

In these cases, however, it is evident that Matthew was taking care to remain as close as possible to his source (Mark), even while significantly altering the sense. These examples illustrate Matthew's *respect for his text and unwillingness to depart from it* more than was absolutely necessary to prevent his audiences drawing the wrong conclusion from the Markan original. But what we encounter in most cases of the diverging Synoptic tradition is *inconsequential* variation. If redaction is the only plausible or recognisable explanation, then we have to infer a *casualness* and *arbitrariness* in the redaction which can only imply a *lack* of respect for the authoritative original.

It was such reflection which led me to look for other or complementary explanations. If the degree of similarity and difference is explainable only in part by the thesis of literary interdependence, then ought we not to look for an alternative or complementary explanation for the other part of the same data of Synoptic interrelationship?

III

As indicated at the beginning of this chapter, an obvious area to look for such an alternative or complementary explanation lies in **the *oral* character of the earliest Jesus tradition**. This has been recognised in principle by not a few Gospel specialists, that there must have been a period before the writing of the Gospels (or their written sources) when the Jesus tradition, or at least the bulk of it, would have circulated and been used only in *oral form*. Unfortunately, when the major investigation into and debate on the sources of the Gospels were being undertaken, there was too little appreciation of the character of oral transmission. Streeter, for example, cautioned against studying the Synoptic Problem 'merely as a problem of literary criticism'. Likewise, he fully recognised the need to look beyond the two sources of Mark and Q to explain the composition of the Synoptic Gospels. Ironically, however, it was he who is particularly recalled for his promotion of 'a four *document* hypothesis'.[8] The oral

8. Streeter, *The Four Gospels* ch. 9 (quotations from 229).

period of transmission was not really examined or any real recognition given to the possibility that oral tradition and transmission might have different characteristics from the literary models which were being assumed in the focus on literary interdependence.

A more hopeful development was the emergence of *Formgeschichte,* or form criticism, as an attempt to reach behind the written Gospels to the oral forms of the tradition which the Evangelists put into writing. For Rudolf Bultmann, indeed, the purpose of form criticism was 'to study the history of the oral tradition behind the gospels'.[9] Hence his focus on identifying the forms on which the Evangelists were able to draw — apophthegms, dominical sayings, miracle stories, etc.[10] However, Bultmann's attempt to illuminate the oral period of the Jesus tradition suffered from two major weaknesses.

First, he assumed that certain *'laws of style'* determined the transmission of the forms. These laws, apparently drawn from some acquaintance with studies in folklore elsewhere,[11] included the further assumptions of an original *'pure'* form, of a natural progression in the course of transmission from purity and simplicity towards greater complexity, and of a development in the tradition determined by form rather than content. But the so-called laws were neither drawn from what was known of folklore at the time,[12] nor were they validated by the character of the tradition in the Gospels themselves.[13]

Second, and more significant, was Bultmann's assumption of a *literary* model to explain the process of transmission. This becomes most evident in his conceptualisation of the whole tradition about Jesus as 'composed of a se-

9. R. Bultmann (with K. Kundsin), *Form Criticism* (1934; ET New York: Harper Torchbook, 1962) 1.

10. R. Bultmann, *The History of the Synoptic Tradition* (1921; ET Oxford: Blackwell, 1963).

11. Bultmann, *History* 6-7.

12. J. Schröter, *Erinnerung an Jesu Worte: Studien zur Rezeption der Logienüberlieferung in Markus, Q und Thomas* (WMANT 76; Neukirchen-Vluyn: Neukirchener, 1997): 'The "pure form" represents a mixture of linguistic and history of language categories, which is to be assigned to an out of date conception of language development' (59; also 141-42). See also G. Strecker, 'Schriftlichkeit oder Mündlichkeit der synoptischen Tradition?', in F. van Segbroeck et al., eds., *The Four Gospels 1992, Festschrift Frans Neirynck* (Leuven: Leuven University Press, 1992) 159-72 (here 161-62, with other bibliography in n. 6).

13. See particularly E. P. Sanders, *The Tendencies of the Synoptic Tradition* (SNTSMS 9; Cambridge: Cambridge University Press, 1969): 'There are no hard and fast laws of the development of the Synoptic tradition. On all counts the tradition developed in opposite directions. It became both longer and shorter, both more and less detailed, and both more and less Semitic. . . .' (272). And further W. H. Kelber, *The Oral and the Written Gospel* (Philadelphia: Fortress, 1983) 2-8.

ries of layers'.[14] The imagined process is one where each layer is laid upon or builds upon another. Bultmann made such play with it because, apart from anything else, he was confident that he could strip off later (Hellenistic) layers to expose the earlier (Palestinian) layers.[15] The image itself, however, is drawn from the *literary* process of *editing*, where each successive edition (layer) is an edited version (for Bultmann, an elaborated and expanded version) of the previous edition (layer). But is such a conceptualisation really appropriate to a process of oral retellings of traditional material? Bultmann never really addressed the question, despite its obvious relevance. He simply assumed that the transmission of oral tradition was no different in character from the transmission of already written tradition.

Since Bultmann, much more attention has been paid to the character of oral tradition and its transmission. I mention what I regard as the most illuminating for us: first, investigation into the early oral, preliterary period in Greek culture, and the recognition both that Homer was recited orally for a lengthy period before being written down and that the written text indicates the character of the oral recitations;[16] second, Birger Gerhardsson's investigation of the oral procedures for preserving and transmitting rabbinical tradition within the most immediate context for the early Jesus tradition;[17] third, very fruitful and illuminating research into oral communities in Africa;[18] and fourth, the impressionistic and anecdotal accounts by Kenneth Bailey of thirty years' experience of oral communities in the villages of Egypt and Lebanon.[19] If the latter two seem remote from first-century Palestine, it should be noted that such village life, in both Africa and the Middle East, is likely to have been largely conservative and unchanging in the ways in which the communities operated as oral societies.

The most striking feature to emerge, and emerge consistently, from these

---

14. R. Bultmann, *Jesus and the Word* (1926; ET New York: Scribner, 1935) 12-13.

15. Bultmann, *Jesus and the Word* 12-13.

16. E. A. Havelock, *Preface to Plato* (Cambridge, MA: Harvard University Press, 1963); A. B. Lord, *The Singer of Tales* (Cambridge, MA: Harvard University Press, 1978).

17. B. Gerhardsson, *Memory and Manuscript: Oral Tradition and Written Transmission in Rabbinic Judaism and Early Christianity* (Lund: Gleerup, 1961, 1998).

18. I refer particularly to J. Vansina, *Oral Tradition as History* (Madison: University of Wisconsin Press, 1985), a revision of his earlier *Oral Tradition: A Study in Historical Methodology* (London: Routledge and Kegan Paul, 1965); R. Finnegan, *Oral Literature in Africa* (Oxford: Clarendon, 1970); and I. Okpewho, *African Oral Literature: Backgrounds, Character, and Continuity* (Bloomington: Indiana University Press, 1992).

19. K. E. Bailey, 'Informal Controlled Oral Tradition and the Synoptic Gospels', *Asia Journal of Theology* 5 (1991) 34-54; also 'Middle Eastern Oral Tradition and the Synoptic Gospels', *ExpTim* 106 (1995) 363-67.

different examples is the characteristic combination of *fixity* and *flexibility*, of *stability* and *diversity*, of *the same yet different*. In oral tradition there is characteristically a *tale* to be told, but told using different words to highlight different aspects in different tellings. In oral tradition there is characteristically a *teaching* to be treasured, but it is formulated variously depending on the emphases the different teachers want to bring out.[20] Oral tradition is oral memory; its primary function is to preserve and recall what is of importance from the past. Tradition, more or less by definition, embodies the concern for continuity with the past, a past drawn upon but also enlivened that it might illuminate the present and future. In the words of Eric Havelock, 'Variability and stability, conservatism and creativity, evanescence and unpredictability all mark the pattern of oral transmission' — the 'oral principle of "variation within the same"'.[21] Or as Alan Dundes puts the same point: '"multiple existence" and "variation" [are] the two most salient characteristics of folklore'.[22]

What excited me when I learned about this characteristic feature of oral transmission was that *it spoke immediately to the character of the Synoptic tradition.* For the character of the Synoptic tradition, the character which had intrigued me from the first, is well caught in the phrase 'the same yet different' — the same story told, but with different introduction and conclusion and different wording, the same teaching but differently worded and differently grouped. It was this Synoptic material, illustrated above, which could now be made sense of in terms of oral tradition. *That material was oral tradition,* its diversity frozen in the differing versions of the Synoptic Gospels. The model of literary interdependence could explain well the Synoptic passages where there was close verbal agreement. But the literary model made little sense of the passages where the verbal agreement was less than 40 percent, sometimes much less. Whereas the model of *oral* tradition seemed to meet the case precisely. The obvious conclusion to be drawn is that *large sections of the Synoptic tradition are the varying oral tradition put into writing.*

20. Gerhardsson makes the same point in regard to rabbinic tradition, not so clearly in his early work, but certainly latterly — most recently in *The Reliability of the Gospel Tradition* (Peabody, MA: Hendrickson, 2001), which includes two other earlier studies. I regret that I did not recognize this sufficiently in *Jesus Remembered* 197-98.

21. Kelber, *Oral* 33, 54; quoting Havelock, *Preface to Plato* 92, 147, 184, *passim*.

22. A. Dundes, *Holy Writ as Oral Lit: The Bible as Folklore* (Lanham, MD: Rowman and Littlefield, 1999) 18-19.

IV

Two important points emerge from this attempt to reappreciate the oral Jesus tradition, with several equally important corollaries. They are important, I believe, for our understanding of the early Jesus tradition, its oral character, the use made of it, its early circulation and its transcription in writing in due course.

The first major point underlines the difference between the model of literary interdependence and oral interdependence. The oral tradition model subverts the idea of an *'original'* version. With minds attuned to the literary paradigm, we envisage an original form, a first edition, from which all subsequent editions can at least in principle be traced by form and redaction criticism. We envisage tradition-history as an archaeological tell where we in principle can dig through the layers of literary strata to uncover the original layer, the 'pure form' of Bultmann's conceptualisation of *Formgeschichte*. But in *oral* tradition each performance is not related to its predecessors or successors in that way. In oral tradition, as Albert Lord particularly observed, *each* performance is, properly speaking, an 'original'.[23]

The point as it applies to the Jesus tradition is *not* that there was no originating impulse which gave birth to the tradition. On the contrary, in many cases we can be wholly confident that there were things which Jesus said and did which made an *impact,* and a *lasting* impact on his disciples.[24] But, properly speaking, the *tradition* of the event is not the *event* itself. And the *tradition* of the saying is not the *saying* itself. The tradition is at best the *witness* of the event, and as there were presumably several witnesses, so there may well have been several traditions, or versions of the tradition, *from the first.* Of an originating *event* we can speak; but we should certainly hesitate before speaking of an original *tradition* of the event. The same is true even of a saying of Jesus. The tradition of the saying attests the impact made by the saying on one or more of the original audience. But it may well have been

---

23. 'In a sense each performance is "an" original, if not "the" original. The truth of the matter is that our concept of "the original", of "the song", simply makes no sense in oral tradition' (Lord, *The Singer of Tales* 100-101). R. Finnegan, *Oral Poetry: Its Nature, Significance, and Social Context* (Cambridge: Cambridge University Press, 1977), also glosses Lord — 'There is no correct text, no idea that one version is more "authentic" than another: each performance is a unique and original creation with its own validity' (65) — and credits Lord with bringing this point home most convincingly (79).

24. In ch. 1 above I put this forward as one of my presuppositions, and in *Jesus Remembered* I emphasise the importance of recognising that Jesus' mission must have made a considerable impact on his disciples.

heard slightly differently by others of that audience, and so told and retold in different versions *from the first*. Moreover, if, as Werner Kelber points out, Jesus himself used his most effective parables and aphorisms on more than one occasion, the ideal of a single original, a single authentic version, reduces once again more to the figment of a literary-moulded mind-set.[25] And who can doubt that Jesus did indeed teach the same message in different ways and words on many occasions — what good teacher ever teaches what is important to him on only one occasion? Which, then, of the various versions of the same teaching was the 'original' version?

From this first point several corollaries immediately follow. First, that we should regard the diversity within the Synoptic tradition much more positively than often has been the case in the past. The *differences* between the Synoptic Gospels within particular pericopes and collections of teaching are *not a problem*. The differences do not indicate 'mistakes' or 'errors' or 'contradictions'. They indicate simply *the different ways that Jesus was remembered and the fact that the Jesus tradition was handled and presented in different contexts*.

A second corollary is that we should not think of *only one* of the differing versions as the original and as having primary authenticity. We should not think of the alternative versions as less authentic, or as corruptions (for devious theological reasons) of the 'original'. We should rather regard them all as 'authentic', as the original actions and teaching of Jesus continued to exert their power on succeeding disciples.

Third, it also follows that the tradition of Jesus' teachings and doings was not regarded as fixed and frozen. It was not like a sacred relic paraded round for devout followers to venerate — 'Ah! This is what Jesus said on August 10, in the year 28; we must reverence and preserve it just as he gave it'. On the contrary, it was *living tradition,* tradition which they celebrated, tradition by which they lived and in the light of which they worshipped. This, I believe, is already evident in the way the Jesus tradition has been absorbed into the ethical teaching of Paul and James, so that it has become an integral part of their own paraenesis without any sense that particular exhortations would only be authoritative if explicitly attributed to Jesus.[26]

Fourth, all this gives us a fresh slant on the concept of the Evangelists' editing of earlier tradition. For in the event, editing was only a more extended example of the variety integral to the whole circulation, use and transmission

25. 'Each oral performance is an irreducibly unique creation'; if Jesus said something more than once, there is no 'original' (Kelber, *Oral* 29; also 59, 62).

26. I have argued this point in regard to Paul on several occasions — particularly in *The Theology of Paul the Apostle* (Grand Rapids: Eerdmans, 1998) 649-58.

of the Jesus tradition.[27] If apostles and teachers had no qualms in repeating stories about Jesus and the teaching of Jesus in their own words, neither, it is evident, did they have any qualms about interpreting some teaching of Jesus in a way which brought out its relevance more forcibly to their own situation or any qualms about drawing a conclusion from their account of one of Jesus' miracles which again showed its relevance to their own hearers. The impact of Jesus' mission thus continued to exercise direct influence on the first-generation embryonic Christian churches.

The second major point which emerges regards in particular the *transition* from *oral* Jesus tradition to *written* Jesus tradition. Regrettably Werner Kelber, who did so much to bring home to us the importance of understanding the oral character of the early Jesus tradition, headed off in a very misleading direction. He argued, in effect, that the oral tradition was itself the only authentic tradition and that the transcription of the oral tradition into writing was a kind of 'fall' from grace, the death of the living (oral) word.[28] But even though recognition of the character of oral tradition liberates us from a mind-set too rigidly controlled by our literary heritage, it would be a mistake to regard the scribalisation of the oral Jesus tradition as changing its character altogether. I will return to this subject in the third chapter, but here I think three points can already be made.

First, I have no doubt that some at least of the Jesus tradition was transcribed at an early stage. It is not that written material would be regarded as more reliable than oral. Such a view is once again an expression of the literary mind-set; we ourselves have become so reliant on written records that our ability to absorb quickly into our memory and to retain even information of first importance to us is much less efficient than in oral societies. In contrast, prior to the reliability of the printing press, written texts were generally regarded as *less* reliable than what the memory retained for itself. Writing would have become a factor when distance was involved; in the same way that letters could serve as a substitute for personal presence. Such writing, however, evidently did not rigidify or imprison the Jesus tradition. Here again we should learn from the Synoptic tradition. The diversity among the Synoptic Gospels again shows that the Evangelists did not regard it as essential that they should convey forms made fixed and rigid by writing. Even though Matthew and Luke evidently knew and used at least one written source (Mark), they did not merely copy what Mark had written, but gave their own version

27. I give some examples in ch. 3 below.
28. Kelber, *Oral* ch. 5.

even of the traditions which Mark conveyed. In other words, *the flexibility of the oral transmission period carried over into the written forms of the tradition.*

One of the major failings of the attempts to resolve the Synoptic Problem in exclusively literary terms was the inference (not usually consciously formulated) that when Matthew or Luke received his copy of Mark's Gospel, that was the first time each had encountered the stories and teaching contained in Mark. But such a scenario is hardly credible. Much or most of the Jesus tradition inscribed by Mark must have been widely circulating and well known in the Christian communities in Syria and beyond. In many cases where Matthew and Mark diverge on the same tradition, the most obvious explanation is that Matthew knew an (oral) version of that tradition different from the Markan version, and that Matthew preferred in these cases to transcribe the other version, which perhaps he knew better. In other words, we probably see in such data evidence of Jesus tradition both oral and written circulating at the same time and among the same churches. Initially the written was essentially a transcription of one version of the oral, or was itself a scribal presentation of Jesus tradition sharing the same characteristics (the same but different) as typical oral presentations.

Second, all this means that the understanding of Q has to be revised. The non-Markan material common to Matthew and Luke should not simply be grouped together on the assumption that it all comes from a single document. As I noted earlier, there is certainly evidence that some of the Q material had been put into writing. But beyond that the evidence will not support the hypothesis of a single written document. Beyond the passages of near-identical wording, the diversity is such that another explanation is much more likely: namely, that such diversity exemplifies the varied sequence or sequences of oral tradition, as used by apostles and teachers in the various Christian assemblies, the varied sequences representative of the typical repertoires many Christian teachers drew from the community store of tradition for which they were particularly responsible. The fact that the Q hypothesis finds it necessary to envisage different versions or different editions of Q simply underlines the myopic character of the literary mind-set at this point. That Matthew and Luke had access to much more material than Mark is clear. That some of it was already in writing is highly probable. But that they also knew the Jesus tradition as living oral tradition, with the sort of diversity we still find in the Synoptic tradition, is equally probable. The attempt to recover a Q document is in many ways admirable.[29] But it has prevented us from re-

---

29. See particularly J. M. Robinson, P. Hoffmann, and J. S. Kloppenborg, *The Critical Edition of Q: Synopsis* (Leuven: Peeters, 2000).

cognising that well into the second half of the first century the Jesus tradition was still well known in oral mode. And by assuming the fixity of written sources the attempt to recover a written Q has lost sight of the living character of the Jesus tradition.

Third, we should not make the mistake of thinking that there was a single transition from oral to written, as though the writing down of the Jesus tradition made an end to the oral tradition, or brought the flexible character of the Jesus tradition to an end. On the contrary, it is evident from the echoes and uses made of the Jesus tradition, for example, in James, 1 Peter and the Apostolic Fathers, that they knew versions of the Jesus tradition alluded to which were different from the versions used by the Gospels.[30] To use such echoes and allusions of Jesus tradition only as evidence in the debates as to whether there was a Q document or whether the canonical Evangelists were already known is once again to lose sight of how widely the Jesus tradition was known in oral form and of its degree of variability. In other words, the oral forms of Jesus tradition continued alongside the written versions into the second century. And here again, as Richard Bauckham has demonstrated with regard to James, the way they drew on the Jesus tradition again evidences the flexibility of the tradition, as they adapted it to the needs they were addressing.[31]

Moreover, textual critics like David Parker and Eldon Epp have been pointing out for some time that the transition to written forms did not kill the flexibility of the tradition.[32] For just as we have seen the inadequacy of thinking in terms of a single original version of items of the Jesus tradition, so these textual critics have moved away from assuming a single original text, alone authentic, with all the variations the result of textual corruption, of scribal error and mistake. On the contrary, what we have in the textual tradition is evidence of different versions of these texts, the different versions which were the NT writings for different churches, often reflecting the differing concerns and needs of their differing communities. In other words, the textual tradition itself attests the continuing flexibility of (in this case) the Jesus tradition.

To sum up, then. How should we envisage the period between Jesus and the Gospels? Not, assuredly, by a great empty space, with Jesus at one end, and

---

30. H. Köster, *Synoptische Überlieferung bei den apostolischen Vätern* (Berlin: Akademie, 1957).

31. R. Bauckham, *James: Wisdom of James, Disciple of Jesus the Sage* (London and New York: Routledge, 1999).

32. D. C. Parker, *The Living Text of the Gospels* (Cambridge: Cambridge University Press, 1997); E. J. Epp, 'The Multivalence of the Term "Original Text" in New Testament Textual Criticism', *HTR* 92 (1999) 245-81.

stories about Jesus and teaching attributed to Jesus suddenly created more or less out of nothing for some reason at the other end. If Jesus proved to be an influential figure, as I assume, then the space was filled by people influenced by him. If Jesus said memorable and controversial things, then, assuredly, the memory of such sayings filled part of that space. If Jesus did remarkable and controversial things, then memory of such events no doubt filled part of the space too. These memories of Jesus would be in the form of oral tradition. These memories would be shared, they would be circulated, they would be interpreted, they would be elaborated, but initially almost entirely in oral forms. The first disciples, apostles and teachers, would tell stories about Jesus in the gatherings of the first believers in Jesus. They would introduce the stories and draw conclusions from the stories of relevance to their own situations. They would recall and repeat his teachings, grouping them in different combinations, drawing out different lessons for different circumstances, for the benefit of followers whose only access to that tradition was through those responsible for maintaining and preserving the oral tradition. It was not like the rote learning or memorisation of sacred texts. Rather it was living tradition, narratives which made their own life story meaningful, teachings by which they lived their own lives. Elsewhere in the New Testament there is little or no effort made to remember it as Jesus tradition as such. Rather in letters of Paul and James, for example, it has been absorbed into the lifeblood of their own ethical teaching.

Why do I find such a portrayal of the gap between Jesus and the Gospels so appealing? For the simple reason that it explains so well the character and content of the Synoptic Gospels themselves. They show how Jesus was remembered during that period between Jesus and the Gospels — the same yet different. They show why Jesus was remembered during that period. They exemplify the ways in which the memories of Jesus, his actions and his teachings, were formulated and used and passed on. They show that the impact of Jesus was not dissipated or covered over by subsequent beliefs and dogmas about Jesus. They show how the Jesus who made an impact during his mission continued to make an impact on those who had never seen him in the flesh through the tradition which embodied the character of his mission so clearly.

CHAPTER 3

The Birth of a New Genre:
Mark and the Synoptic Gospels

One of the major developments over the first forty or so years of Christianity was the transition from the oral Jesus tradition to the written Gospel. For the history of Christianity, the importance of this development can hardly be exaggerated. We are talking about the establishment of a new genre within ancient literature, the *'Gospel'*, or, more precisely, the Christian Gospel. Still more important, this new genre was one which both defined, distinguished and characterised the new movement within Second Temple Judaism as no other development did.

The Gospel before the Gospel

The noun 'gospel, good news' *(euangelion)* is one of several terms which Christianity owes to Paul; sixty of its seventy-six occurrences in the New Testament appear in the Pauline corpus. A strong body of New Testament scholarship believes that Paul borrowed the term 'gospel' from its political use in relation to Caesar. And it is certainly true that the word *euangelion* (usually in the plural) was used for the good news of Caesar Augustus's achievements. So one can argue with some plausibility that Paul deliberately described his message as 'gospel' *(euangelion)* in order to set his good news of Christ in opposition to the Roman Empire's good news of Caesar. The peace brought by Christ (Rom. 5.1) was a more profound 'gospel' than the *Pax Romana*. However, the fact is that the word *euangelion* was in wider use than simply the good news of Caesar;[1] so a direct challenge to the political power and authority of Caesar was not immediately obvious in Paul's usage.

More to the point, the decisive influence on Paul's choice of *euangelion* to denote his message probably came from elsewhere. I refer to the direct and strong influence of Isaiah's language evident at many points of early Christian tradition — and Paul especially.[2] So I regard it as much more likely that Paul was influenced by the Hebrew Bible use of *bsr* to speak of the bringing of good news, especially of God's saving deeds,[3] and especially as used by Isaiah.[4] Two of these Isaiah passages were evidently influential in the Jewish theological reflection in Second Temple Judaism prior to Jesus and Paul. *Pss. Sol.* 11.1 clearly echoes Isa. 52.7:

> Isa. 52.7 — 'How beautiful upon the mountains are the feet of the messenger who announces *(euangelizomenou)* peace, who brings good news *(euangelizomenos agatha),* who announces salvation, who says to Zion, "Your God reigns"'.

> *Pss. Sol.* 11.1 — 'Sound in Zion the signal trumpet of the sanctuary; announce in Jerusalem the voice of one bringing good news *(euangelizomenou)*'.

And 11QMelch 2.15-24 makes explicit exposition of Isa. 52.7, applying it to the sect's own situation. Of the various allusions to Isa. 61.1 in the Qumran scrolls, the same 11QMelch passage also draws on Isa. 61.1-3, identifying 'the messenger' as the one 'anointed' by the Spirit (Isa. 61.1). And in a remarkable parallel to Matt. 11.5/Luke 7.22, 4Q521 draws similarly on Isa. 61.1, in expectation of God's Messiah who will preach good news to the poor:

> [1]. . . [the hea]vens and the earth will listen to his messiah. . . . [5]For the Lord will consider the pious *(hasidim)* and call the righteous by name, [6]and over the poor his spirit will hover, and he will renew the faithful with his power. [7]For he will glorify the pious upon the throne of an eternal kingdom. [8]He who liberates the captives, restores sight to the blind,

---

1. LSJ 705; *NDIEC* 3.13-14; other examples in H.-J. Klauck, *The Religious Context of Early Christianity: A Guide to Graeco-Roman Religions* (1995; ET Edinburgh: T. & T. Clark, 2000) 328-29.

2. That Paul was himself heavily influenced by Isaiah is well known; see e.g. J. R. Wagner, *Heralds of the Good News: Isaiah and Paul in Concert in the Letter to the Romans* (Leiden: Brill, 2002).

3. Pss. 40.9; 68.11; 96.2; also 2 Sam. 18.31.

4. Isa. 40.9; 52.7; 60.6; 61.1; similarly Nah. 1.15. See further O. Schilling, *TDOT* 2.313-16.

straightens the b[ent]. . . . ¹¹And the Lord will accomplish glorious things which have never been as [ ]. ¹²[For] he will heal the wounded, and revive the dead and preach good news to the poor.

It is no surprise, then, that Jesus was remembered as similarly seeing in Isa. 61.1-2 ('to bring good news [*euangelisasthai*] to the poor') a foreshadowing of his own ministry. This is implied in two passages shared by Luke and Matthew (Q passages),[5] and is explicit in Luke 4.17-21. Nor should it cause any surprise that Paul explicitly quotes Isa. 52.7 in a passage explaining his understanding of the commission to preach the gospel — Rom. 10.15.[6] But the fact that Isaiah's talk of one who would preach good news was so much reflected on does greatly increase the probability that Paul made a deliberate choice to use the term *euangelion* to characterise his message; and that he did so precisely because he believed Isaiah's hope of one who would preach good news (*euangelizomenos*) to the poor *had been realised in Jesus*, a claim which was recalled as having been made by Jesus himself.

None of this is to deny that Paul and his audiences would have been aware that Paul was offering a very different 'good news' from that of Caesar. But for us there is a much more important deduction to be drawn from the evidence just reviewed. This is that it was *Paul himself* who introduced into Christian vocabulary the term 'gospel' *(euangelion)*, and that he did so by using the noun form of the verb familiar to him both from Isaiah and from the Jesus tradition.

How does Paul use the term 'gospel'? What was the good news for Paul? In fact, Paul himself usually speaks of the 'gospel' without specifying its content. It is 'the gospel of God',[7] and more commonly 'the gospel of Christ'.[8] This latter phrase probably means 'the good news about Christ', including his Davidic descent (Rom. 1.1-3; 2 Tim. 2.8), and particularly his death and resurrection.[9] And especially in Galatians Paul vigorously defends his gospel as good news also for Gentiles.[10] Does this imply that Paul limited his use of the

5. Luke 6.20/Matt. 5.3; Matt. 11.5/Luke 7.22.
6. See further my *The Theology of Paul the Apostle* (Grand Rapids: Eerdmans; Edinburgh: T. & T. Clark, 1998) 164-69.
7. Rom. 1.1; 15.16; 2 Cor. 11.7; 1 Thess. 2.2, 8, 9; also 1 Pet. 4.17.
8. Rom. 1.9; 15.19; 1 Cor. 9.12; 2 Cor. 2.12; 9.13; 10.14; Gal. 1.7; Phil. 1.27; 1 Thess. 3.2; 2 Thess. 1.8.
9. Rom. 1.4; 1 Cor. 1.23; 15.1-5; Gal. 3.1. By 'resurrection' I refer to the earliest Christian belief that God had raised Jesus from the dead.
10. Gal. 1.6, 7, 11; 2.2, 5, 7, 14; also Rom. 1.16; 15.16; Eph. 3.6.

term to the acts of Jesus decisive for salvation, particularly his death and resurrection? Such was a much favoured conclusion at the end of the nineteenth century: that Paul had turned the message *of* Jesus into a message *about* Jesus; that the good tidings of Jesus' proclamation of the kingdom had been transformed into a message of redemption from sin.

So an interesting issue arises of relevance to us. How does the word 'gospel' move from Paul's focus on Jesus' death and resurrection to a biographical account of Jesus' mission? At what point does the Jesus tradition itself begin to be regarded as 'gospel'? Indeed, we might well ask, When did *the Jesus tradition* itself become 'gospel'? The issue is posed since, as we shall see, it seems to have been Mark who introduced the noun *euangelion* into the Jesus tradition itself. Apart from the possible exceptions of Mark 13.10 and 14.9, there are no indications that Jesus himself used an equivalent Aramaic form. The term *euangelion* as such never appears in the Q material within the Jesus tradition.

However, even if Paul did focus his gospel on the good news of Jesus' death and resurrection, that should not mislead us into thinking that he *excluded* tradition of Jesus' life and mission from 'the good news about Christ'.

- The very fact that Paul used *euangelion* implies his awareness of Jesus' use of Isa. 61.1-2 in self-reference to refer to his own mission. It is hardly likely that it would even have occurred to Paul to bracket out the tradition of Jesus' mission from the gospel he preached.
- The good news about Jesus must have included some narrative explaining who Jesus was and recounting something at least of the character of what he had said and done during his mission. The gospel which converted so many Gentiles could hardly have been simply that an unidentified 'X' had died and been raised from the dead. On the contrary, since new believers in Paul's gospel were beginning to be called 'Christians' (Acts 11.26), baptised 'in the name of Christ' (1 Cor. 1.12-15), that would inevitably have prompted them to ask more about this 'Christ', not least so that they could give an answer to any questions as to why they had changed their lives and now based them on this 'Christ'.
- It is also the case that Paul must have conveyed a good deal of Jesus tradition to the churches he founded. He refers on several occasions to the traditions he passed on to the new churches he established[11] — mostly ethical traditions, and in all probability including a good deal of what was remembered as Jesus' own teaching.[12] Certainly Paul's allusions to

11. 1 Cor. 11.2; 2 Thess. 2.15; 3.6.
12. Explicitly 1 Cor. 7.10 — Matt. 5.32; 1 Cor. 9.14 — Luke 10.7.

the Jesus tradition in his exhortations presuppose a web of knowledge of Jesus' teaching,[13] no doubt set reverberating for many or most of his audiences by such allusions.[14]

- Apart from anything else, various tracts of the Jesus tradition must have been known round the earliest churches. As already noted, we can hardly assume that the tradition known as Q or the traditions on which Mark drew were submerged for forty years, or remembered and cherished only by a very small band of original disciples (apostles). The various groups of teaching materials which make up Q most likely included or formed the repertoires for many church teachers.[15] And Mark seems to have been able to draw on blocks of stories told about Jesus and blocks of Jesus' teaching.[16] It is not credible that these materials were regarded as sharply distinct from the gospel that Paul and others preached. To make such a case is to argue *e silentio* and to ignore basic historical probabilities.

- Worth recalling is the fact that the earliest memories of Jesus seem to have included an element of narrative structure, beginning with John the Baptist, taking in Jesus' mission and message and climaxing in his death and resurrection. In Acts 10.36-40 this whole narrative seems to be summed up as 'the word *(logos)* which God sent to the sons of Israel preaching the good news *(euangelizomenos)* of peace through Jesus Christ' (10.36).[17] It is hardly likely that such usage was strange to Paul. On the contrary, Paul's formulation of the Christian message as 'gospel' took place during the period when the Jesus tradition was still predominantly in oral form. And the Acts 10 tradition also harks back to the period of oral tradition. So we may infer that *the shaping of the Jesus tradition as 'gospel'*, and in the shape that Mark was to provide (or consolidate), *was already beginning to take place during that period*

13. E.g. Rom. 12.14; 13.9; 16.19; 1 Cor. 9.4; 13.2; Gal. 5.14; Phil. 4.6; 1 Thess. 5.2, 13, 15.

14. E.g. Rom. 6.17; 15.3; Col. 2.6; Gal. 6.2. See further my *Christianity in the Making*, vol. 1, *Jesus Remembered* (Grand Rapids: Eerdmans, 2003) 181-84.

15. See further e.g. my 'Q[1] as Oral Tradition', in M. Bockmuehl and D. A. Hagner, eds., *The Written Gospel*, G. N. Stanton FS (Cambridge: Cambridge University Press, 2005) 45-69.

16. Mark 1.21-38 (twenty-four hours in the ministry of Jesus); 2.1–3.6 (Jesus in controversy in Galilee); 4.2-33 (parables of Jesus); 4.35–5.43 (miracles of Jesus round the lake); 10.2-31 (marriage, children and discipleship); 12.13-37 (Jesus in controversy in Jerusalem); 13.1-32 (the little apocalypse); 14.1-15 (the passion narrative). Mark 2.1–3.6 provides a good example of how one of the Twelve or an early disciple may have grouped a number (five) of *controversy stories* together to form a dramatic sequence culminating in a plot to do away with Jesus (3.6).

17. See further my *Christianity in the Making*, vol. 2, *Beginning from Jerusalem* (Grand Rapids: Eerdmans, 2009) #21.3c.

when the Jesus tradition was still being told in oral form. Certainly we should avoid the unjustified and misleading impression that the Jesus tradition existed orally only in fragmentary aphoristic forms or small collections of teaching material or of stories about Jesus.[18] Of course, Christian teachers variously combined their material for their teaching purposes. In which case it becomes entirely plausible that the earliest tradents regularly retold the Jesus tradition conscious of the 'gospel shape' of the material as a whole. And probably they often provided mini-Gospel presentations, as are still evident in the Acts 10 tradition, perhaps also in a pre-Markan block like Mark 2.1–3.6, as well as in the passion narrative.[19]

In short, if, as seems most probable, a body of Jesus tradition was part of the message Paul delivered to his converts, part of the foundation on which he sought to build his churches, it most naturally follows that Paul and his converts would have seen such material as at least complementary to the gospel, if not itself integral to the gospel.[20] We need not argue over terms used, but it is most likely that Paul thought of the information about Jesus and the passing on of the teaching of Jesus as integral to the process by which he became father of many new children 'through the gospel' (1 Cor. 4.15).

Thus the importance of what Paul did and of the influence he exercised in summarising his message as 'gospel' was not that he excluded the traditions of Jesus' mission and teaching from the gospel. Rather the importance of his use of that term is that he *centred* the decisive gospel significance of Jesus' mission on his death and resurrection. It was Mark's Gospel which took the next logical step of giving the title 'Gospel' to his account of Jesus' mission — 'Gospel' as an account which climaxed in Jesus' death and resurrection.

---

18. One of the key mistakes made by the Jesus Seminar; see my *Jesus Remembered* 245-48.

19. C. H. Dodd, *Historical Tradition in the Fourth Gospel* (Cambridge: Cambridge University Press, 1963), suggested that the transitional passages and topographical notices in John were 'traditional data summarizing periods in the ministry of Jesus, with indications of the places where they were spent' (243).

20. 'We should probably already presuppose this Christological connection of a narrative about Jesus and proclamation with the term *euangelion* in a large number of communities even before the composition of Mark's work' (M. Hengel, *Studies in the Gospel of Mark* [London: SCM, 1985] 54); Hengel goes on to attempt to detect a particular Petrine link informing Mark's use of *euangelion* (54-56).

The Gospel of Mark

I have already indicated the broad consensus in scholarship on the New Testament and earliest Christianity that Mark's Gospel is the earliest of the canonical Gospels to have been written. The consensus includes a large measure of agreement that Mark was most probably written either in the late 60s or early 70s. It was written possibly from Rome, or perhaps more likely in Syria, and in either case it reflected something of the crisis of the first Jewish revolt leading up to the destruction of the Jerusalem Temple in 70. Three features of Mark, the first Christian Gospel, call for immediate attention.

Mark's Use of Euangelion

It is an immediately intriguing consideration that Mark seems to have introduced the term *euangelion* into the Jesus tradition. He uses it seven times;[21] in contrast, Matthew uses it only four times,[22] and Luke and John do not use it at all.[23] What is notable is that Mark's use seems to be consistently his own — either his own use in narrative (1.1, 14), or as an addition to the forms of Jesus-tradition passed down to him.

- So, only Mark summarises Jesus' preaching as a call to 'repent and *believe in the gospel*' (Mark 1.15), whereas Matt. 4.17 has only the call to 'Repent'. Similarly, the mission of the disciples to preach the same message, that the kingdom of God has drawn near, calls only for repentance (Luke 10.1-16).
- Again, in the word which all three Synoptics share, that 'He who loses his life for my sake shall save it', only Mark inserts 'He who loses his life for my sake *and the gospel's* shall save it' (Mark 8.35 pars.).
- Likewise, in the promise to those who have left home and family 'for my sake', that they will receive a hundredfold, only Mark adds '*and for the sake of the gospel*' (Mark 10.29 pars.).

In these cases, the fact is clear that Matthew and Luke, as they drew on Mark, nevertheless omitted Mark's reference to the 'gospel', even when they stayed

---

21. Mark 1.1, 14, 15; 8.35; 10.29; 13.10; 14.9; also 16.15.
22. Matt. 4.23; 9.35; 24.14; 26.13.
23. Though Luke uses the verb, *euangelizesthai*, fairly frequently (ten times); John uses neither verb nor noun.

close to what Mark otherwise wrote. That fact is probably best explained by the hypothesis that Matthew and Luke were aware that the references to the 'gospel' had been added to the tradition, that is, were a peculiarity of Mark's version of the tradition.[24]

Only in two cases does Matthew follow Mark in attributing the term 'gospel' to Jesus himself. One is Mark 13.10 ('The gospel must first be proclaimed to all the nations'), followed by Matt. 24.14. However, it is generally agreed that the verse is a Markan interpretative addition to the 'little apocalypse' (Mark 13) in the light of the much more extensive Gentile mission already well under way.[25] The second is the story of the woman anointing Jesus in Mark 14. Both Mark and Matthew have Jesus affirming, 'Truly, I say to you, wherever the gospel is proclaimed in the whole world, what she has done will be told in remembrance of her' (Mark 14.9/Matt. 26.13). However, given Mark's predilection for the term 'gospel', it is more than likely that the usage here too betrays Mark's hand. In this case we may envisage Mark's own rendering of tradition which came to him (again reflecting the more universal character of the gospel already apparent in Mark's time). And Matthew this time simply followed suit.[26]

Notwithstanding the ambiguity of Mark 13.10 and 14.9, then, it is clear enough that *euangelion* is Mark's term which he has introduced into the Jesus tradition at several points.[27] In so doing, of course, and particularly in the case of Mark 14.9, Mark shows that in the circles where the Jesus tradition was known and cherished, *stories about Jesus and accounts of his preaching were thought of as part of the 'gospel'*.

Euangelion *as Gospel*

The second point which demands attention is the fact that Mark begins his Gospel with the words 'The beginning of the gospel of Jesus Christ *(archē tou euangeliou Iēsou Christou)*' (Mark 1.1). Here again the implication is clear: that it was entirely appropriate for Mark to use the term *euangelion* to refer not only to the preaching of the cross, but also to the account of Jesus' mission

---

24. See further my 'Matthew's Awareness of Markan Redaction', in F. Van Segbroeck, ed., *The Four Gospels: Festschrift for Frans Neirynck* (Leuven: Leuven University Press, 1992) 1349-59.

25. See further *Jesus Remembered* 435-36.

26. M. Casey, *Aramaic Sources of Mark's Gospel* (SNTSMS 102; Cambridge: Cambridge University Press, 1998), makes no effort to render Mark 13.10 and 14.9 back into Aramaic.

27. This was one of the major conclusions of the first redactional study of Mark — W. Marxsen, *Mark the Evangelist* (ET Nashville: Abingdon, 1969) 117-50.

and record of *his* preaching. It is not just that recollection of the Jesus tradition was complementary to the gospel as preached by Paul. The Jesus tradition here is itself *euangelion*.

But the significance of Mark 1.1 goes still further. For in this use of *euangelion* we probably see the transition from 'gospel' as Jesus tradition, 'details recounting the life and mission of Jesus', to 'Gospel' as 'a book dealing with the life and mission of Jesus'.[28] Here *euangelion* moves from 'content' of a message to the *book* which conveys the message. As the Jesus tradition is no longer conceived (if it ever was) as supplementary to the gospel, but as gospel itself, so the writing which contains the Jesus tradition is not to be regarded as merely a container of the gospel, but is itself the Gospel. Almost consciously and deliberately, Mark in effect was introducing a new genre to the literature of the ancient world. This is no longer simply a biography *(bios)* of a great man, but a *Gospel*, the account of a particular man's mission which made salvation possible, a book which itself is a means to salvation. It is Mark who, whether knowingly or intentionally or not, made the transition from 'gospel' to 'Gospel'.[29]

This development should not be seen as some sort of radical departure from the oral gospel tradition. As already noted, such a thesis was argued by Werner Kelber when he drew fresh attention to the oral gospel.[30] The thesis was unfortunate since it obscured the importance of what he was saying about the oral phase of the Jesus tradition and its character as oral. But there is no reason to press for such a sharp transition between oral and written. On the contrary, there is much to be said for regarding Mark's Gospel as a natural development of the oral phase. Almost certainly it was written not for an individual to read privately, but for an audience to hear being read aloud.[31] It uses the

---

28. So in effect BAGD 403; see further L. E. Keck, 'The Introduction to Mark's Gospel', *NTS* 12 (1966) 352-70 (358-60), and particularly R. Guelich, 'The Gospel Genre', in P. Stuhlmacher, ed., *Das Evangelium und die Evangelien* (WUNT 28; Tübingen: Mohr Siebeck, 1983) 183-219 (here 204-16). See also R. A. Burridge, *What Are the Gospels? A Comparison with Graeco-Roman Biography* (Grand Rapids: Eerdmans, ²2004) 186-89.

29. Hengel, *Studies* 82-83; 'It is likely that the practice of referring to the four works as "Gospels" ultimately derives from Mark' (A. Y. Collins, *Mark* [Hermeneia; Minneapolis: Fortress, 2007] 3).

30. Kelber, *The Oral and the Written Gospel* (Philadelphia: Fortress, 1983): for example, 'the gospel signals a disruption of the oral synthesis' (92); it constituted an 'indictment of oral process and authorities', an 'alienation from the oral apparatus', 'emancipation from oral identity'; Mark 'repudiates oral representatives' (98).

31. As Hengel pointed out in the same year — *Studies* 52: 'The Second Gospel probably developed out of living oral teaching and was composed for solemn reading in worship. The short cola, often with a rhythmic shape, point to oral recitation in the assembled community. The Gos-

same tricks and techniques of the oral performance of tradition.[32] It was in effect a written version of an oral recitation of Jesus tradition. An important corollary should not be missed: that what a whole generation of scholars has regarded as (literary) redaction was in the first instance little more than the variation which different oral teachers would give to the tradition they were teaching, to bring out its relevance to the situation of the particular audience. In Mark's Gospel, of course, the variation and application were no doubt more sustained through what was in effect a very full performance of the tradition. But at least it is important to be aware that any redactional adaptation of earlier tradition was not part of some fundamental transition from oral to written, but something most congregations would be familiar with from long experience of the Jesus tradition being celebrated and expounded.

A Passion Narrative with an Extended Introduction

It was Martin Kähler who, in a famous note, described the Gospels as 'passion narratives with extended introductions'.[33] This description was particularly apposite for Mark, the earliest written Gospel.

- The basic fact is that the passion narrative, covering the last week of Jesus' life and the discovery of his empty tomb (Mark 11.1–16.8), takes up more than one-third of the Gospel of Mark.
- Mark's Gospel is structured so that Peter's confession of Jesus as Messiah near Caesarea Philippi (8.27-30) is the centre and turning point of the Gospel. It is both the geographical turning point (the region is the most northerly point of Jesus' mission in the Galilee) and the dramatic turning point in the Gospel (thereafter Jesus heads south towards Jerusalem and his destiny there).
- The point is marked by the first of Jesus' explicit teachings on the necessity of his suffering (8.31), a passion prediction which is repeated starkly two more times in the following chapters (9.31; 10.33-34).

pel was written for the audience to listen to . . .' (52); though Hengel also speaks of 'the revolutionary innovation of writing a gospel' (52).

32. See particularly J. Dewey, 'Oral Methods of Structuring Narrative in Mark', *Interpretation* 43 (1989) 32-44; also 'The Gospel of Mark as an Oral-Aural Event: Implications for Interpretation', in E. S. Malbon and E. V. McKnight, eds., *The New Literary Criticism and the New Testament* (JSNTS 109; Sheffield: Sheffield Academic, 1994) 145-63.

33. M. Kähler, *The So-Called Historical Jesus and the Historic Biblical Christ* (1896; Philadelphia: Fortress, 1964) 80 n. 11.

- The thrust of Mark's strategy is clear from the allusions to and foreshadowings of Jesus' death from early on in his Gospel.
  - Jesus likens his mission to the bridegroom's presence at the wedding feast, when fasting is inappropriate. But then he adds, 'The days will come when the bridegroom is taken away from them, and then they will fast' (2.20).
  - Mark concludes a sequence of adversity stories (2.1–3.5): 'The Pharisees went out and immediately conspired with the Herodians against him, how to destroy him' (3.6) — a decision to do away with Jesus which comes surprisingly early in Mark's narrative.
  - The account of the summary execution of John the Baptist, Jesus' precursor, is surprisingly lengthy and rather ominous (6.17-29).
  - In the buildup to the passion narrative itself, we should note also Jesus' talk of his having to drink the cup (of suffering) and to be baptised with a baptism of death (the image of being drowned) (10.38-39).
  - The parable of the tenants of the vineyard climaxes in the tenants killing the son and heir of the vineyard owner (12.1-9), and the rejected stone testimony is added (12.10-11; Ps. 118.22-23). The addition is probably earlier than Mark himself,[34] as also the conclusion that the parable incited more virulent opposition to Jesus (Mark 12.12).
  - The ominous predictions of suffering, persecution and death for Jesus' followers (13.9-13) imply a fate consequent upon similar rejection of Jesus himself.
  - Note also the anointing of Jesus' body by the woman in Bethany, 'beforehand for its burial' (14.8); Jesus' prediction of his betrayal (14.18-20); and the institution of the Lord's Supper, betokening a broken body and spilled blood (14.22-24).
  - On the Mount of Olives Jesus warns of the imminent striking of the shepherd (14.27), and in the garden of Gethsemane the anguish of anticipation of an agonising death is briefly sketched in stark terms (14.33-36).

In calling his life of Jesus a 'Gospel', Mark, then, was not leaving behind Paul's understanding of why the message about Jesus counted as 'gospel'. On the contrary, by climaxing his account of Jesus' mission with the passion narrative he reinforced Paul's point. The good news of Jesus was primarily the good news of his death and resurrection. The message about Jesus was good

---

34. Dunn, *Jesus Remembered* #23 at n. 97.

news, not simply because of his teaching and not because he was a great healer and miracle-worker, but because his death and resurrection brought forgiveness of sins and life from the dead.

At the same time, however, by naming the account of *the whole of Jesus' mission,* and not just his death and resurrection, as *Gospel,* Mark ensured that the two could not be pulled apart. The point of Jesus' mission could not be grasped apart from his death and resurrection; but neither could the full significance of Jesus' death and resurrection be grasped outside the context of his mission as a whole. To treasure Jesus' mission apart from his death and resurrection would be to misappropriate it. But to treasure the account of Jesus' death and resurrection apart from his mission as a whole would be equally to misappreciate it. The gospel of Jesus' passion was the central but not the only part of the Gospel of the mission of the Galilean who proclaimed and lived out his message of the kingdom of God.

Mark's Particular Emphases in His Retelling the Gospel

Within this passion-climaxed Gospel Mark makes several distinctive points.

For Mark, Jesus is particularly 'the Son of God'.

- This is the voice which Jesus hears when he is baptised by John: 'You are my beloved Son, with you I am well pleased' (Mark 1.11).
- The unclean spirits also hail him, 'You are the Son of God' (3.11); as does the Gerasene demoniac, 'Jesus, Son of the Most High God' (5.7).
- On the Mount of Transfiguration, the heavenly voice announces, 'This is my Son, the beloved, listen to him' (9.7), echoing the promise of a prophet like Moses in Deut. 18.15.
- In the parable of the dishonest tenants, the vineyard owner finally sends his 'beloved son' (Mark 12.6).
- In the hearing before the council, Jesus' fate is sealed by his affirmative reply to the high priest's question, 'Are you the Messiah, the Son of the Blessed?' (14.61-62).
- Most strikingly of all, Mark's Gospel climaxes with the confession of the Roman centurion who has just seen the crucified Jesus breathe his last: 'Truly this man was God's Son' (15.39).

We should at once add that Mark headlines his whole Gospel as 'the Gospel of Jesus Christ' (1.1). And he may have added, 'of Jesus Christ, the Son of God'. That last phrase ('the Son of God'), it is true, is not present in some of the earliest manuscripts of Mark. So it was probably added by later scribes.[35] But if so, it must be because they recognised how central was the theme of Jesus as 'the Son of God' to Mark's Gospel. In other words, those who added the phrase may simply have brought out more clearly and explicitly what was already quite clear for those who read Mark's Gospel carefully.

The point is, once again, that for Mark Jesus is not to be understood as God's Son as one might speak of a king or a great philosopher as a son of God. Jesus' sonship is attested by heaven as a special sonship — 'my Son, the beloved'. Nor is Jesus' sonship to be understood as one might understand the sonship of Hanina ben Dosa or Honi the Circle-Drawer — as one whose prayers had special effect. Jesus' sonship for Mark is as one condemned to death. The superb irony for Mark is that it is the Roman centurion who is the only human being who confesses Jesus as God's Son. And the one he confesses as God's Son has just died on a cross (15.39).

This brings into prominence another facet of Mark's Gospel. I refer to the fact that the first half of the Gospel is largely dominated by accounts of Jesus' very effective healing and miracle-working mission. It is only in the second half that we begin to hear, but to hear repeatedly, of Jesus' expected suffering, with the climax in the account of Jesus' passion. In the middle decades of the twentieth century this encouraged several scholars to argue that Mark so organised his Gospel to correct what he regarded as a lopsided and misleading presentation of Jesus simply as one who spoke with divine authority and executed extraordinary miracles, what is sometimes described as a 'divine man' *(theios anēr)* Christ.[36] That is, when Mark presents Peter as confessing Jesus to be the Messiah, Mark immediately goes on to show that Jesus spoke of his imminent suffering (8.29-31). And that when Peter protested, Jesus even denounced Peter as the mouthpiece of Satan (8.32-33). In other words, the implication may be that Peter was confessing Jesus as a triumphalist Messiah, the one who, according to popular hope, would soon liberate Israel from Roman domination (as in *Pss. Sol.* 17.21-24). On this thesis, then, the function of the intense focus on Jesus as the son of man who must suffer and be rejected was precisely to correct such views of Jesus which may have still been circulating, on the basis of the miracles which he wrought and the authority with which he taught.

I am less convinced by this argument. But what we can say is that Mark's

35. See e.g. Collins, *Mark* 130.

36. See T. J. Weeden, *Mark: Traditions in Conflict* (Philadelphia: Fortress, 1971) 52-69; but R. T. France, *The Gospel of Mark* (NIGTC; Grand Rapids: Eerdmans, 2002), justifiably notes that the concept of the *theios anēr* is more like a twentieth-century construct than a category recognised in the first century (21).

account of Jesus' response to the Caesarea Philippi confession of Peter was a way of shifting the focus from Jesus as Messiah to Jesus as the suffering Son of Man. This strategy presumably included a shift from any claim that the significance of Jesus was to be assessed in terms of the extent to which Jesus had fulfilled the popular hope for a military leader who would liberate Israel from Roman domination. Jesus' significance as Messiah and Son of Man could not be appreciated without reference to his death and resurrection.

A further important motif in Mark's Gospel is the failure of Jesus' disciples to understand him.[37] This is part of what has been traditionally known in Markan scholarship as 'the Messianic secret', a motif which fascinated scholars of the Gospels for most of the twentieth century.[38] This motif is to be seen most clearly in episodes when Jesus, having healed someone, at once instructs the healed person to tell no one about it — that is, to keep Jesus' healing success a secret.[39] Whether Mark introduced the motif or simply highlighted a facet of the Jesus tradition as it came to him, the point of the motif is clear. It is that a false impression of Jesus could easily arise from what he did. Even Jesus' disciples were unable to understand Jesus when still in the midst of his mission. They could not understand him until they had witnessed the completion of his mission, that is, until he had been killed and raised again from the dead. Recognition of this is what points to Mark 9.9 as a key to the motif: during the descent from the Mount of Transfiguration Jesus ordered his disciples 'to tell no one about what they had seen, until after the Son of Man had risen from the dead' (9.9). Once again, the key to understanding Jesus' mission, including his messianic status, was to be found only in his death and resurrection. As much as with Paul, so with Mark, Jesus' death and resurrection were the heart of the gospel, what made Jesus' whole mission 'good news'.

The Date and Circumstances in Which Mark Was Written

As already noted, the date of Mark's writing is usually estimated to be in the late 60s or early 70s. This of course would set Mark in the period of the Jewish revolt (66-70) or immediately afterwards. Without going into all the considerations, there is one verse in Mark's Gospel which above all others may provide the key. The verse is Mark 13.14: 'When you see the desolating sacrilege set up where it ought not to be (let the reader understand), then those in Judea must

---

37. Mark 4.13; 6.52; 7.18; 8.17, 21; 9.5-6, 32.
38. W. Wrede, *The Messianic Secret* (1901; ET Cambridge: James Clarke, 1971).
39. Mark 1.25, 34, 44; 3.12; 5.43; 7.24, 36; note also 8.30 and 9.9.

flee to the mountains'. There is a strong possibility that the wording reflects the earlier crisis caused by the emperor Gaius Caligula's insistence on his statue being erected within the Temple (in 39). But the note to the reader ('let the reader understand') looks like a Markan insertion, an instruction to the one who would be responsible for reading the Gospel to an assembled congregation. In which case, it is certainly plausible that the Gospel was written sometime after the start of the Jewish revolt against Rome, presumably after the murderous factions within the revolt had seized the Temple and in effect desecrated it by their bloodthirsty tactics. Joel Marcus, for example, observes that the prediction of 'false messiahs and false prophets' who 'produce signs and omens' and lead astray others (13.22) well reflects the circumstances recorded by Josephus in the buildup to the Jewish revolt and during the revolt itself.[40] And he refers to the use of the word 'brigands' in Jesus' 'cleaning of the temple' — 'you have made it a den of brigands *(lēstōn)*' (11.17) — noting that 'brigands' was 'Josephus' term of opprobrium for the revolutionaries who in his view hijacked the Jewish people into the disastrous conflict with the Romans'.[41] These suggestions would fit with what is known as the Pella tradition, that is, the early Christian tradition that the believers in Jerusalem fled from the city and crossed the Jordan to the Perean city of Pella before the Roman legions made that impossible.[42] That would suggest a date for the writing of the Gospel in 68 or 69, perhaps during the 'wars and rumours of wars' (13.7) following the death of Emperor Nero and before Vespasian was able to establish his authority.[43]

Alternatively, it is hardly implausible to envisage the Gospel being written in the wake of the revolt, while Jewish (and Christian?) communities within the Roman Empire were still reeling at the outcome.[44] The Gospel's stress on the suffering which disciples of Jesus could expect to endure (8.34-37; 13.9-13) could equally reflect that situation. And in those circumstances, 13.14 would serve as a comfort and reassurance that Jesus had predicted the destruction of the Temple so clearly.

All this suggests in turn a close knowledge of the Jewish revolt and its antecedents shared by the writer and the recipients of the Gospel — that is,

---

40. J. Marcus, 'The Jewish War and the *Sitz im Leben* of Mark', *JBL* 111 (1992) 441-62 (here 457-59), referring to Josephus, *War* 2.433-434, 444, 652; 6.313; 7.29-31.

41. J. Marcus, *Mark 1-8* (AB 27; New York: Doubleday, 2000) 35.

42. Eusebius, *Ecclesiastical History* 3.5.3; Epiphanius, *Refutation of All Heresies* 29.7.7-8; 30.2.7; *Treatise on Weights and Measures* 15.

43. Hengel, *Studies* 28; R. A. Guelich, *Mark 1-8:26* (WBC 34A; Dallas: Word, 1989) xxxi-xxxii; Collins, *Mark* 13-14.

44. Josephus records further attempts to foster revolt in the Jewish communities of Alexandria and Cyrene (*War* 7.409-419, 437-441).

somewhere close to the land of Israel, probably Syria. Our knowledge of Christian communities in Israel-Syria during and immediately after the war is almost nonexistent. But it is certainly plausible to allow the possibility that someone who had endured some of the early hardships of the revolt wrote his Gospel for the benefit of Jesus-Messianists who were still in Judea and when his note to the reader in 13.14 would still have relevance. Or, alternatively in the wider region of Syria, when there would be many readers or auditors who had experienced the war and who resonated with its warnings and encouragement.

The Gospels of Matthew and Luke

a. One of the most striking features of the Gospels of Matthew and Luke,[45] as has been well appreciated for more than a century, is that they are heavily dependent on Mark's Gospel. As already pointed out, I strongly caution against seeing the interdependence of the Synoptic Gospels in exclusively literary terms. Nevertheless, the near identical wording of much of the tradition which Matthew and Luke share with Mark is most obviously to be explained by the very strong probability that Matthew and Luke had the written Gospel of Mark to hand when they composed their Gospels.[46] They evidently composed their own Gospels either by interweaving other Jesus tradition with Mark or by using Mark as a framework for their own Gospels. This includes, preeminently, the fact that in doing so *they took over the character of 'Gospel' which Mark's structure established* — a passion narrative with an extended introduction.

We find this to be the case when we look at Matthew and Luke. They not only take over Mark's structure; they also take over the turning point of Peter's confession,[47] the passion predictions,[48] the correction of any inferences drawn too easily from Jesus' miracles, and the various foreshadowings of Jesus' final sufferings and death.[49] These are not simply cases of 'copy and paste'. But the very fact that Matthew and Luke follow Mark's pattern so closely, even when using the Jesus tradition in their own way or using other versions of Jesus tradition known to them, underlines the commitment Matthew and Luke in ef-

---

45. The major consensus dates these Gospels ten to twenty years after Mark's. Within the space constraints of the present study, I will be able to deal with them only briefly.

46. Dunn, *Jesus Remembered* ##4.4, 7.3.

47. Matt. 16.13-20; Luke 9.18-21.

48. Matt. 16.21; 17.22-23; 20.18; Luke 9.22, 44; 18.32-33.

49. Mark 2.20 pars.; 3.6 pars.; 6.17-29 par. (not Luke); 10.38-39 pars.; 12.6-12 pars.; 13.9-13 pars.; 14.8 par. (Luke has a different version); 14.18-20, 22-24 pars.; 14.27 par. (not Luke); 14.33-36 pars.

fect took upon themselves — that is, *a commitment to use Mark's Gospel genre* for their own retelling the story of Jesus and to follow the pattern of Mark's buildup of his Gospel to the climax of Jesus' death and resurrection.

Integral to this compositional plan was the incorporation of the Q material into the framework provided by Mark. The non-Markan material shared by Matthew and Luke, we recall, is commonly designated as Q, on the hypothesis that Matthew and Luke were both able to draw on a second source, that is, on the same source. The argument, we may also recall, is on whether the Q material was drawn from a written document. I have pointed out that the similar feature of nearly identical Q passages in Matthew and Luke indicates a similar conclusion as regards the near-identical passages when Mark is involved. That is, the likelihood is that some of the Q material was already in Greek and already in writing when Matthew and Luke drew on it. But I have also pointed out in chapter 2 that the equally common feature of shared material which is quite diverse and far from being nearly identical points away from Matthew and Luke being dependent on a written Q source. The more likely solution to the conundrum of shared but very diversely worded tradition is that there were various oral versions of Jesus tradition circulating among the early churches and that in such passages Matthew and Luke knew and used diverse versions of the same tradition.

The point here, however, is that the Q material, when disentangled from Matthew and Luke, can*not* be described as 'a passion narrative with an extended introduction'. It does not have a passion narrative. The Q material consists almost exclusively of Jesus' teaching. Moreover, the Q material lacks almost all the various structural features and foreshadowings of the passion narrative which are such a feature of Mark. Some indeed argue that the hypothesised Q document expressed a Christology different from and antithetical to Mark's passion Gospel. I remain unconvinced.[50] The Q material is better seen as varied collections of Jesus tradition serving as the repertoire for teachers responsible for preserving the Jesus tradition and for instructing gatherings of believers in that tradition of Jesus' mission and teaching. The Q

50. See my *Jesus Remembered* 147-60.

51. Notably Matt. 10.38/Luke 14.27 ('whoever does not take up his cross and follow me cannot be my disciple'); Matt. 23.37-39/Luke 13.34-35 and Matt. 23.34-36/Luke 11.49-51 (the implication that Jesus is included among the 'prophets and messengers' killed); Matt. 5.11-12/Luke 6.22-23 (similarly, suffering as the lot of disciples as of prophets). See further J. Kloppenborg Verbin, *Excavating Q: The History and Setting of the Sayings Gospel* (Minneapolis: Fortress, 2000) 369-74.

52. Matt. 10.32/Luke 12.8; Matt. 23.37-39/Luke 13.34-35. See further Kloppenborg Verbin, *Excavating Q* 374-79.

tradition contains some allusions to Jesus' death[51] and vindication.[52] However, the allusions fit well with material which served a different function from proclamation of the gospel but which was complementary to proclamation focused on Jesus' death and resurrection.

The key fact, however, is that *in Matthew and Luke the Q material is encased within the structure provided by Mark.* In Matthew and Luke the Q tradition becomes part of a fuller version of the account of Jesus' mission climaxing in his passion. Moreover, the Q material was evidently not retained independently, as a single, coherent block, by the churches which Matthew and Luke represent and for whom they wrote their Gospels. In the Christian church-life which picks up from one or more of the canonical Gospels, there is subsequently no hint that a Q document, distinct from the Gospels, was valued. Knowledge of oral Jesus tradition is still clear, but there is no evidence of a document consisting solely of Jesus' teaching being cherished as such in such churches.

These findings yield important conclusions:

- First, it was only as held within the framework of a story of Jesus' mission climaxing in his death and resurrection that the tradition of Jesus' teaching was preserved in the mainstream Christian churches.
- Second, in these churches it was only as held within Mark's passion framework that Jesus' teaching was retained and valued as itself 'gospel', as part of the Gospel.
- Third, if the Markan framework, taken over by Matthew and Luke, determines and defines what is a Gospel, then it is *inappropriate and misleading to speak of Q, the hypothesised Q document, as a Gospel.*
- It also follows that other documents which have appeared from within the milieu of early Christianity, documents which contain only teachings attributed to Jesus, have too casually been entitled 'Gospel' — the *Gospel of Thomas,* the *Gospel of Judas,* etc. Mark's Gospel not only begins the new genre of 'Gospel', but also defines what may be properly called 'Gospel'. And it is not simply collections of teaching. If we follow Mark, as early Christianity did, only an account of Jesus' mission and teaching which climaxes in the passion narrative of his death and resurrection should be called a 'Gospel'.

b. Equally striking about *the Gospel of Matthew* is that it slants its own version of the Gospel to take part in what was evidently an ongoing debate with the Judaism which survived the disaster of the destruction of Jerusalem and its Temple — the rabbinic Judaism which came to clearest expression in the Mishnah some generations later (c. 200). Such a dispute between Matthean Christianity and the post-70 rabbis is strongly suggested by Matt. 23 — Jesus' trenchant denunciation of 'scribes and Pharisees' for what is clearly regarded as their wrong and false priorities. The point to be noted, however, is that the Jesus of Matthew engages in much more constructive debate and argument with the Pharisees than the Jesus of the other Synoptic Gospels.

Matthew was evidently concerned to demonstrate his (and his community's) *loyalty to the Torah*. To the Pharisees with whom he was in conflict, Jesus says in effect, We are as loyal to the law as you: 'Do not think that I have come to abolish the law or the prophets; I have not come to abolish but to fulfill. For truly I tell you, until heaven and earth pass away, not one letter, not one yodh, will pass from the law until all is accomplished. Therefore, whoever breaks one of the least of these commandments, and teaches others to do the same, will be called least in the kingdom of heaven; but whoever does them and teaches them will be called great in the kingdom of heaven' (Matt. 5.17-19). Indeed, the claim is that the followers of Jesus are *more* devoted to what the law demands. For example:

- In the same paragraph, Jesus continues: 'For I tell you, unless your righteousness exceeds that of the scribes and Pharisees, you will never enter the kingdom of heaven' (5.20).
- So in the rest of chapter 5, Jesus goes on to penetrate below the wording of various commandments to their deeper meaning. The commandment against murder is more fully to be understood as a warning against anger and insult and denigration of a brother (5.21-22); the commandment against adultery is more fully to be understood as a warning against lust (5.27-28).
- Like Hillel, the Matthean Jesus is ready to sum up the law in a single word — 'In everything do to others what you would have them do to you' (7.12) — a positive version of 'the golden rule', where Hillel's was a negative form. Similarly, like Mark, Matthew depicts Jesus as summing up the law and the prophets by referring to the Shema ('You shall love the Lord your God with all your heart, and with all your soul, and with all your mind'), and by pulling out Lev. 19.18 from the sequence of commandments in Lev. 19 ('You shall love your neighbour as yourself') to give it a unique primacy: 'On these two commandments hang all the law and the prophets' (Matt. 22.37-40).
- In Matt. 15.1-20 Matthew takes up the same tradition as Mark, where Jesus teaches about purity, that the impurity of the heart is more serious

than the impurity of the hands. But where Mark infers from this that Jesus thus abolished the distinction between clean and unclean foods (Mark 7.15, 19), Matthew simply underlines that inner cleanliness is much more important than the cleanliness of some foods (Matt. 15.17-20).

- Matthew's version of Jesus' teaching on divorce is also significant. In Mark 10.1-9 Jesus seems to deny the legitimacy of divorce, and thus overrules the Mosaic ruling which permits divorce (Deut. 24.1-4). In Matthew, however, Jesus' teaching is presented as a contribution to the debate about how Deut. 24.1, 3 should be interpreted (Matt. 19.3-9). The Matthean Jesus in effect participates in the debate between the schools of Hillel and Shammai, and seems to side with the more rigorous Shammaite ruling, that divorce is only permitted in the case of adultery.

- In the denunciation of 'scribes and Pharisees' in Matt. 23, Jesus commands his followers to 'do whatever they teach you and follow it; but do not do as they do, for they do not practise what they preach' (23.3). And later his denunciation is that the scribes and Pharisees 'tithe mint, dill, and cumin, and have neglected the weightier matters of the law: justice, mercy and faith. It is these you ought to have practised without neglecting the others' (23.23) — a prophetic word very much in the spirit of Amos and Micah.

- In the same vein we should note that only in Matthew does Jesus quote Hos. 6.6, and does so twice: 'Go and learn what this means, "I desire mercy, not sacrifice"' (Matt. 9.13; also 12.7).

- A final example is the addition Matthew makes to the warning of Mark 13.18, 'Pray that the catastrophe may not happen in winter'. Matthew's version reads, 'Pray that it may not happen in winter or on a Sabbath' (Matt. 24.20). Clearly implied is the fact that the Matthean community continued to observe the Sabbath; Jesus had not called for the Sabbath law to be abrogated.

A striking feature of Matthew's Gospel at this point is his use of two words distinctive of his own vocabulary. He is the only Gospel writer to speak of *anomia*, 'lawlessness'.[53] Clearly this is Matthew's own word. In warning against 'lawlessness', as Jesus does in these passages, Matthew was clearly proclaiming Jesus' loyalty to the law, and his own and the gospel's loyalty to the law at the same time. Almost as distinctive of Matthew's vocabulary is his use

53. Matt. 7.23; 13.41; 23.28; 24.12.
54. Matt. 3.15; 5.6, 10, 20; 6.1, 33; 21.32.

of the word 'righteousness', *dikaiosunē*.[54] Note again 5.20: 'Unless your righteousness exceeds that of the scribes and Pharisees, you will never enter the kingdom of heaven'.

Equally worthy of note is the way Matthew presents Jesus as a new Moses, or as the fulfilment of Israel's divinely intended purpose.

- The infant Jesus is spared from the murderous wrath of King Herod (Matt. 2.16-18), just as the infant Moses had been saved from the murderous command of the pharaoh (Exod. 1–2).
- Jesus' return from Egypt is understood by Matthew as a fulfilment of Hos. 11.1 — 'Out of Egypt have I called my son'.
- The temptation of Jesus in the wilderness after his forty-day fast is interpreted by reference to passages from Deut. 6 and 8, evoking the parallel with Israel's wilderness wanderings.
- Only Matthew gathers Jesus' various teachings into five blocks or sermons, the first (the Sermon on the Mount) when he had gone up a mountain, presumably in some echo of the five books of Moses.[55]
- On a broader scale we might simply note the repeated 'fulfilment of scripture' theme in Matthew. Things happen to Jesus and Jesus acts again and again 'in order that what had been said (by Moses or one or more of the prophets) might be fulfilled'.[56]

All this suggests a Gospel written where rabbinic Judaism was already well established and growing in influence. Most think this favours an origin in mixed Jewish/Christian communities in Syria, probably about 90.

We should note, then, that Matthew's taking over of the Gospel format from Mark did not mean that he saw the gospel of Jesus as set in antithesis to the law. Matthew would not have welcomed the antithesis between gospel and law which the Lutheran Reformation read too quickly into Paul. And he certainly would not have welcomed the suggestion that Christianity had abandoned its Jewish heritage. The Gospel for him was a thoroughly Jewish gospel — entirely in the spirit of the law and the prophets. There was disagreement between Jesus' followers and the rabbis on how the law and the prophets should be interpreted. But there was a basic agreement with the rabbis that the law and the prophets were central. And the clear implication is that the gospel, like Jesus himself, was in direct continuity with the law

---

55. The blocks are marked by the repeated ending, 'When Jesus had finished these words/instructing/parables' (7.28; 11.1; 13.53; 19.1; 26.1).

56. Matt. 1.22-23; 2.5-6, 15, 17-18, 23; 4.14-16; 5.17; 8.17; 12.17; 13.35; 21.4; 26.54, 56; 27.9.

and the prophets, and should be understood as fulfilment of the law and the prophets. To make this clear was evidently one of the prime purposes of Matthew's Gospel.

c. *The Gospel of Luke* has many interesting features. Here, as with Matthew, I focus particularly on the positive continuity between Israel and the gospel which Luke sought to make clear. But as in other aspects of Luke's theology, we need to bear in mind that Luke wrote two books, and that he saw them as closely connected. Moreover, it is sufficiently clear that when he wrote his Gospel, Luke already had the intention to write a second volume. That is to say, he did not intend his Gospel to be complete in itself, as we might say Mark and Matthew saw their Gospels as complete in themselves. Rather Luke saw his two volumes as two parts of the one story. So he began his second volume by referring to his first volume (his 'first word') as the narrative of 'what Jesus began to do and teach' (Acts 1.1). The point is that themes and motifs run through both volumes. Their development is only half-completed by the end of the Gospel. Consequently, if we are to fully appreciate Luke's concern to draw out the continuity between Israel's expectations and the gospel about Jesus, we cannot stay with the Gospel alone and must be prepared to trace it on into the Acts of the Apostles.

We see the importance of this more or less immediately in the opening chapters of the Gospel.

- The narrative in these chapters begins and ends in the Jerusalem Temple (Luke 1.5-23; 2.25-50).
- The chief characters are entirely admirable in terms of Jewish piety: particularly, Zechariah, the father of John the Baptist, descended from Aaron, 'righteous before God, living blamelessly according to all the commandments and regulations of the Lord' (1.5-6); Mary, mother of Jesus, highly favoured by God (1.30); Simeon, 'righteous and devout, looking forward to the consolation of Israel' (2.25); and Anna, who 'never left the Temple but worshipped there with fasting and prayer night and day' (2.37).
- The songs sung by Mary and Zechariah are typical of traditional Jewish piety. Mary's song, the Magnificat (Luke 1.46-55), is modeled closely on Hannah's prayer in 1 Sam. 2.1-10. It ends with the words:

> He has helped his servant Israel, in remembrance of his mercy,
> according to the promise he made to our fathers,
> to Abraham and to his descendants together.

Likewise the song of Zechariah, the Benedictus (Luke 1.68-79), echoes psalmist and prophet in every line. For example,

> Thus he has shown the mercy promised to our fathers,
> and has remembered his holy covenant, the oath that he swore
>   to our father Abraham. . . .
> [John the Baptist] will go before the Lord to prepare his ways,
> to give knowledge of salvation to his people by the forgiveness
>   of their sins.

- Likewise Simeon in his prayer, the Nunc Dimittis (Luke 2.29-32), praises God for the salvation which he has seen in the child Jesus, the salvation 'which you have prepared in the presence of all peoples, a light for revelation to the Gentiles and for the glory of your people Israel'. The echo of Isaiah's commission of the Servant — 'I have given you as a covenant to the people, a light to the nations' (Isa. 42.6); 'I will put salvation in Zion, for Israel my glory' (Isa. 46.13); 'I will give you as a light to the nations, that my salvation may reach to the end of the earth' (Isa. 49.6) — is certainly deliberate and foreshadows the consistent thrust Luke maintains through his two volumes.
- In his Gospel Luke gives particular emphasis to two of the themes of Jesus' mission present in the Jesus tradition which he received — first, Jesus' mission as mission to and for 'sinners' *(hamartōloi)*.[57] It is striking that he makes so much of Jesus' protest against the categorisation (by Pharisees?) of fellow Jews as 'sinners'. He makes a point of Jesus' acceptance and forgiveness of a woman whom his Pharisaic host disowns as a 'sinner' (Luke 7.39-50). And he introduces the three parables of lost sheep, lost coin, and lost son by noting that 'sinners' drew near to listen to Jesus in the face of the criticism of Pharisees and scribes that 'This man welcomes sinners and eats with them' (15.1-2).[58]
- Equally significant is the added emphasis Luke gives to Jesus' mission to and for 'the poor' *(ptōchoi)*.[59] Here a feature particularly worth noting is the repeated emphasis in Luke 14.13, 21 that those to be invited to the banquet of the new age are 'the poor, the crippled, the lame and the blind'. The language echoes the list of those who are excluded from the priestly community of Qumran[60] — and echoes it so closely that it

---

57. Luke 5.8, 30, 32; 7.34, 37, 39; 15.1-2, 7, 10; 18.13; 19.7.

58. I return to this and the following feature in chapter 5 below.

59. Luke 4.18 (citing Isa. 61.1); 6.20 and 7.22 (echoing Isa. 61.1); 14.13, 21; 16.20, 22; 18.22; 19.8; 21.3.

60. 1Q28a 2.3-10; 1QM 7.4-6; 4QCD⁶; 11QT 45.12-14.

must be regarded as probable that Luke recalls Jesus as rejecting such exclusion from the divine presence. Neither sinners nor the disabled are to be treated as unfit to feast with the saints and worship with the angels.

- Like Mark, Luke emphasises that the gospel comes to focus in Jesus' suffering and death. Like Mark, he stresses that Jesus fulfilled the role purposed for him by his suffering and death. In the encounter of two disciples with the risen Jesus, the two disciples express their disappointed hope 'that Jesus was the one to redeem Israel' (Luke 24.21). But Jesus responds by pointing to the scriptures, the law, the prophets and the psalms, which forewarn 'that the Messiah is to suffer and to rise from the dead on the third day' (24.46). And the theme of Jesus' suffering and vindication becomes a major theme in the sermons in Acts,[61] in fulfilment of the divine purpose.[62] Typical is the account of Paul's mission in Greece, 'explaining and proving (from the scriptures) that it was necessary for the Messiah to suffer and to rise from the dead' (Acts 17.2-3).
- Luke's second volume begins with the disciples asking the risen Jesus, 'Lord, is this the time when you will restore the kingdom to Israel?' (Acts 1.6), a concern which Jesus does not dismiss. And it ends with Paul claiming that 'it is for the hope of Israel' that he has been imprisoned (28.20).
- In the conclusion of Peter's first sermon in Jerusalem, Peter says the promise (of the Spirit from the Father God) is 'for you, for your children, and for all who are far off, everyone whom the Lord our God calls to him' (2.39). Those who are 'far off' are probably the Jews of the diaspora, and the echo is of Isa. 57.19.
- In his second sermon Peter looks for 'times of refreshing' to come from God and 'the time of universal restoration' that God announced through the prophets (Acts 3.20-21). He goes on to identify Jesus as the prophet like Moses promised by Moses (Deut. 18.15-20; Acts 3.22-23). And he concludes by reminding the Jerusalemites that 'You are the descendants of the prophets and of the covenant that God gave to your fathers, saying to Abraham, "And in your descendants all the families of the earth shall be blessed"' (Gen. 12.3; Acts 3.25).
- In Acts 10–11 Peter learns that the laws of clean and unclean do not mean that he should regard any person as profane or unclean (10.28).
- Finally we should note how James, the brother of Jesus, and leader of

---

61. Acts 2.23-24; 3.14-15; 4.10; 5.30; 8.32-33; 10.39-40; 13.28-30.
62. Acts 2.23; 3.18; 17.3.

the Jesus messianists in Jerusalem, resolves the problem of the increasing number of non-Jews who were coming to faith in Messiah Jesus, but without being circumcised. He resolves the problem in two steps. First, he quotes from Amos 9.11-12:

> Afterwards I will return and I will rebuild the tent of David
> that has fallen down,
> and I will rebuild its ruins and I will raise it up,
> in order that the rest of humanity may seek the Lord,
> even all the Gentiles upon whom my name has been named.
> (Acts 15.16-17)

• And then James issues what has become known as 'the apostolic decree'. This requires Gentile believers in Jesus to 'abstain from things polluted by [contact with] idols, from fornication *(porneia)*, from that which is strangled *(pnikton)*, and from blood [the kosher laws]'. What has often been missed here is that the principal source of 'the apostolic decree' seems to be the legislation regarding 'the resident alien', that is, the non-Jews who were permanently resident in the land of Israel, 'in the midst of' the people (Lev. 17.8-9, 10-14; 18.26).[63] This was presumably the solution to 'the Gentile problem' which Luke himself approved, and probably the Jerusalem church. That is, to treat such Gentiles in effect as 'resident aliens', Gentiles in the midst of the people, while retaining their identity as Gentiles.

Here then was an insistence by Luke that the gospel is not foreign to Israel. The gospel is not in opposition to Israel, is not to be set in antithesis to the law. On the contrary, the gospel looks for the restoration of Israel, for the fulfilment of the hopes of Israel's prophets, and for the inclusion of Gentiles within and as part of that fulfilled hope. Unlike Mark, the Gospel of Luke does not focus on the discontinuities between the law and a message fully open to Gentiles. Unlike Matthew, the Gospel of Luke is not fighting with the rabbinic survivors of the catastrophe of 70 over the inheritance from Moses and the prophets. For Luke, *the Gospel is not gospel except as it works for the fulfilment of Israel's hope, as including Gentiles within that hope.*

The only other canonical Gospel, the Gospel of John, is more complex. So much so that it requires separate and more extensive treatment. To that task we turn in the fourth lecture.

---

63. See further my *Beginning from Jerusalem* 461-69.

CHAPTER 4

A Very Different Version!
John as a Source for the Historical Jesus

I began this series of lectures, first, by arguing that Jesus made a considerable impact on his disciples. This impact, I believe, is clear from the Jesus tradition of the Gospels, and is expressed in greater or smaller degree in the tradition itself. From the impression made by Jesus, as expressed in the first place by the tradition shared by the first three Christian Gospels, we are able to discern a clear outline of the mission and person who made that impact. Second, we looked carefully at these traditions, the traditions shared by the Gospels of Matthew, Mark and Luke, the Synoptic tradition. We noted that Jesus was remembered in somewhat diverse ways, as expressed in 'the same yet different' character of the Synoptic tradition. The shared impact of Jesus was expressed differently. The shared tradition took different forms in divergent tellings of the same material. Third, we noted that Mark's Gospel, probably the earliest of the Christian Gospels, gave or established a 'gospel' shape to the tradition. Mark told the story of Jesus as a passion narrative with an extended introduction. He did not remember Jesus only as a great teacher, or a great wonder-worker. He remembered a story which moved steadily towards the climax of Jesus' suffering, death and (as Christians believed) resurrection. This was the 'gospel-shape'. He was probably the first to give to this new form of biography the title 'Gospel'. He created a new genre. And in this he was followed by the two other Synoptic Gospels, the Gospels of Matthew and Luke. Each in his own way helped establish the remembrance of Jesus as a passion narrative with an extended introduction as the form of that remembrance to be called 'Gospel'. Whatever other form is used to recollect what Jesus did or taught, it is not 'Gospel' without the climax of the death and resurrection of Jesus.

What, then, about the other New Testament Gospel — the Fourth Gospel, the Gospel of John? This is generally agreed to be the latest of the four New Testament Gospels — written probably sometime in the 90s. Among the papyri findings a century or so ago, one of the most exciting was a fragment of John's Gospel which can be dated to about 125 in Egypt. This implies that John's Gospel must have been copied and circulated quite widely and rather quickly. When we turn to this Gospel, however, we immediately run into some problems. For John's Gospel is different from the other three. The formula which so well describes the Synoptic tradition ('the same yet different') does not seem to fit John's Gospel in its relation to the other three New Testament Gospels. 'Different' certainly, but 'the same'? Different certainly, but in what sense or in what degree 'the same'? On any reckoning, the contrast between the first three canonical Gospels and the fourth, the Gospel of John, is striking. It can be typified in the terms used in the table on page 72. Older harmonising explanations were keen to affirm that John's Gospel is as historical in its presentation as the Synoptics. So they tried to explain such differences in terms of the different audiences to whom Jesus spoke — for example, the Synoptics recalling Jesus' teaching to the crowds, John recalling Jesus' teaching to his disciples.[1] But as was pointed out long ago,[2] the style of Jesus' speech in John's Gospel is consistent, whether Jesus is depicted as speaking to Nicodemus, or to the woman at the well, or to 'the Jews', or to his disciples. And the style is very similar to that of the Baptist, as indeed to that of 1 John. The inference is inescapable that the style is that of the *Evangelist* or of the Evangelist's tradition, rather than that of *Jesus*.[3]

What are we to make of this? If, for example, the Synoptic tradition provides good evidence of the impact made by Jesus, then how do we take best account of the different character of John's Gospel? If the Synoptic tradition provides good evidence of the speech forms in which the earliest memories of

---

1. Cf. e.g. those referred to in my 'Let John Be John', in P. Stuhlmacher, ed., *Das Evangelium und die Evangelien* (WUNT 28; Tübingen: Mohr Siebeck, 1983) 309-39 (here 314 n. 11); P. N. Anderson, *The Fourth Gospel and the Quest for Jesus* (London: T. & T. Clark, 2006) 61. More discriminating is C. L. Blomberg, 'The Historical Reliability of John', in R. T. Fortna and T. Thatcher, eds., *Jesus in the Johannine Tradition* (Louisville: Westminster John Knox, 2001) 71-82. The relation of history to theology in John is the main theme of P. N. Anderson et al., eds., *John, Jesus, and History*, vol. 1, *Critical Appraisals of Critical Views* (SBLSymS 44; Atlanta: Society of Biblical Literature, 2007).

2. D. F. Strauss, *The Life Critically Examined* (ET 1846; Philadelphia: Fortress, 1972) 384-86.

3. As Anderson recognises (*Fourth Gospel* 58-59). See further J. Verheyden, 'The De-Johannification of Jesus: The Revisionist Contribution of Some Nineteenth-Century German Scholarship', in Anderson et al., *John, Jesus, and History* 1.109-20.

SYNOPTICS	JOHN
Matthew and Luke begin with virgin conception/birth of Jesus	Begins with incarnation of preexistent Logos/Word
Jesus goes to Jerusalem only for the last week of his mission; only one Passover mentioned	Jesus is active in Judea for a large part of his mission; his mission extends over three Passovers
Jesus speaks little of himself — nothing quite like John's 'I am's'	Jesus speaks much of himself — notably the 'I am' statements[4]
Jesus calls for faith in God	Jesus calls for faith in himself[5]
The central theme of Jesus' preaching is the kingdom of God[6]	The kingdom of God barely features in Jesus' speech
Jesus speaks of repentance and forgiveness quite often	Jesus never speaks of repentance and of forgiveness only in 20.23
Jesus speaks typically in aphorisms and parables	Jesus engages in lengthy dialogues and circuitous discussion
Jesus speaks only occasionally of eternal life	Jesus speaks regularly of eternal life[7]
Jesus shows strong concern for the poor and sinners	Jesus shows little concern for the poor and sinners[8]
Jesus is notable for his ministry of exorcism	John narrates no exorcisms

Jesus were formulated by the first disciples of Jesus, and of the way in which the Jesus tradition was used and transmitted in the earliest churches, then what are we to make of the *very different* character of Jesus' speech in John's Gospel? If the first three Gospels can be described as 'remembering Jesus', can John's Gospel be described in the same way, as also *remembering* Jesus? The debate is complex, and I can focus on only three features, before asking what John was trying to do with his Gospel. We should note:

4. Particularly John 6.35, 41, 48, 51; 8.12, 58; 10.7, 9, 11, 14; 11.25; 14.6; 15.1, 5; 18.6.

5. E.g. John 3.15-18; 5.46; 6.29, 35, 40; 7.38; 8.24; 9.35; 11.25-26; 12.44, 46.

6. See ch. 5 n. 3 below.

7. Mark 10.30 pars.; Matt. 25.46; John 3.15-16, 36; 4.14, 36; 5.24, 39; 6.27, 40, 47, 54, (68); 10.28; 12.25, 50; 17.2-3.

8. Texts like Matt. 5.3/Luke 6.20; Matt. 11.5/Luke 7.22, and Mark 10.21, 12.42-43 ('the poor'), and Mark 2.15-17 pars. and Matt. 11.19/Luke 7.34 ('sinners') have been sufficient to indicate to most of the last two generations' treatments of the historical Jesus that these were strong concerns of Jesus. John 12.5-8 and 13.29, and 9.16, 24-25, 31 would never have given that impression.

- first, that John's Gospel follows Matthew and Luke in using the Gospel format provided by Mark;
- second, that although Jesus' discourses in John are very different from the way Jesus teaches in the Synoptics, we can see that the discourses are rooted in Synoptic-like tradition; and
- third, that it becomes clear that John has filled some gaps left by the other Gospels.

The Gospel Format

Given the differences between John and the Synoptic Gospels, it is very striking that John nevertheless has used *the same Gospel format* given to the Jesus tradition by Mark. John has set his Gospel within the same framework — a passion narrative with an extended introduction — even though his 'extended introduction' is so very different in content and character from the 'extended introductions' of the Synoptics. If we reckon the 'passion narrative' as extending from Jesus' entry into Jerusalem, covering Jesus' final week there and climaxing in his trial, execution and resurrection, then John's passion narrative extends from John 12 to the end of the Gospel; that is, it takes up about 40 percent of the Gospel as a whole.

What may we infer from this? Not that John knew Mark's Gospel as such, as some have argued. The absence of the sort of closely identical passages, which point to the literary interdependence of a good deal of the Synoptic Gospel material, still remains the decisive consideration at this point. What it probably does mean is that the Markan step of labeling the story of Jesus' whole mission as itself *euangelion*, 'Gospel', quickly became the established way of thinking about the story of Jesus' mission. Matthew and Luke, following Mark's example, attest the same probability, and these further two 'Gospels' will themselves have strengthened and circulated more widely the conviction that the way to use and reflect on the Jesus tradition was in the narrative form of 'Gospel'.

This is all the more significant, since, as we shall see, the different account John gives of the Jesus tradition could so easily have pushed in a different direction. A Jesus who came as (primarily) a revealer, and whose teaching was characterised by lengthy discourses, could have focused the Gospel's presentation of Jesus precisely on these features or narrowed its presentation to such features, as we see in the subsequent Gnostic presentations of Jesus' teaching.[9] Neverthe-

---

9. See further e.g. P. Perkins, *Gnosticism and the New Testament* (Minneapolis: Fortress, 1993) ch. 9.

less, John follows what had been the pattern set by the earlier 'Gospels' by setting his version of Jesus' mission and revelation within the same framework, beginning with John the Baptist and climaxing in Jesus' passion and resurrection. For all the freedom the Fourth Evangelist displays in his presentation of Jesus and despite all the differences from the Synoptics, John's Gospel is far closer to them than it is to the apocryphal Gospels.

What is all the more striking in John's Gospel is the way he makes the imminent passion of Jesus suffuse the whole of his account. Even more than Mark, the 'extended introduction' foreshadows and prepares for the climax of Jesus' death and resurrection.

- Uniquely in the Gospel tradition, John the Baptist hails the one to come as 'the lamb of God who takes away the sin of the world' (John 1.29, 36). John also dates Jesus' execution to the time when the Passover lambs would have been slaughtered in the Temple (18.28), and explicitly identifies Jesus' death with that of the Passover lamb (19.36; Exod. 12.46).[10] That must mean that John saw Jesus' death in terms of the Passover sacrifice, now seen also as a sin offering.[11]
- John relocates the account of Jesus' 'cleansing of the Temple' to a much earlier phase of Jesus' mission (John 2.13-22), presumably to serve as a headline for Jesus' whole mission. In it he includes the memory of Jesus speaking about the destruction of the Temple (cf. Mark 13.2; 14.58): 'Destroy this temple, and in three days I will raise it up' (John 2.19). But then he adds the explanatory note: Jesus 'was speaking about the temple of his body', that is, about his death and resurrection (2.21).
- Other early signals of the passion climax include:
  - the miracle of the water turning into wine at the wedding in Cana happening 'on the third day' (2.1);
  - the talk of resurrection and of Jesus as the source of life in 5.21-29;
  - the powerful interpretation of the feeding of the five thousand in terms of Jesus himself as 'the bread of life', his flesh to be eaten and his blood to be drunk as the source of life (6.32-58);
  - the increasing number of attempts to do away with Jesus, heighten-

10. The fact that the soldiers did not (have to) break the crucified Jesus' legs (John 19.33) fulfilled the scripture, 'None of his bones shall be broken' (19.36), one of the regulations for the Passover lamb — 'you shall not break any of its bones' (Exod. 12.46).

11. The Passover was not originally thought of as a sin offering, but the Passover was probably already associated with atonement in Ezek. 45.18-22; and in the Synoptics Jesus' last supper with his disciples is associated both with the Passover and with the thought of Jesus' 'blood poured out for many' (Mark 14.24 pars.).

ing the sense of the ever more imminent crisis,[12] matched by Jesus' increasing reference to his imminent departure.[13]

- Not surprisingly, as the passion narrative draws closer, Jesus talks of the good shepherd who lays down his life for the sheep (10.11, 15, 17-18), of his imminent burial (12.7), and of the wheat grain that must die if it is to bring forth fruit (12.24).

- Particularly notable is the drumbeat of references to Jesus' 'hour'.[14] Initially it sounds as a still-distant or yet-to-happen event: certain eventualities could not happen because Jesus' hour 'had not yet come'.[15] There have been hints as to what the 'hour' will bring forth, but only when the passion narrative proper has begun does it become clear that the 'hour' is the hour of Jesus' death. 'The hour has come for the Son of Man to be glorified. Very truly, I tell you, unless a grain of wheat falls into the earth and dies, it remains just a single grain; but if it dies, it bears much fruit' (12.23-24).[16] The drama of the steadily mounting climax should not be missed.

- Equally notable is John's adaptation of the concept of Jesus' 'glorification' *(doxasthēnai),* where it again becomes steadily clearer that what is in view is not, or not simply, Jesus' exaltation following his death. What is in view is Jesus being 'glorified' in his death *and* resurrection[17] — particularly, again, 12.23-24. Since the 'glory' (and 'glorifying') of Christ is such an important feature of John's Gospel,[18] it is also to be noted that it is the 'signs' of water transformed into wine, and of life from death (2.11; 11.4), which most clearly reveal that glory — that is, actions which foreshadow the glory of his death and resurrection and what they achieve. This factor, it should be noted, affects all references to Jesus' glory, from the first mention of 'the glory as of the Father's only son', which the Johannine witness attested (1.14). The 'glory' of the only Son which the disciples had witnessed was not in terms of the Synoptic Gospels' scene of Jesus' transfiguration (Mark 9.2-8 pars.). For John the Son's glory was most clearly attested in Jesus' death and resurrection. His Gospel was never simply a Gospel of incarnation but of incarnation-death-resurrection.

---

12. John 5.18; 7.1, 19-20, 25, 30, 32, 44; 8.37, 40; 10.31-33, 39; 11.8, 52-54, 57.

13. John 7.33; 8.14, 21; 13.3, 33, 36; 14.4, 28; 16.5, 10, 17.

14. John 2.4; 7.30; 8.20; 12.23, 27; 13.1; 17.1.

15. John 2.4; 7.30; 8.20; alternatively as Jesus' *kairos* ('critical or right time') (7.6, 8).

16. See also John 12.27; 13.1; 17.1.

17. John 7.39; 12.16, 23; 13.31-32; 17.1.

18. John 1.14; 2.11; 8.50, 54; 12.41; 14.13; 16.14; 17.1, 5, 10, 22, 24.

• The same point is made in John's talk of Jesus being 'lifted up' *(hypsōthēnai)*. As is now generally recognised, John uses this word not only for Jesus' lifting up on the cross, but also for his lifting up to heaven, that is, his ascension.[19] For John, Jesus' decisive saving act was a unitary conceptual whole, Jesus' dying, rising and ascending a single upward sweep. To be correlated with this is also John's adaptation of the Son of Man tradition to include talk of the Son of Man ascending as well as descending.[20] Jesus evidently could not be adequately understood except when both were held together, within that Gospel framework.

Wherever John derived his Gospel format from, then, it is clear that he was firmly wedded to that format as the structure within which his more distinctive portrayal should be held. He could have presented Jesus as the great revealer of God and of the mysteries of heaven. The Fourth Evangelist could have developed his mode of presenting the teaching of Jesus even more extensively than he did — Jesus, the divine agent from on high who brought the secret meaning of human existence to those born of the flesh and imprisoned in darkness. Others took that option. But for John it was integral to the message he sought to promote that Jesus had been executed and had been raised from the dead, and not simply as an episode in his life or incidental to his revelation. On the contrary, Jesus' death and resurrection was central to the message of Jesus, a fundamental element in his message, without which the message could not be adequately grasped and would be misappropriated. In terms of our present discussion, and although John never uses either noun *(euangelion)* or verb *(euangelizesthai),* we can justifiably say that John affirmed and strongly stressed the *sine qua non* of his message about Jesus as Gospel.

The Johannine Discourses of Jesus

The teaching material in John provides one of the most striking contrasts between John's Gospel and the Synoptics. The other three Gospels depict Jesus as a sage typically teaching by means of *meshalim,* aphorisms and parables. In contrast, John depicts Jesus engaged in lengthy back-and-forth discussions in various settings. In fact, however, in more or less every chapter of John's Gospel there are particular sayings or part-sayings which echo Synoptic material

19. John 3.14; 8.28; 12.32-34. See e.g. R. E. Brown, *The Gospel according to John* (2 vols.; AB 29; New York: Doubleday, 1966) 1.145-46.
20. John 3.13; 6.62; also 20.17; and cf. 1.51.

or form different versions of the Synoptic tradition.[21] Some see in this evidence that John knew one or more of the earlier Gospels. But in my view the thesis of literary dependence of John on the Synoptics is a further example of a post–printing press literary mind-set which is totally anachronistic. It assumes that any parallel can be (plausibly) explained only by literary dependence. And it takes too little account of the oral character of ancient society, including the early Christian communities. In my view, the data is best explained in terms of John's knowledge of oral Jesus tradition, that is, of Synoptic-like material.[22] The oral Jesus tradition, we can safely assume, was much more widely known before it began to be put into writing by the earlier Gospels. And it no doubt continued to be more widely known even as knowledge and use of the earlier written Gospels began to spread more widely. So, of course, the Fourth Evangelist and his church(es) knew Jesus tradition quite apart from the earlier written Gospels as such. Moreover, the fact that we can recognise such tradition in John's Gospel, precisely because of the parallels with sayings in the Synoptic Gospels, is a further indication that the substance of so much of the Jesus tradition remained constant within the process of oral transmission and use. John's discourses, I maintain, are rooted in the memories of what Jesus taught during his mission, in Galilee or in Judea.

Let me give some examples to demonstrate my argument.[23]

- Jesus speaks of entry into the kingdom as dependent on being born again/from above (John 3.3, 5). This looks like a sharper expression of the Matt. 18.3 tradition: entry into the kingdom is dependent on becoming like children. Interestingly, John 3.3, 5 are the only kingdom references in John which come close to the Synoptic kingdom of God motif.
- Jesus' presence is likened to the presence of the bridegroom (John 3.29); and this is a mark of the difference between Jesus and the Baptist. Here we see an echo of Mark 2.19 pars. (also Mark 2.21-22 pars.).

---

21. See my 'John and the Oral Gospel Tradition', in H. Wansbrough, ed., *Jesus and the Oral Gospel Tradition* (JSNTS 64; Sheffield: Sheffield Academic Press, 1991) 351-79 (here 356-58), drawing particularly on C. H. Dodd, *Historical Tradition in the Fourth Gospel* (Cambridge: Cambridge University Press, 1963). See also C. M. Tuckett, 'The Fourth Gospel and Q', and E. K. Broadhead, 'The Fourth Gospel and the Synoptic Sayings Source', in Fortna and Thatcher, *Jesus in the Johannine Tradition* 280-90 and 291-301 respectively. About seventy verses in the Johannine discourses can be said to have Synoptic parallels.

22. For the discussion see particularly D. M. Smith, *John among the Gospels: The Relationship in Twentieth-Century Research* (Minneapolis: Fortress, 1992).

23. See also my 'John and the Oral Gospel Tradition' 369-73 for brief treatment of John 2.18 and 6.30; 4.35-38, 44; 12.15; 13.20, 21, 38 and 20.23.

- The great bread of life discourse — 'I am the bread of life' (John 6.26-58) — is most obviously to be understood as a reflection on Jesus' words at the Last Supper — 'This (bread) is my body' (Mark 14.22-25 pars.). Although John dates the episode to the time of the Passover (John 6.4), his presentation focuses not so much on the Passover significance of Jesus' words as on the contrast with Moses and with the manna of the wilderness.
- The good shepherd theme in John (John 10) most obviously takes up the memory of Jesus' apparently quite frequent use of the same imagery in his teaching.[24]
- John's principal theme of presenting Jesus as the incarnate Word who reveals God most fully (John 1.14-18) forms a consistent theme of Jesus' discourses:
  - Jesus' repeated talk of himself as *the Son* to God as Father is an obvious elaboration of the much more limited early memory of Jesus' praying to God as 'Abba', perhaps already elaborated in the Synoptic tradition.[25]
  - Similarly Jesus' repeated talk of his having been *sent* by the Father (John 4.34; 5.24, 30, 37; 6.38-39, 44; etc.) is an obvious elaboration of the memory of Jesus' occasional self-reference in similar terms.[26]
  - Similar is the elaboration of Jesus' undoubted talk of 'the Son of Man' by adding the thought of his *descent and ascent* (John 3.13; 6.62; cf. 1.51) and of his *being lifted up glorified* (3.14; 8.28; 12.23; 13.31).
  - The '*Amen, Amen*' formula introducing Jesus' teaching is regularly used by John and is obviously drawn from the tradition, well known in the Synoptics, of Jesus introducing a saying with 'Amen'.[27]
  - The noteworthy 'I am's' of John's Gospel[28] are certainly formulations unknown to the earlier Synoptic tradition (what Evangelist could have omitted such sayings of Jesus?); but equally it is likely that the memory of some awe-inspiring assurances of Jesus (Mark 6.50 pars.; John 6.20) provided the stimulus for the uniquely Johannine forms.[29]

---

24. Matt. 18.12/Luke 15.4; Mark 6.34; Matt. 10.6; 15.24; Luke 12.32.

25. Jeremias noted the tremendous expansion of references to God as 'Father' in the words of Jesus within the Jesus tradition — Mark 3, Q 4, special Luke 4, special Matthew 31, John 100 (J. Jeremias, *The Prayers of Jesus* [ET London: SCM, 1967] 30, 36).

26. Mark 9.37 pars.; 12.6 pars.; Matt. 15.24; Luke 4.18; 10.16.

27. See further R. A. Culpepper, 'The Origin of the "Amen, Amen" Sayings in the Gospel of John', in Fortna and Thatcher, *Jesus in the Johannine Tradition* 253-62; see also ch. 1 above.

28. John 6.35, 41, 48, 51; 8.12, 24, 28, 58; 10.7, 9, 14; 11.25; 13.19; 14.6; 15.1, 5; 18.5-8.

29. Cf. Anderson, *Fourth Gospel* 56-58.

This rootage of the Johannine discourses, in tradition which echoes and parallels Synoptic tradition, suggests the most plausible way to understand these discourses. That is, *many if not most of the principal themes of the Johannine discourses are the fruit of lengthy meditation on particular sayings of Jesus or of characteristic features of what he said and of how he acted.* These are discourses and themes which not only emerge out of and express the developed Christology of John and the Johannine churches, but also express the reflection over some time on things Jesus said and taught, reflection in the light of the richer Christology which Jesus' resurrection and exaltation had opened up to them.[30] In other words, they exemplify not simply the passing on of Jesus tradition, but the way that tradition stimulated their understanding of Jesus in the light of what had happened subsequently.

John himself attests and justifies this very process.

- Twice he explicitly notes that Jesus' disciples did not understand what Jesus was saying or doing, but that they remembered these details and later understood them in the light of Jesus' resurrection and glorification.[31] This makes precisely the point that the claims regarding Jesus were rooted in Jesus' own mission as illuminated by Easter. His immediate disciples already had a true knowledge of Jesus during his mission (John 6.69; 17.7-8), but they did not fully understand; their knowledge was still imperfect.[32]

- To the same effect is the role ascribed to the Spirit/Paraclete. During Jesus' mission 'the Spirit was not yet', that is, presumably, not yet given (7.39). But when the Spirit came he would teach Jesus' disciples everything and remind them of all that Jesus had said to them (14.26); he would guide them into all truth and declare more of Jesus' truth that they were as yet unable to bear (16.12-13). This is the same balance between revelation already given and received, and fuller revelation still to

30. Tom Thatcher, 'The Riddles of Jesus in the Johannine Dialogues', in Fortna and Thatcher, *Jesus in the Johannine Tradition* 263-77, notes the substantial body of riddles in the Johannine dialogues. Since riddles are a widely attested oral form, he suggests that at least some of these sayings circulated orally in Johannine circles before the Fourth Gospel was written, and that some of the larger dialogues may also have circulated orally as riddling sessions (he refers particularly to John 8.12-58).

31. John 2.22; 12.16; similarly 13.7; 14.20; 16.4.

32. John 8.28, 32; 10.6, 38; 13.28; 14.9. See also T. Thatcher, 'Why John Wrote a Gospel: Memory and History in an Early Christian Community', in A. Kirk and T. Thatcher, eds., *Memory, Tradition, and Text: Uses of the Past in Early Christianity* (Semeia Studies 52; Atlanta: SBL, 2005) 79-97 (particularly 82-85); also *Why John Wrote a Gospel: Jesus — Memory — History* (Louisville: Westminster John Knox, 2006) 24-32.

come, a fuller revelation which makes the revelation already given clearer and which enables it to be more fully grasped.[33]

In short, it is hard to doubt that *John's version of Jesus' teaching was an elaboration of aphorisms, parables, motifs and themes remembered as characteristic of Jesus' teaching, as attested in the Synoptic tradition.* At the same time, John's version was not pure invention, nor did it arise solely out of Easter faith. Rather it was elaboration of typical things that Jesus was remembered as saying. Unlike the later 'Gospels', John does not attribute the fuller insight into who Jesus was to secret teaching given to a few following Jesus' resurrection. Rather, he roots it in the Jesus tradition which he shared with the other churches and which was itself rooted in the memory of Jesus' mission. This was the truth of Jesus for John — not a pedantic repetition of Synoptic-like tradition, but the significance of that tradition brought out by the extensive discourses which John or his tradition drew out of particular features of Jesus tradition as exemplified in the Synoptic tradition. To criticise John's procedure as inadmissible is to limit the task of the Evangelist to simply recording deeds and words of Jesus during his mission. But John evidently saw his task as something more — the task of drawing out the fuller meaning of what Jesus had said (and done) by presenting that fuller understanding as the Spirit both *reminding* Jesus' disciples of what Jesus had said and *leading them into the fuller understanding of the truth* made possible by Jesus' resurrection and ascension.

Filling Up Some Gaps

The most striking gap which John fills relates to the *beginning of Jesus' own mission* (John 1–3). John seems to have been able to draw on tradition which the early Gospel writers had either set to one side or did not know about. The other Gospels all begin Jesus' mission *after* John the Baptist had been imprisoned by Herod Antipas (Mark 1.14 pars.) — perhaps, as I have already suggested, because they found the beginning of Jesus' mission within the circle of the Baptist's disciples somewhat embarrassing. In contrast, the Fourth Evan-

---

33. The dialectic of the Johannine conception of revelation here is summed up in the word *anangellō*, which John uses three times in 16.13-15, and which can have the force of 'reannounce', 'reproclaim', but also denote the announcing of new information/revelation in 16.13. Arthur Dewey, 'The Eyewitness of History: Visionary Consciousness in the Fourth Gospel', in Fortna and Thatcher, *Jesus in the Johannine Tradition* 59-70, speaks of 'anticipatory memory' (65-67).

gelist does not hesitate to include reference to a period prior to the Baptist's imprisonment (John 3.24). During that period *Jesus' mission overlapped with the Baptist's* (3.22-36). Moreover, it was apparently of the same character as the Baptist's (3.22-26), though John takes care to deny that Jesus himself practised baptism (4.2).[34] This tradition almost certainly goes back to Jesus' first disciples, since it includes the detail that *some of Jesus' own key disciples had earlier been the Baptist's disciples* (1.35-42).[35] Neither detail nor emphasis was likely to have been invented given the degree of embarrassment indicated elsewhere in the Jesus tradition over the extent to which Jesus could be counted as himself a disciple of the Baptist.[36]

The different ways that early Christian tradition handled the relation between John the Baptist and Jesus are very interesting, then. The Synoptic Gospels omitted a not unimportant aspect of the tradition, presumably to prevent any confusion between the two missions and to highlight the distinctiveness of Jesus' mission. John's Gospel retains the memory of Jesus' emergence from the Baptist's circle and of the period of overlap of the two missions. But he focuses on the Baptist's role as the one who bore most clear and explicit witness to Jesus and to his significance (1.6-9, 19-34; 3.25-36). So we certainly cannot resolve the tensions between the first three Gospels and the Fourth Gospel by assuming that the Synoptic tradition is always more reliable than John's. In this case for sure we can be sufficiently confident that the Johannine tradition too goes back to the first disciples. Indeed, in this case, John has retained a clearer memory of the overlap period than we could have deduced from the Synoptic tradition.

Another of the most striking differences between the Synoptics and John is that whereas the Synoptics focus on Jesus' mission in Galilee, the bulk of John's narrative *focuses on Judea and Jerusalem* — 2.13–3.36; 5.1-47; 7.10 onwards. It is not unlikely that Jesus did pay more visits or spend longer time in Judea and Jerusalem than the Synoptic tradition allows.

- The early period of overlap between the missions of the Baptist and Jesus suggests early mission in Judea (cf. John 3).
- Luke records the close discipleship of Mary and Martha (Luke 10.38-42), and though he locates them in a village passed through on the jour-

34. A. T. Lincoln, '"We Know That His Testimony Is True": Johannine Truth Claims and Historicity', in Anderson et al., *John, Jesus, and History* 1.179-97, suggests that there may be 'slightly fewer difficulties' with the hypothesis 'that the discussion of Jesus baptizing is the result of the creativity of the Fourth Evangelist or his tradition' (187-91).
35. See also Dodd, *Historical Tradition* 279-87, 302-5.
36. Note again particularly Matt. 3.14-15; and see further above, ch. 3.

ney to Jerusalem, John is clear that the village was Bethany, close to Jerusalem (John 11.1, 18; 12.1-8).[37]

• John's geographical locations are generally reckoned to be evidence of firm historical rootage — for example, John 1.28 (Bethany across the Jordan); 3.23 (Aenon near Salim); 5.2 (pool of Bethzatha with its five porticoes); 11.54 (town called Ephraim).

• That Jesus had close disciples in Jerusalem or in the near environs is suggested by the (secret?) disciples who provided the donkey for his entry into Jerusalem (Mark 11.2-3 pars.) and the room for the Last Supper (Mark 14.12-16 pars.).

In that case, why did the Synoptic tradition ignore or set to one side Jesus' earlier Jerusalem visits? The fact that they deliberately excluded the overlap period with the Baptist is evidence enough that they felt free to do so. Perhaps Mark or the tradition on which he drew wanted to make the (final) visit to Jerusalem the climax of the Jesus story; and Matthew and Luke simply followed him (or their main stream of tradition) in doing so. Since the leadership of the earliest Jerusalem community of believers in Messiah Jesus were all Galileans, one could understand why the tradition which they began and taught focused on the Galilean mission.

John, of course, does not ignore the Galilean mission, even though Jesus' coming and going to Galilee in the early chapters of his Gospel do read rather awkwardly.[38] The two miracles included in that material are in fact the closest to the Synoptic miracle tradition — healing the royal official's son (John 4.46-54; cf. Matt. 8.5-13/Luke 7.2-10) and the feeding of the five thousand (John 6.1-13; cf. Mark 6.32-52 pars.). But the likelihood grows throughout John's Gospel that John had a source for the mission of Jesus which was different from, or rather in addition to, the remembrances of Peter. Here I have in mind the figure indicated (and obscured) by the reference to him as 'the one whom Jesus loved' (John 13.23; 19.26; 21.7).[39] If that disciple is also re-

---

37. Jesus lodged in Bethany during his last week (Mark 11.11-12 par.; 14.3 par.). The depiction of Martha and Mary in John 12.1-2 (Martha served; Mary focused attention on Jesus) echoes the similar presentation of Luke 10.39-42; on the fuller story (John 12.1-8) see Dodd, *Historical Tradition* 162-73, and my 'John and the Oral Gospel Tradition' 365-67.

38. John 2.1, 12, 13; 4.1-3, 43-46; 5.1; 6.1, 59; 7.1, 9, 10.

39. See particularly R. Bauckham, *Jesus and the Eyewitnesses: The Gospels as Eyewitness Testimony* (Grand Rapids: Eerdmans, 2006) 358-411; also 'The Fourth Gospel as the Testimony of the Beloved Disciple', in R. Bauckham and C. Mosser, eds., *The Gospel of John and Christian Theology* (Grand Rapids: Eerdmans, 2008) 120-39. M. Hengel, *The Johannine Question* (ET London: SCM, 1989), argues that the Fourth Evangelist had been a resident in Jerusalem, was an

ferred to in 1.35-39, then he would have been a good source for the overlap period between the Baptist's and Jesus' missions (including the recruitment of the Baptist's disciples to become followers of Jesus). Similarly if that disciple is also referred to in 18.15-16, then he had good contacts in Jerusalem (he was known to the high priest!). This suggests that this disciple could have known or cherished memories of Jesus' mission in Jerusalem on one or another of his brief visits to the capital, as also episodes and contacts (like Nicodemus and Joseph of Arimathea) which the other tradents largely ignored,[40] since the Galilean tradition was more familiar and so full in itself.[41] With only John's attestation for the Judean mission, and given the freedom with which the tradition he uses or draws upon has represented the memories of Jesus' overall mission, it is difficult to draw firm conclusions. But the most likely explanation is that John has drawn on good memories of one or two, or some, visits to Jerusalem by Jesus, even if he has treated them in his own distinctive parabolic or symbolic terms.

John's Christology

The most helpful way to understand what the Fourth Evangelist was trying to do with his Gospel is to set it in the context of late Second Temple Judaism, or, perhaps more precisely, post–Second Temple Judaism, or very early rabbinic Judaism. We don't know with any assurance where John's Gospel emerged from, but it may reflect a situation in northern Galilee or southern Syria in the decades following the disaster of the first Jewish revolt against Rome. What we do know is that the communities which John's Gospel represents were in a situation of antagonism or schism with the Jewish authorities. Half of the references to 'the Jews' in John are hostile or reflect deep suspicion.

eyewitness of Jesus' death and a member of the earliest community, emigrated to Asia Minor in the early 60s and founded a school; he there wrote his Gospel in his old age, 'in which typical "Jewish Palestinian" reminiscences are combined with more "Hellenistic", "enthusiastic" and indeed even Pauline approaches into a great synthesis [in which] the christological doctrinal development of primitive Christianity reached its climax' (134). See also R. A. Culpepper, *John: The Son of Zebedee; The Life of a Legend* (Edinburgh: T. & T. Clark, 2000) ch. 3; T. Thatcher, 'The Legend of the Beloved Disciple', in Fortna and Thatcher, *Jesus in the Johannine Tradition* 91-99; Lincoln, 'We Know' 180-83.

40. Joseph is mentioned by all the Gospels at the end (Mark 15.43 pars.; John 19.38), but Nicodemus appears only in John (3.1-9; 7.50; 19.39).

41. Similarly with regard to any missioning in Samaria (John 4), whereas the Synoptics show why such a mission might have been excluded (Matt. 10.5; Luke 9.52-54). O. Cullmann, *The Johannine Circle* (London: SCM, 1976), made much of John 4.38 at this point (47-49).

There is talk more than once of the Johannine group having been or expecting to be 'expelled from the synagogue' — *aposynagōgos* (John 9.22; 12.42; 16.2). But most of the other half of the references to 'the Jews' are to the crowd of Jews debating about Jesus, about his significance. Where does he come from?[42] Is he Messiah?[43]

The inferences which should be drawn from this are probably twofold. One is that John's Gospel probably reflects a situation where Jews who had come to believe in Jesus as Messiah were becoming increasingly unacceptable within at least some (probably many) post-70 synagogues. We should not envisage 'the parting of the ways' between emerging Christianity and post-70 rabbinic Judaism as something clear-cut, finished and done. The overlap between these two heirs of Second Temple Judaism continued for many decades, even centuries, despite repeated attempts by the leaders of both movements to achieve and insist on a complete break. Such overlap is quite evident in rabbinic references to various *minim* and in Christian writings from the second century onwards.[44] But the strains between the two movements are already evident in the late first century, and not least in John's Gospel.

The other inference to be drawn, however, is that the Fourth Evangelist still had hopes of persuading more Jews that Jesus was indeed Israel's Messiah. Although well aware of the moves to expel Jesus' followers from the synagogue, John still saw the issue of Jesus' origin and status as Messiah to be a real subject of debate with and among 'the Jews' whom he had in mind when writing his Gospel. The hope may, in the event, have been a vain hope. But it still seems to be a major concern behind the writing of John's Gospel.

The key for us is probably to recognise the importance John attached to presenting Jesus as the one who above all others had brought *revelation* from God, as the one, indeed, who *had revealed God most clearly*. This theme provides a key, since similar concerns regarding divine revelation were widely shared in late Second Temple Judaism. That is to say, we can probably see in this theme *the central subject matter of the debate/dispute between the Johannine Christians and their Jewish contemporaries,* both rabbinic leaders and

---

42. John 7.26-27, 41-42, 52; 8.48; 9.29; 19.9.

43. John 4.25-29; 7.27-31, 41-42; 10.24; 12.34.

44. See e.g. my 'Two Covenants or One? The Interdependence of Jewish and Christian Identity', in H. Lichtenberger, ed., *Geschichte — Tradition — Reflexion: Festschrift für Martin Hengel. III. Frühes Christentum* (Tübingen: J. C. B. Mohr, 1996) 97-122 = 'Zwei Bünde oder Einer? Die wechselseitige Abhängigkeit der jüdischen und christlichen Identität', in P. Fiedler and G. Dautzenberg, eds., *Studien zu einer neutestamentlichen Hermeneutik nach Auschwitz* (Stuttgarter biblische Aufsatzbände 27; Stuttgart: KBW, 1999) 115-54.

their fellow Jews more generally. Let me try to elaborate this way of looking at John's Gospel within its historical context a little more fully.[45] I start with three observations.

First, we know that both Jewish apocalyptic writings and merkabah mysticism were characterised precisely by their claim to direct knowledge of heavenly mysteries — either by means of a vision or, more frequently, by means of an ascent into heaven. Such ascents to heaven are attributed not only to Enoch and Abraham, but also to Adam, Levi, Baruch and Isaiah.[46] Most of the reports of these heavenly ascents are roughly contemporary with or predate the time of John's Gospel.[47] So too, the account of Moses' ascent of Mount Sinai (Exod. 19.3; 24.18) evidently encouraged several circles within Judaism to view it as an ascent to heaven.[48] Similarly with the practice of merkabah mysticism — by means of meditation, particularly on the chariot vision of Ezek. 1 (but also other visions, notably Isa. 6 and Dan. 7.9-10), such practitioners aspired to experience for themselves a mystical ascent to or revelation of the throne of God. The practice itself seems to have become already well established in our period. It may be reflected already in *1 En.* 14, is hinted at in Sir. 49.8, and is clearly attested in the so-called angelic liturgy, or *Songs of the Sabbath Sacrifice* of Qumran (4Q400-407).[49] Not least of relevance here is the appearance in some of these visions of a glorious heavenly being, and the motif of the transformation into angel-like form of the one who ascends, no-

45. I draw on my earlier 'Let John Be John — a Gospel for Its Time', in *Das Evangelium und die Evangelien* (ed. P. Stuhlmacher; Tübingen: J. C. B. Mohr) 309-39 = 'Let John Be John: A Gospel for Its Time', in P. Stuhlmacher, ed., *The Gospel and the Gospels* (Grand Rapids: Eerdmans, 1991) 293-322.

46. Enoch — *1 En.* 14.8-25; 39.3-8; 70-71; *2 En.* 3-23

     Abraham — *T. Ab.* 10-15; *Apoc. Ab.* 15-29

     Adam — *Life of Adam and Eve* 25-29

     Levi — *T. Levi* 2-8

     Baruch — *2 Bar.* 76; *3 Baruch*

     Isaiah — *Ascen. Isa.* 7-10

47. For fuller detail see A. F. Segal, 'Heavenly Ascent in Hellenistic Judaism, Early Christianity, and Their Environment', *ANRW* 2.23.2 (Berlin: De Gruyter, 1980) 1352-68.

48. Philo, *On the Life of Moses* 1.158; *Questions and Answers on Exodus* 2.29, 40, 46; Josephus, *Antiquities* 3.96; *2 Bar.* 4.2-7; Ps-Philo 12.1; *Memar Marqah* 4.3, 7; 5.3; cf. *Ezekiel the Tragedian* in Eusebius, *Preparation for the Gospel* 9.29.5-6; 4 Ezra 14.5; *2 Bar.* 59. In Targum Neofiti, Deut. 30.12-14 is elaborated thus: 'The law is not in the heavens, that one should say, Would that we had one like Moses the prophet who would go up to heaven and fetch it for us'.

49. J. Strugnell, 'The Angelic Liturgy at Qumran', in VTSup 7 (1959) 318-45; C. A. Newsom, *Songs of the Sabbath Sacrifice* (Atlanta: Scholars, 1985); J. R. Davila, *Liturgical Works* (Grand Rapids: Eerdmans, 2000) 83-167.

tably Moses and Isaiah, and especially Enoch.[50] It is probably significant that it was just in the same period (post-70) that we find the Dan. 7.13-14 vision of 'one like a son of man' becoming a focus of speculation in both Jewish and Christian apocalyptic literature (4 Ezra 13; Rev. 1.13).[51] In Daniel's vision the manlike figure represented the saints of the Most High in their vindication after horrendous suffering. So in the aftermath of the fall of Jerusalem it would have been natural for Jewish apocalypticists to look to this figure for inspiration after the catastrophe of 70. The common concern in all these cases was *the revelation of divine mysteries* which these visions and heavenly ascents provided.

Second, we should also note that *both early Christianity and the Yavnean sages were not unaffected by such tendencies within Judaism*. Paul's account of a visionary ascent to the third heaven (2 Cor. 12.2-4) may well support the view that Paul himself was familiar with the practice of merkabah mysticism.[52] And the vision of John the seer (Rev. 1.13-16) has some striking points of contact with the earlier visions of Ezek. 1, Dan. 7.9-14 and Dan. 10.5-6. As for the rabbis, there is evidence that Yohanan ben Zakkai, who played such a leading role in initially reestablishing rabbinic Judaism at Yavneh after 70, was himself greatly interested in the chariot chapter of Ezek. 1 and probably practised meditation on it (*t. Hagigah* 2.1ff. pars.).[53] More striking is the indication that the 'two powers heresy' was dated back to much the same period — to the vision of the chariot throne of God (probably) by four rabbis, including the famous Akiba (*b. Hagigah* 15a; *t. Hagigah* 2.3-4). It will be recalled that one of the four, Elisha ben Abuyah, took the glorious figure on the throne (Metatron in *3 En.* 16) to be a second power in heaven.[54]

---

50. Moses — Sir. 45.2; Josephus, *Antiquities* 3.96-97; 4.326

   Isaiah — *Ascen. Isa.* 9.30

   Enoch — *Jub.* 4.22-23; *1 En.* 12-16; *2 En.* 22.8.

51. Probably also *1 En.* 37–71, since the 'Similitudes of Enoch' do not appear in the Dead Sea Scrolls, and since the early Jesus tradition shows no evidence of knowledge of the 'Son of Man' as featured by the Similitudes. But the issue is greatly disputed in Jewish and Christian scholarship.

52. J. Bowker, '"Merkabah" Visions and the Visions of Paul', *JSS* 16 (1971) 157-73; see also J. D. Tabor, *Things Unutterable: Paul's Ascent to Paradise in Its Greco-Roman, Judaic, and Early Christian Contexts* (Lanham, MD: University Press of America, 1986). But see also the cautionary remarks of P. Schäfer, 'New Testament and Hekhalot Literature: The Journey into Heaven in Paul and Merkavah Mysticism', *JJS* 35 (1985) 19-35.

53. See J. Neusner, *A Life of Johanan ben Zakkai* (Leiden: Brill, ²1970) 134-40; I. Gruenwald, *Apocalyptic and Merkabah Mysticism* (Leiden: Brill, 1980) 75-86; C. Rowland, *The Open Heaven: A Study of Apocalyptic in Judaism and Early Christianity* (London: SPCK, 1982) 282-305.

54. See R. T. Herford, *Christianity in Talmud and Midrash* (London: Williams and

One of the starting points for this 'two powers heresy' seems to have been speculation on the plural 'thrones' in Daniel's vision (Dan. 7.9). For there is also the tradition that even Akiba was rebuked for his speculation as to the occupant of the second throne in Dan. 7.9 (*b. Hagigah* 14a; *b. Sanhedrin* 38b). This evidence strengthens the hypothesis suggested above, that in the period between the two Jewish revolts (70-132) the vision(s) of Dan. 7.9-14 were a focus of considerable reflection in the hope that they might provide a source of insight and inspiration in the crisis confronting Judaism during that period.

Third, we know that *there were already strong reactions against some of these tendencies in apocalyptic and merkabah speculation, in both Jewish and Christian circles.* Sir. 3.18-25 can be readily understood as an exhortation to refrain from speculations involving visionary experiences.[55] 4 Ezra 8.20-21 seems to be directed against claims to be able to see and describe God's throne.[56] And the Mishnah prohibits the use of Ezekiel's passage about the chariot as a prophetic reading in the synagogue (*m. Megillah* 4.10), and even discussion of the passage in private, unless with a sage already familiar with the subject (*m. Hagigah* 2.1). In Christian circles we may recall the strong warnings against angel worship in Heb. 1–2 and possibly Col. 2.18,[57] and the early churches' hesitation over granting too much authority to the book of Revelation. Similarly the rabbinic polemic against angelology probably goes back to our period.[58] And the apostasy of Elisha ben Abuyah is a notorious fact elsewhere in rabbinic tradition.[59] We should also note how frequently subsequent rabbinic polemic against *minim* consists in a defence of monotheism, the unity of God.[60]

Within this context the Fourth Gospel's presentation of Jesus precisely in terms of divine revelation becomes luminously significant.

For example, the prologue to John's Gospel ends with the highest claim for the revelatory significance of Jesus. 'No one has ever seen God; the only

---

Norgate, 1903) 262-66; A. F. Segal, *Two Powers in Heaven: Early Rabbinic Reports about Christianity and Gnosticism* (Leiden: Brill, 1977).

55. Gruenwald, *Apocalyptic and Merkabah Mysticism* 17-18.

56. Rowland, *The Open Heaven* 54-55.

57. Col. 2.18 can be understood as referring to worship of angels, or, more probably, to participation in the worship of God by angels, as in the *Songs of the Sabbath Sacrifice, T. Job* 48–50 and *Ascen. Isa.* 7.13–9.33; see my *Colossians and Philemon* (NIGTC; Grand Rapids: Eerdmans, 1996) 177-85.

58. P. S. Alexander, 'The Targumim and Early Exegesis of "Sons of God" in Gen 6', *JJS* 23 (1972) 60-71.

59. E.g. Rowland, *The Open Heaven* 331-39.

60. See e.g. Herford, *Christianity in Talmud* 291-307; and further E. E. Urbach, *The Sages: Their Concepts and Beliefs* (Jerusalem: Magnes, 1979) 24-30.

begotten God . . . has made him known' (1.18). The claim is no less than that the invisible God has made himself visible in and through Jesus. Worth noting is a further detail in 3.1-15. The conversation with the sympathetic 'teacher of Israel', Nicodemus, is about how one can 'see' and 'enter the kingdom of God' (3.3, 5). But Jesus explicitly denies that such knowledge can be attained by an ascent to heaven: '*no one* has ascended into heaven' (3.13). This sweeping assertion can hardly be other than a polemic against the current belief in the possibility of such heavenly ascents, through contemplation on the divine chariot or otherwise.[61] Such knowledge of heavenly things is possible, claims the Johannine Jesus, *only* for him who *descended* from heaven, the Son of Man (3.13). A similar contrast is made in John 6 and pressed further. To think of Jesus as simply another prophet, even a prophet like Moses, is to miss the point of contrast. The prophet may think to ascend into heaven to 'listen in' on the heavenly council.[62] But Jesus as 'him whom God sent' does not gain his knowledge of God by such heavenly ascent. His knowledge is his because he descended from heaven. As one 'from above', his revelation of the divine mysteries transcends that of the prophets, also John the Baptist (3.31), and even that of Moses himself. Only 'the one who comes from God' 'has seen the Father' (6.46), the bread of life come down from heaven (6.41-51).

John's claims for Jesus are clearest in his presentation of Jesus as Wisdom. It has long been recognised that the language of the Johannine prologue is considerably dependent on the Wisdom theology of Second Temple Judaism. John speaks of the divine Word *(logos)*, but the language echoes the Wisdom reflection of Israel's sages, as also Philo's reflection on the Logos.

- As with Wisdom in Prov. 8 and Wis. 9.9, the Logos of John was in the beginning with God (John 1.1).
- As in *1 En.* 42, Wisdom sought a dwelling place among the children of men, and found no dwelling place, so the Johannine Logos 'came to his own home, and his own people received him not' (John 1.11).
- As in Sir. 24.8, Wisdom 'set up her tent in Jacob', so the Johannine Logos 'pitched his tent among us' (John 1.14).
- John's talk of Jesus descending from heaven has its closest parallels in such Wisdom passages.[63]

61. See e.g. H. Odeberg, *The Fourth Gospel* (Uppsala: Almqvist & Wiksell, 1929) 72-98; W. A. Meeks, *The Prophet-King: Moses Traditions and the Johannine Christology* (NovTSup 14; Leiden: Brill, 1967) 295-301.

62. See further J. A. Bühner, *Der Gesandte und sein Weg im 4. Evangelium* (Tübingen: Mohr Siebeck, 1977).

63. Wis. 9.16-17; Bar. 3.29; *1 En.* 42.

- The 'I am' claims of the Johannine Jesus are closely paralleled in the first-person singular speech of Wisdom in Prov. 8 and Sir. 24.
- That Wisdom is not just another intermediary or angelic agent, but is a way of speaking of God himself in his self-revelation, lies behind John 12.45 and 14.9: 'He who sees me sees him who sent me' (12.45); 'He who has seen me has seen the Father' (14.9).
- In a similar vein, 12.41 — Isaiah 'saw his glory and spoke of him'. Jesus is identified with the glory/Shekinah of God, the presence of God visible to Isaiah in the Temple (Isa. 6).
- Hence the charge laid by 'the Jews' in John's Gospel against Jesus: he makes himself equal with God (John 5.18); he, though a man, makes himself God (10.33).

What we see in all this is John engaging with many of his fellow Jews in reflection about whether and how God reveals himself to his people. Many of them were content to rest on the testimony of Moses and the prophets. John replies by asserting that Moses and the prophets wrote of Jesus (5.46). The grace and truth through Jesus transcended the law that had come through Moses (1.17). The water of life gave a more lasting satisfaction than the well of Jacob (4.5-14). The bread of life come down from heaven far transcended the manna in the wilderness (6.31-40). Many sought deeper revelation through apocalyptic vision and heavenly journey. John replies that it is not those who ascend to heaven who bring true knowledge of God, but the one who has descended from heaven, Jesus. The sages were not slow in identifying the divine wisdom by which God created the world, the divine wisdom which he offered to his people. They identified the Wisdom of God with *the Torah*. 'All this [Wisdom's hymn in praise of herself] is the book of the covenant of the Most High God, the law that Moses commanded us' (Sir. 24.23). 'She [Wisdom] is the book of the commandments of God, the law that endures forever' (Bar. 4.1). John replies by claiming that this divine Wisdom is not so much to be found in the Torah as in *Jesus* (John 1.14-18). We may say that Israel's sages *inscripturated* Wisdom in the Torah. Whereas John *incarnated* Wisdom in Jesus. As the sages had found God's Wisdom nowhere more clearly expressed than in the Torah, so the Johannine Christians claimed that they had found the same Wisdom nowhere more clearly expressed than in Jesus.

We can see, then, why the Fourth Gospel is so different from the other three New Testament Gospels. The Synoptic Evangelists were recording the memories of Jesus' teaching and mission within a Gospel framework. They were concerned to show that what Jesus taught and the way Jesus taught were wholly of a piece with the gospel of his death and resurrection. They were concerned to show that what Jesus did and how he did what he did, again, were fully part of the gospel. It was important that their interpretation of Jesus' mission and teaching was largely limited to organising their traditions and to what we might call 'performance variations'. For it was important to show that the character of Jesus' mission and of his teaching was entirely consistent with and part of the gospel, that the gospel of Jesus' death and resurrection could not be fully told without being attached to the story of his mission.

With John, however, it was different. The first three Gospels, we may say, had made their point, and established it firmly. No wedge could be pushed between the mission and teaching of Jesus in Galilee and the gospel of Jesus' death, resurrection and exaltation to God's right hand. But repeated performances of the Jesus story, as told by the Synoptic Gospels, could not bring out the full significance of his mission. And with fresh questions being raised about whether God reveals himself as fully or more fully than he did to Moses on Mount Sinai, and how God reveals the mysteries of heaven to visionaries and mystics, more could and should be said — so we may envisage the motivation behind the Fourth Gospel. It was never a matter of abandoning the Gospel format that Mark had provided. But it was a matter of addressing a new situation, of tuning the Gospel format to be heard by those seeking to know God and the secrets of heaven more fully. It was never a matter of ignoring and leaving behind the memories of what Jesus had said and done. On the contrary, it was a matter of demonstrating that Jesus' miracles were 'signs' of great significance, that Jesus' teaching had a depth which spoke both rebukingly and invitingly to those wanting to know more of God. It was a matter of depicting Jesus as the Logos of God incarnate, as God's self-revelation in its fullest form. Where the Torah had previously been identified with Wisdom, as embodying Wisdom most fully, now John could present Jesus as the even fuller identification of God's Wisdom, as the bodily incarnation of God's self-revelation in Wisdom.

The attempt was bold. It went too far for most Jews — as far as the two-powers heresy, we might say.[64] But at the time of writing, John's Gospel was

64. D. Boyarin, *Border Lines: The Partition of Judaeo-Christianity* (Philadelphia: University of Pennsylvania Press, 2004). Boyarin argues that Christianity's developing Logos Christology should be seen as closely parallel to Judaism's (the Targums') Memra theology. He argues, indeed, that 'Logos theology (and hence trinitarianism) emerges as a difference between Judaism and Christianity only through the activities of heresiologists on both sides of the divide'. Rabbinic theology chose to name what had been the traditional Logos (or Memra) doctrine of God as a heresy, indeed, *the* heresy, the archetypal 'two powers in heaven' heresy, and thus in effect labeled Christianity a heresy. The Christian heresiologists for their part named Monarchianism and Modalism a heresy by calling it 'Judaism' (92, 145-46)!

part of a debate which had still to be resolved within post-70 Judaism. The resolution of the debate may not have been as satisfactory as it might have been if more good will had ensued on both sides. And perhaps a return to that debate, before positions became hardened and denunciations and excommunications followed, would have been of salutary significance for both sides. Rebecca's children may have much more to ponder and to share than is usually recognised.[65]

For Christians, in the face of the contrasts between the Gospels, it is important always to remember that the titles of the four Gospels are not 'the Gospel of Matthew', 'the Gospel of Mark', 'the Gospel of Luke' and 'the Gospel of John'. But 'the Gospel according to Matthew', 'the Gospel according to Mark', 'the Gospel according to Luke', and 'the Gospel according to John'. These are not different Gospels, but the same gospel. There may be four Gospels, but for Christians there is only one gospel. And that includes the distinctive variation of John's Gospel from the rest. It is still the same gospel, now expressed by John in his own distinctive way. The point being that the gospel is not a rigid form or format. There is no single canonically valid form of the gospel. The gospel of and about Jesus Christ needs ever to be expressed variously, as new and previously unforeseen situations and issues arise. The gospel remains the same by constantly changing its form and delivery. No Gospel shows that more clearly than 'the Gospel according to John'.

---

65. A. F. Segal, *Rebecca's Children: Judaism and Christianity in the Roman World* (Cambridge, MA: Harvard University Press, 1986). More strongly, Boyarin: 'Judaism is not the "mother" of Christianity; they are twins, joined at the hip' (*Border Lines* 5).

PART TWO

FROM JESUS TO PAUL

CHAPTER 5

From Jesus' Proclamation to Paul's Gospel

Introduction

The gap between Jesus and Paul has been an increasing problem for students of the New Testament and the beginnings of Christianity for most of the last two centuries. For nearly eighteen centuries of Christianity's history there was no problem, because there was no gap. The line of continuity from Jesus to Paul was seen as straightforward and unbroken. The Christ of Paul's theology was easily identified with the Jesus of the Gospels. But then questions began to rise. Why does Paul say so little about Jesus' mission in Palestine? If we had to depend on Paul for our knowledge of Jesus' life and mission, how little would we know, how bare would be our picture of Jesus. So, how much did Paul know about Jesus' mission? How much did he care to know about it? How important was it for Paul?

The problem began to be serious when the quest of the historical Jesus became a major concern. For the message of Jesus seemed to be so different from the gospel of Paul. And as the Jewishness of Jesus became steadily clearer for those engaged in the quest for the historical Jesus, the problem became still more severe. For Jesus could be understood in characteristically Jewish terms — Jesus as a prophet,[1] Jesus as a Jewish teacher, Jesus as engaged

---

1. See e.g. the summary treatment of one of the leading contributors to the quest of the historical Jesus — J. P. Meier, 'From Elijah-like Prophet to the Royal Davidic Messiah', in D. Donnelly, ed., *Jesus: A Colloquium in the Holy Land* (New York: Continuum, 2001) 45-83.

in mission for the restoration of Israel.[2] Whereas Paul, on the other hand, was characteristically understood as the one who broke with his Jewish past, as the one who abandoned the Torah, as the one who turned what began as a Jewish messianic sect into a predominantly Gentile religion, as one who began to transpose the very Jewish message of Jesus into the language of Greek idiom and philosophy, as one who transformed the morality of Jesus into a religion of bloody sacrifice and redemption.

The gap, or should we say gulf, between Jesus and Paul can be documented on several fronts.

1. *Jesus proclaimed the kingdom of God; Paul preached Jesus.* In the first three Gospels Jesus is not at the centre of his own message; his message is focused on God's kingdom and is summed up in the headline text of Mark: 'The time is fulfilled, and the kingdom of God has come near; repent, and believe in the good news' (Mark 1.15).[3] In Paul, however, the kingdom of God features hardly at all,[4] and his gospel focuses on Christ crucified and risen from the dead,[5] on Jesus as Lord,[6] and on the vital importance of being 'in Christ'.[7]

2. *Jesus' message was primarily for Israel; Paul's mission was primarily for the Gentiles.* Jesus did respond positively to the one or two Gentiles he encountered. But he is also recalled as sending his disciples on mission only 'to the lost sheep of the house of Israel' (Matt. 10.6), and as saying to the Syrophoenician woman, 'I was sent only to the lost sheep of the house of Israel' (Matt. 15.24). Paul, however, understood himself and is remembered precisely as 'an apostle to the Gentiles' (Rom. 11.13). And his mission to the Gentiles became a festering sore close to the heart of the mother church in Jerusalem, as attested by Luke's account of Paul's

---

2. The restoration of Israel has been a major theme in recent studies of Jesus — B. F. Meyer, *The Aims of Jesus* (London: SCM, 1979); E. P. Sanders, *Jesus and Judaism* (London: SCM, 1985); N. T. Wright, *Jesus and the Victory of God* (London: SPCK, 1996).

3. 'The kingdom of God' appears regularly on Jesus' lips in the Synoptic Gospels — Mark 13 times; Q 9 times; special Matthew 28 times; special Luke 12 times; a total of about 105 times in all.

4. Pauline corpus 14 times, usually in the formulaic talk of 'inheriting the kingdom' (1 Cor. 6.9-10; 15.50; Gal. 5.21; cf. Eph. 5.5) or with similar future eschatological reference (1 Thess. 2.12; 2 Thess. 1.5; cf. Col. 4.11; 2 Tim. 4.1, 18).

5. See ch. 3 above at n. 9.

6. In the undisputed Paulines (i.e. not including Ephesians and the Pastoral Epistles) *kyrios* is used of Jesus about 200 times.

7. In the Pauline corpus 'in Christ' occurs 83 times, and 'in the Lord' a further 47 times; to which should be added many 'in him/whom' references.

final visit to Jerusalem, where James, the Lord's own brother, informs him of the common opinion among the Jerusalem believers that Paul was an *apostate* from Israel (Acts 21.20-21).[8]

3. *Jesus was a local Jewish teacher; Paul was influenced by the religions and politics of his day.* Late-nineteenth-century liberalism characterised Jesus as preaching the simple message, to love God and one's neighbour.[9] The *religionsgeschichtliche Schule* maintained that Paul borrowed the myth of the dying and rising god of the mystery cults to proclaim Jesus as the dying and rising Saviour or as the divine redeemer of the Gnostic redeemer myth.[10] Late-twentieth-century liberalism has revived its predecessor's thesis in a new guise. Jesus was essentially a wisdom teacher, seeking to restore communal harmony within the villages of Galilee.[11] Paul is now characteristically portrayed as working in the very different setting of the cities of the Mediterranean world and presenting Jesus as Lord in direct challenge to the lordship of the Roman emperor.[12]

The issues thus posed are well summed up in William Wrede's famous description of Paul as the 'second founder of Christianity' who has, 'compared with the first, exercised beyond all doubt the stronger — not the better — influence'.[13] So, is Paul the real founder of Christianity? And is the message and mission of Jesus an accidental antecedent of Paul, of little actual relevance to the Christianity to which Paul gave enduring shape?

Alternatively, what are the continuities between Jesus and Paul? To what extent was Paul's gospel itself shaped by Jesus' mission and message? Was Paul inspired only by Jesus' death and resurrection, or also by the mission of Jesus which preceded his passion? I believe more can be said on this than is usually thought to be the case. I focus here on three important features of both their messages and argue that the similarity of emphasis is not coincidental but is

8. I return to this issue in chs. 6 and 7 below.

9. A. Harnack, *What Is Christianity?* (London: Williams and Norgate, 1900; ET 1901, ³1904).

10. H. Gunkel, *Zum religionsgeschichtlichen Verständnis des Neuen Testaments* (Göttingen: Vandenhoeck & Ruprecht, 1903); R. Bultmann, *Theology of the New Testament*, vol. 1 (London: SCM, 1948; ET 1952).

11. Particularly J. D. Crossan, *The Historical Jesus: The Life of a Mediterranean Jewish Peasant* (San Francisco: Harper, 1991).

12. Particularly R. A. Horsley, ed., *Paul and Empire: Religion and Power in Roman Imperial Society* (Harrisburg, PA: Trinity, 1997); also *Paul and Politics: Ekklesia, Israel, Imperium, Interpretation* (Harrisburg, PA: Trinity, 2000); also *Paul and the Roman Imperial Order* (Harrisburg, PA: Trinity, 2004).

13. W. Wrede, *Paul* (London: Philip Green, 1907) 180.

best explained by the enduring impact made by Jesus' own mission prior to his death and resurrection.[14]

1. The Openness of God's Grace

1.1. The Distinctives of Jesus' Message

There is no doubt, as already indicated, that Jesus proclaimed the kingdom of God, God's kingly rule. This was itself distinctive within the Judaism of his time. Of course, for the Jewish contemporaries of Jesus, the imagery of God as king and of God's kingdom was familiar. But in the scriptures and postbiblical writings of Second Temple Judaism, the phrase 'the kingdom of God' is hardly attested, and the theme of God's kingship is not particularly prominent.[15] So Jesus' focus on the kingdom of God was distinctive in itself. But the really distinctive features of his message were threefold.

a. *Jesus taught that God's kingly rule was already being experienced in and through his own ministry.* The hope that God's kingdom would come soon was not unusual. Indeed, the second petition of the prayer taught by Jesus, 'May your kingdom come' (Matt. 6.10/Luke 11.2), echoes what was probably an early form of the Jewish Kaddish prayer: 'May he let his kingdom rule in your lifetime . . . and in the lifetime of the whole house of Israel, speedily and soon'.[16] In contrast, however, it was Jesus' emphasis that Israel's ancient hope was *already* being fulfilled which so marked out his message. 'The time is fulfilled' (Mark 1.15), claimed Jesus. The people to whom Jesus ministered were blessed, because they were seeing and hearing what many prophets could only long to see and hear (Matt. 13.16-17/Luke 10.23-24). In response to John the Baptist's question, 'Are you the one who is to come?' Jesus answered: 'Go and tell John what you hear and see: the blind receive their sight, the lame walk . . . and the deaf hear, the dead are raised and the poor have good news brought to them' (Matt. 11.3-5/Luke 7.19, 22). These were hopes for the age to

14. My focus is on Jesus' message and teaching. The issue of whether an implicit Christology can be discerned in Jesus' mission (the issue of messiahship, his sense of sonship to God, the authority with which he spoke) which links into Pauline Christology is a further stage in the discussion which I pursue in *The Partings of the Ways between Christianity and Judaism* (London: SCM, 1991, ²2006) ch. 9.

15. See above, ch. 1 n. 21.

16. More detail in my *Christianity in the Making*, vol. 1, *Jesus Remembered* (Grand Rapids: Eerdmans, 2003) 409-10.

come, especially as expressed by Isaiah;[17] but in Jesus' ministry they were already coming about. Jesus' exorcisms were evidence that 'the kingdom of God has come upon you' (Matt. 12.28/Luke 11.20). The present reality of God's kingdom, the active experience of God's kingly rule here and now, marked off Jesus' preaching of God's kingdom and made his mission truly distinctive.

b. *Good news for sinners.* Jesus is remembered as claiming that 'I came not to call the righteous but sinners' (Mark 2.17 pars.). This was in response to the criticism of certain Pharisees that he ate with tax collectors and sinners (Mark 2.16). Evidently this was such a feature of his mission that he became notorious for it, as indicated by the popular jibe directed against Jesus: 'Look, a glutton and a drunkard, a friend of tax collectors and sinners' (Matt. 11.19/Luke 7.34). And Luke's Gospel recalls that Jesus told his parables of the lost things (the lost sheep, the lost coin and the lost son) in response to Pharisaic grumbling: 'This fellow welcomes sinners and eats with them' (Luke 15.2).

Now the significance of this is frequently missed, and because it is so important to our theme I will draw out that significance, even if I can do so here only in somewhat simplified terms.[18] 'Sinners', of course, are simply those who break the law or who fail to keep the law.[19] This does not mean, however, that Jesus was notorious for keeping company with criminals. The clue is given by the contrast between 'the righteous' and 'sinners', when Jesus says, 'I came not to call the *righteous* but *sinners*' (Mark 2.17). For this points us to the fact that 'sinners' was *a factional term* within the Second Temple Judaism of Jesus' time. Let me explain.

Second Temple Judaism was characterised and almost torn apart by different factions. The most obvious factions were the Sadducees, the Pharisees, and the Essenes, assuming, as almost everyone does, that the Qumran community was a branch of the Essenes. In addition, we have to include what may well have been a fairly coherent movement whose views were expressed in the Enoch literature;[20] and others behind the *Psalms of Solomon*. What made these groups distinctive factions within Second Temple Judaism? It was their conviction that *their* understanding of what it meant to be Israel, God's covenant community, was the correct understanding — the *only* correct understanding, so that only they were conducting themselves as faithful Israelites

17. Isa. 26.19; 29.18; 35.5-6; 42.7, 18; 61.1.
18. See more fully my *Jesus Remembered* #13.5.
19. E.g. Exod. 23.1; Deut. 25.2; Pss. 1.1, 5; 10.3; 28.3; 37.32; 50.16-18; 71.4; 82.4; 119.53, 155; Prov. 17.23; Ezek. 33.8, 11, 19; Sir. 41.5-8.
20. Emphasised particularly by G. Boccaccini, *Beyond the Essene Hypothesis* (Grand Rapids: Eerdmans, 1998).

should act. They each interpreted the law in their own way and practised the law in accordance with their interpretation. *Halakhah,* we should recall, comes from *halakh,* 'to walk'; their *halakhoth* (interpretative rulings) determined how they should walk, how they should conduct their lives. Inevitably they disagreed with other interpretations and in some cases tried to persuade their fellow Jews of the correctness of their particular interpretations, of *their halakhoth.* Among the Dead Sea Scrolls, the sectarian letter to the leaders of Israel, known as 4QMMT, is a very good example of this. The letter was written by the early sectarians to inform the leaders of Israel of their own particular rulings, their *halakhoth,* governing, for example, purity and sacrifice. It was because their rulings disagreed with the way the law was practised in Jerusalem that they had separated themselves from the rest of the people (4QMMT C7). In writing thus their hope was to persuade the Jerusalem leadership of the rightness of the sect's rulings, their 'works of the law' (C26-27). They were sure that if the leadership were persuaded by their letter, and began to practise 'the works of the law' as the sect understood them, it would be counted to those who so acted for righteousness (C28-32).

More to the point, such groups naturally tended to regard themselves as 'the *righteous*'. They were righteous because they were observing the law as it should be observed. But the inevitable corollary was that those who disagreed with such factional *halakhoth,* and who thus did not practise the law properly, were lawbreakers, 'sinners'. We find such usage running through the literature of the period from 1 Maccabees[21] onwards. So the Enoch sectarians regarded themselves as 'righteous', and they regarded others who calculated the Jewish feasts by a different calendar as 'sinners'.[22] The Dead Sea Scrolls refer to their opponents, that is, other Jews, in similar terms.[23] And in the *Psalms of Solomon* 'the righteous' repeatedly denounce the 'sinners', that is, probably the Hasmonean Sadducees who controlled the Temple cult.[24] In all these cases the term 'sinners' does not denote nonpractising, law-defiant Jews, those who would be regarded by all as lawbreakers, but Jews who practised their Judaism *differently* from the writer's faction. They were 'sinners', that is, lawbreakers, but only from a sectarian viewpoint, and only as judged by the sectarians' interpretation of the law.

Now we can see what Jesus was accused of: he was sharing table-fellowship not with blatant criminals, but with those whom the 'righteous'

---

21. 1 Macc. 1.34; 2.44, 48.
22. *1 En.* 1.7-9; 5.4, 6-7; 22.9-13; 82.4-7; and 94-104 *passim.*
23. 1QpHab 5.1-12; 1QH 10.10-12; 12.34; CD 2.3; 11.18-21; 19.20-21; 4QFlor (4Q174) 1.14.
24. *Pss. Sol.* 1.8; 2.3; 7.2; 8.12-13; 17.5-8, 23.

Pharisees regarded as unfaithful to the law. And we can see better why Jesus said, 'I came not to call the righteous, but sinners' (Mark 2.17). *He was reacting against that Pharisaic factionalism.* The factions of his day had, as it were, been drawing internal boundaries within Israel. They were drawing the definition of who should be counted a faithful member of the covenant people more tightly round themselves, excluding others, denying in effect that these others were recipients of God's covenant grace. To this Jesus reacted strongly. He refused to agree with that attitude. He broke through the boundaries the Pharisees were in effect erecting within Israel. The good news of God's kingdom was not least for 'sinners'. Here we should also remember that the name 'Pharisees' had almost certainly started as a kind of nickname, 'the separated ones', *perushim,* from the Hebrew *parash,* 'to separate'.[25] That is, they separated themselves from those who would make them unclean, prevent them from being holy. They ate their meals as though they were priests in the Temple.[26] They believed that to be holy, set apart to God, they had to separate themselves and to eat separately from others. This was what Jesus objected to — the belief that faithfulness to the law required such separation, the conviction that failure to observe such Pharisaic *halakhoth* cut people off from God's covenant mercy. For Jesus it was of fundamental importance that God's grace was *open,* and above all open to those whom the religious regarded as beyond that grace. He broke through the boundaries between factions which limited the grace of God within Israel. He shared his table with the irreligious, with those regarded by the righteous as 'sinners'.[27]

c. *Good news for the poor.* A third distinctive feature of Jesus' mission was that he saw one of his priorities to be to bring the good news of God's kingdom to the poor.[28] Poverty here should not be spiritualised, as Matthew's version of the first Beatitude may seem to suggest: 'Blessed are the poor in spirit' (Matt. 5.3). For Luke makes it clear that Jesus' blessing was for the poor, that is, the materially poor: 'Blessed are you poor' (Luke 6.20). But the difference between Matthew and Luke should not be overemphasised. For it had long been Israel's experience that poverty had many dimensions — material, social and

25. See E. Schürer, *The History of the Jewish People in the Age of Jesus Christ* (rev. and ed. G. Vermes and F. Millar; 4 vols.; Edinburgh: T. & T. Clark, 1973-87) 2.396-97; S. J. D. Cohen, *From the Maccabees to the Mishnah* (Philadelphia: Westminster, 1987) 162; A. J. Saldarini, *Pharisees, Scribes, and Sadducees in Palestinian Society* (Edinburgh: T. & T. Clark, 1988) 220-25.

26. Emphasised particularly by J. Neusner, *From Politics to Piety: The Emergence of Rabbinic Judaism* (Englewood Cliffs, NJ: Prentice-Hall, 1973). See further below, ch. 8 at n. 2.

27. Dunn, *Jesus Remembered* #14.8.

28. In what follows I again draw on *Jesus Remembered* #13.4.

spiritual. That is why Israel's prophets had denounced the ruthlessness and heartlessness with which the rich disregarded and exploited the materially poor. That is why the psalmist could be so confident that God was preeminently the God of the poor,[29] and why the psalmist and his community could identify themselves as the poor and needy.[30]

It is clear from the echoes of Isa. 61.1 in Jesus' preaching that Jesus drew from that passage an understanding of his mission.[31] Luke simply gives more explicit expression of this in his portrayal of Jesus' sermon in the synagogue of Nazareth. There he tells us that Jesus read from Isaiah, 'The Spirit of the Lord is upon me, because he has anointed me to bring good news to the poor' (Isa. 61.1). And then Jesus went on, 'Today this scripture has been fulfilled in your hearing' (Luke 4.17-21). As Jesus' first Beatitude also makes clear, the good news for the poor was that 'the kingdom of God is yours' (Matt. 5.3/ Luke 6.20). The kingdom of God is misunderstood unless it is seen to be for beggars.[32] And other episodes in Jesus' mission make the same point. To the rich (young) man he says, 'Go sell what you possess and give to the poor, and you will have treasure in heaven' (Mark 10.21). And he goes on to warn, 'How hard it will be for those who have riches to enter the kingdom of God' (Mark 10.23). Elsewhere he warns, 'Where your treasure is there will your heart be also' (Matt. 6.21/Luke 12.34); and, 'No one can serve two masters, for either he will hate the one and love the other, or be devoted to one and despise the other; you cannot serve God and Mammon' (Matt. 6.24/Luke 16.13). The point is clear: precisely because wealth creates a false sense of security, a trust which should be placed only in God,[33] it all too quickly and too often becomes the most serious alternative to God. Good news for the poor and warnings for the rich are two sides of the same coin.

29. Pss. 9.18; 10.14, 17; 12.5; 14.6; 22.24-26; 35.10; 40.17; 41.1; 68.5, 10; 69.33; 70.5; 72.12-13; 102.17; 113.7; 132.15; see also 1 Sam. 2.8; 2 Sam. 22.28; Job 34.28; 36.6; Prov. 3.34; Isa. 11.4; 14.32; 29.19; 41.17; 49.13; 61.1; Jer. 20.13; Sir. 21.5; *Pss. Sol.* 5.11; 15.1.

30. 'I am poor and needy' (Pss. 40.17; 70.5; 86.1; 109.22); see also Pss. 18.27; 37.14; 68.10; 69.32; 72.2, 4; 74.19, 21; 140.12; Isa. 54.11. See further E. Gerstenberger, *TDOT* 11.246-47, 250.

31. Matt. 5.3-4/Luke 6.20-21 and Matt. 11.5/Luke 7.22 both clearly echo Isa. 61.1-2. See further *Jesus Remembered* 516-17, 662.

32. See further my *Jesus Remembered* #13.4.

33. 'Mammon' is usually explained as deriving from *'mn* (to trust), that is, something relied on (in contrast to God); 'the word signifies "resources", "money", "property", "possessions"' (W. D. Davies and D. C. Allison, *The Gospel according to Saint Matthew* (ICC; Edinburgh: T. & T. Clark, 1988) 1.643; see also J. P. Meier, *A Marginal Jew*, vol. 3, *Companions and Competitors* (New York: Doubleday, 2001) 589 nn. 92, 93.

1.2. *The Distinctives of Paul's Gospel*

The distinctives of Paul's gospel can be readily matched with those of Jesus' message.

a. *God justifies the ungodly now.* As the kingdom of God can be seen as the distinctive of Jesus' message, so for many the distinctiveness of Paul's gospel is most clearly seen in his theology of *justification by faith.* The imagery of justification is that of the law court. The judge justifies, that is, acquits those charged with wrongdoing. The most common use of the imagery of God as Judge in Israel's scriptures is with reference to the last judgment. Israel's hope was that in the final judgment its faithfulness to God's covenant and law would be recognised, and Israelites would be acquitted and enter into the life of the age to come. Paul knows that imagery well. He draws on it in various places. For example, he warns the overconfident of 'the day of wrath, when God's righteous judgment will be revealed. For God will repay according to each one's deeds. . . .'[34] For it is not the hearers of the law who are righteous in God's sight, but the doers of the law will be justified' (Rom. 2.5-13). Here already we find an echo of Jesus' warning to 'the righteous' of his day, that his message of the kingdom was not good news to them. But it is the unexpected *presentness* of God's justification which I want to emphasise here.

So Paul writes to the Corinthians, quoting Isaiah, rather as Jesus had quoted Isaiah: '"At an acceptable time I listened to you, and on a day of salvation I have helped you" [Isa. 49.8]. See, *now* is the acceptable time; see, *now* is the day of salvation' (2 Cor. 6.2). Or to the Roman Christians he can write, 'Therefore, having been justified from faith [that is, already justified from faith], we have peace with God, through our Lord Jesus Christ, through whom also we have access into this grace in which we stand' (Rom. 5.1-2). They have *already* been justified. Already they have access into the inner sanctum of God's presence, which only the high priest could enter (the holy of holies), and only on one day of the year (the Day of Atonement), and which for Israelites generally could only be a visionary hope for a visionary future. And later in Romans Paul paints his own picture of the final law court. 'Who' on that day, he asks scornfully, 'will bring any charge against God's elect? It is God who justifies. Who is to condemn? It is Christ who died, rather was raised, who also is at God's right hand, who also intercedes on our behalf' (Rom. 8.33-34). Here the matter has already been set-

---

34. The quotation is from Ps. 62.12 and Prov. 24.12; but the theme is often taken up in Jewish writings; for further detail, see my *Romans* (WBC 38; Dallas: Word, 1988) 85, 97-98.

tled. It is what has already happened in Christ's death and resurrection that is decisive.

In other words, there is a *strong similarity* between Jesus' message and Paul's gospel. *Jesus* spoke of God's kingly rule already effective in and through his ministry. *Paul* saw Jesus' death and God's act of raising Jesus from the dead as similarly enacting what had hitherto been thought of as belonging only to the future — the resurrection of the dead leading into the final judgment (as, classically, in Dan. 12.1-3). As in Jesus' mission the kingdom of God was already present, so in Jesus' resurrection the *final* resurrection had already begun, and that which would determine the final judgment has already happened. The openness of God's grace through Jesus' mission became still more open through Jesus' death and resurrection. Such a coincidence is hardly accidental. It was the same openness of grace, the same realisation that what hitherto could only have been hoped for is already present, and active, and able to be experienced here and now. And it was the same Jesus: the line of continuity between the message of Jesus' mission and the significance of Jesus' death and resurrection is clear.

b. *Good news for Gentile sinners.* There is no doubt that a major contribution of Paul to the development of Christianity, perhaps his major contribution, was his opening out of the mission to the Gentiles. Without Paul the messianic sect of the Nazarenes may have remained a renewal sect within Judaism, destined to fade away or to be reabsorbed into rabbinic Judaism some generations later. It was primarily Paul whose mission to non-Jews transformed the Jewish sect into an ethnically diverse religion, into what became a predominantly Gentile religion. That claim requires a lot more elaboration than I can give it now. Here the point I want to make is that Paul's outreach to the Gentiles was so much like Jesus' mission on behalf of sinners that some knowledge of Jesus' mission almost certainly influenced Paul's understanding of his vocation to take the good news of God's Son to the Gentiles (Gal. 1.16). As in the case of Jesus, the two key features are the appearance of the term 'sinners' and the importance of table fellowship with sinners.

For the righteous who regarded other nonobservant *Jews* as 'sinners', even more deserving of the title 'sinners' were *Gentiles*. Gentiles by definition were outside the chosen people; in the words of Ephesians, they were 'aliens from the commonwealth of Israel, and strangers to the covenants of promise' (Eph. 2.12). They were by definition outside the law which defined Israel, they were literally law-less, out-laws. So, by definition, they were 'sinners'.[35] Paul

35. Ps. 9.17; Tob. 13.6; *Jub.* 23.23-24; *Pss. Sol.* 1.1; 2.1-2; Luke 6.33 *(hoi hamartōloi)* = Matt.

reacted to this very Jewish attitude toward 'Gentile sinners' in the same way that Jesus reacted to Pharisees' condemnation of nonobservant Jews as 'sinners'. This becomes clearest in the incident in Antioch which Paul recalls in Gal. 2.11-17.[36]

In the church in Antioch Peter had readily eaten with the incoming Gentile believers. But, Paul says, when a group came from James in Jerusalem, Peter and the other Jewish believers 'separated' from the Gentile believers (2.12) — that word 'separate' again. Paul rebuked Peter publicly for distorting and departing from 'the truth of the gospel'. Why? Because, says Paul, Peter in effect was trying to 'compel the Gentiles to live like Jews' (2.14). And he continues his appeal to Peter: 'We are Jews by nature and not Gentile sinners, and we know that no one is justified by works of the law but only through faith in Jesus Christ' (2.15-16). The issue is clear. Peter had reverted to the view that Gentiles were sinners by nature, and that Jews, in order to remain faithful to the covenant, had to separate from Gentiles. That meant, in particular, to eat separately from Gentiles, to maintain the laws of clean and unclean (Lev. 20.22-26),[37] to avoid all trace or taint of Gentile idolatry. So once again, it was *table fellowship* which was the test — the test of recognising and living out the openness of God's grace. The test of the gospel was whether people could eat at the same table, fully accept the other, and not limit the wideness of God's mercy by making his love too narrow with false limits of our own.[38]

In short, as Jesus broke through the boundaries *within* Israel, Paul broke through the boundary *round* Israel. And in the same terms: nonobservance of law and tradition, however sacred, did not put anyone beyond God's grace. And in the same way: by sharing the meal table with those whom the religious traditionalists would exclude. This again was surely no coincidence, but attests a clear continuity between Jesus and Paul.

c. *Obligation to help the poor.* Paul also stressed the importance of assisting the poor. This is again often neglected in treatments of Paul. But we know it is the one obligation which he had no hesitation in agreeing to in the Jerusalem council (Gal. 2.10) — *not* in addition to the agreed gospel, but as *integral* to it.

5.47 *(hoi ethnikoi)*; Mark 14.41 pars.; cf. K. H. Rengstorf, *TDNT* 1.325-26, 328. See further below, ch. 8 at n. 12.

36. I have reflected on this passage for thirty years and sum up my findings most recently in my *Christianity in the Making*, vol. 2, *Beginning from Jerusalem* (Grand Rapids: Eerdmans, 2009) ##27.4-5.

37. Cited below in ch. 8.

38. I echo the hymn of Frederick William Faber, 'There's a Wideness in God's Mercy'.

And we know that the collection he made among his churches for the poor in Jerusalem was his main concern in the last phase of his mission.[39] To deliver this collection was the only reason that Paul returned to Jerusalem, knowing that it might cost him his life (Rom. 15.31), as indeed it did. And what is so striking is that in his letters on the subject he uses words which characterise his gospel. Contributing to the collection will be a *charis,* an act of 'grace'.[40] It would be an expression of *koinōnia,* of 'shared experience' of that grace.[41] In Romans he includes 'sharing/giving' and 'acts of mercy' in the charisms which are the functions of the body of Christ (Rom. 12.8). And in Gal. 6.2 he counts 'bearing one another's burdens' as fulfilling 'the law of Christ'. By this he almost certainly refers back to what these Christian communities knew about Christ, how Jesus had interpreted the law. 'The law of Christ' was probably Paul's way of referring to their knowledge of Jesus' own priorities — to bring good news to the poor.

2. Eschatological Tension and the Spirit

2.1. Characteristic of Jesus' Message

I have emphasised the distinctiveness of Jesus' gospel as the proclamation of the kingdom as already present and active in and through his ministry. But as we also noted, Jesus also looked for the future coming of the kingdom, that is, presumably, of the full revelation of God's kingly rule. He taught his disciples to pray, 'May your kingdom come' (Matt. 6.10/Luke 11.2). What deserves notice now is the tension he maintained in his message of the kingdom, the eschatological tension of the kingdom.

a. *Living in the light of the coming kingdom.* The double aspect of Jesus' proclamation has caused much confusion. How could Jesus preach that God's kingdom was already present, yet still to come? Many scholars have found the two emphases to be so incompatible that they must regard one or the other as a later addition to the Jesus tradition.[42] But such a solution simply fails to re-

39. Rom. 15.25-28; 1 Cor. 16.1-3; 2 Cor. 8–9. For more detail see *Beginning from Jerusalem* #33.4.

40. 2 Cor. 8.1, 4, 6, 7, 9, 16, 19; 9.8, 14, 15 (also 1 Cor. 16.3).

41. 2 Cor. 8.4; 9.13.

42. E.g. E. Käsemann, 'The Beginnings of Christian Theology', in *New Testament Questions of Today* (London: SCM, 1969) 82-107, argued that the irreconcilable contradiction between the two emphases could be explained only by postulating that the 'already present' em-

cognise the character of grace: as something already given in its fullness, but also as something always pointing forward to its fuller realisation. The child can always be confident of the parents' love while still looking forward to maturity. So Jesus, we may infer, had no difficulty in recognising the fulfilment that was happening through his ministry, while looking forward to a still richer consummation of God's rule. This in fact is the most obvious way to interpret the tension between Jesus' proclamation of fulfilled hope (Mark 1.15) and the prayer he taught his disciples to pray for the kingdom to come (Matt. 6.10). In his own ministry he resolved the tension by living his life and relationships *in the light of the kingdom*. We have already mentioned his concern for sinners and the poor. We could add his recognition of the need for forgiveness and to forgive (Matt. 6.12, 14-15)[43] and his insistence that final judgment will take account of whether the hungry were fed, the thirsty given drink, the stranger welcomed, the naked clothed, and the sick or imprisoned visited (Matt. 25.31-46). To live by kingdom values had an extensive impact on the way life was lived.

b. *The Spirit as the present power of the kingdom.* Jesus apparently did not speak much about the Holy Spirit. But what he did say is very much to the point here. For when he spoke of God's kingly rule as already active in his ministry, he was thinking primarily of the Spirit of God working through his ministry. This is implicit in the passages already referred to which indicate that Jesus believed himself to have been anointed with the Spirit and thus commissioned to preach the good news to the poor (Isa. 61.1). It was this anointing with the Spirit — we may think of Jesus' anointing at the Jordan after his baptism by John (Mark 1.10 pars.) — which empowered Jesus for his mission (Acts 10.38). It was this anointing of the Spirit which signalled the beginning of the fulfilment which his mission expressed. The link between the kingdom already active and the Spirit of God is most explicit when Jesus attributed his success in exorcism to the Spirit (Matt. 12.27-28 par.). He acknowledges that there were several other successful exorcists in his time (12.27). But he stresses that the *distinctiveness* of his ministry is that he exorcises by the power of the Spirit. The emphasis in the Greek lies on the first and the last phrases: 'Since it is by *the Spirit of God* that I cast out demons, then has come upon you *the kingdom of God*' (12.28). The power of the Spirit is the presentness of the kingdom, God's kingly rule already in evidence.

---

phasis was authentic and the 'still to come' emphasis reflected the teaching of the early communities (101-2).

43. Dunn, *Jesus Remembered* #14.6.

2.2. *The Already and Not Yet in Paul*

The same twofold emphasis is present in Paul's teaching. This is regularly expressed as the 'already and not yet' in his understanding of the process of salvation. Salvation itself is the end of the process;[44] those in the process are 'those who are being saved'.[45] There has been a decisive beginning — all that baptism speaks of, a dying and being buried with Christ (Rom. 6.3-4). But there is also a not-yet — an outworking of the death of Christ in the wasting away of the old nature and a final sharing in Christ's resurrection.[46] What is often missed, once again, however, is the degree to which Paul's already-not-yet emphasis is *the same eschatological tension as in Jesus' mission*.

a. *The future tense of justification.* The centrality of Paul to Reformed theology has tended to focus only on the already aspect of Paul's teaching on justification — what we briefly discussed earlier. In so doing it has also tended to ignore the *future* tense of justification. For though, as we have seen, Paul does emphasise that through faith we can know justification, acceptance by God here and now, he also emphasises that final judgment will take place. And he emphasises that final judgment will depend to at least some extent on the way lives are led — and that includes believers. 'We must all appear before the judgment seat of Christ, so that each may receive recompense for what has been done in the body, whether good or evil.'[47] This 'all' assuredly includes believers! For Paul, as for Jesus, final judgment will be 'according to works'.[48] In Paul, as with Jesus, the imagery of reward for achievement or good deeds (works) is not lacking.[49] For Paul, like Jesus, salvation (eternal life) is in some degree conditional on faithfulness.[50] Paul and Jesus share the *same* double emphasis, the *same* eschatological tension. Is that too accidental, or do we see evidence here of further influence of Jesus' mission, its character and emphases reaching beyond Jesus to Paul through channels no longer obvious to us?

---

44. Rom. 5.9-10; 11.26; 13.11; Phil. 1.19; 2.12; 1 Thess. 5.8-9.

45. 1 Cor. 1.18; 15.2; 2 Cor. 2.15.

46. E.g. 2 Cor. 4.16–5.5; Phil. 3.10-11; see further my *The Theology of Paul the Apostle* (Grand Rapids: Eerdmans; Edinburgh: T. & T. Clark, 1998) #18.

47. Rom. 2.12-13; 2 Cor. 5.10; see further my *The New Perspective on Paul* (WUNT 185; Tübingen: Mohr Siebeck, 2005; revised, Grand Rapids: Eerdmans, 2007) ch. 1 ##4.2(10) and 4.3(11).

48. Matt. 16.27; John 5.28-29; Rom. 2.6-11; 1 Cor. 3.8; 2 Cor. 5.10; 11.15; Col. 3.25; Rev. 20.11-15.

49. E.g. Matt. 6.1-6; 10.41-42; 25.34-40; 1 Cor. 3.14; 9.24-25; Phil. 3.14; Col. 3.24; 2 Tim. 4.8.

50. E.g. Mark 13.13; Rom. 8.13; 1 Cor. 15.2; Gal. 6.8; Col. 1.23.

b. *The Spirit as the* arrabōn *and* aparchē. An even more striking feature linking Paul to Jesus is the same realisation that the Spirit is the key to understanding the tension between the already and the not yet. For with the coming of the Spirit — we may think of Luke's story of Pentecost (Acts 2) — another of Israel's eschatological hopes had been realised. As the prophets had expected, the Spirit had been poured out in the last days.[51] As Jesus' resurrection marked the beginning of the end-time resurrection, so the Pentecost baptism in the Holy Spirit marked the fulfilment of God's final purpose for his people. Paul rejoiced in that Spirit as much as any of the first Christians. But Paul did not go overboard on this, in a wave of wild spiritual enthusiasm — as has so often been the case when individuals have experienced a rich outpouring of the Spirit. For it is Paul who emphasised that the Spirit is the *arrabōn,* the first instalment that guarantees full and final payment (2 Cor. 1.22); and that the Spirit is the *aparchē* (Rom. 8.23), the first fruits which signal the start of the final harvest. For Paul the Spirit is the power of God which transforms believers into the image of their Lord degree by degree (2 Cor. 3.18). The Spirit is the power which, again as the prophets had hoped,[52] enables the obedience which fulfils the law (Rom. 8.4) and bears the fruit of a transformed character (Gal. 5.22-23). The Spirit is the power which in the end will complete the lifelong process of salvation by changing our bodies of humiliation to conform them to Christ's body of glory.[53]

This is why, no doubt, for Paul, as for others of the earliest Christians, the Spirit of God can now be recognised as *the Spirit of Christ.*[54] For the power which anointed Jesus, which gave Jesus' mission its power and effectiveness, is the *same* power that believers now experience. That power bears the character of Jesus, and is distinguished from all false or misleading spiritual powers by the character of Jesus which it nurtures and grows in the believer. For Paul, 'discernment of spirits' (1 Cor. 12.10), testing of the Spirit's gifts (1 Thess. 5.21), was always necessary. And the primary test was whether the manifestation of the Spirit, the effect of the Spirit, was Christlike in character and Christ-forming in effect.[55] Paul could never have employed that test had he not known a lot more about Jesus' mission than his letters reveal. And no doubt it was his knowledge of the impact which the Spirit had had on Jesus which helped shape and determine Paul's pneumatology. As he himself says,

---

51. Acts 2.17-21 quotes Joel 2.28-32; see also Isa. 32.15; 44.3; Ezek. 39.29.

52. Jer. 31.31-34; Ezek. 11.19; 36.26-27.

53. Rom. 8.11; 1 Cor. 15.42-49; Phil. 3.21.

54. Rom. 8.9; Gal. 4.6; Phil. 1.19. Note also 1 Cor. 15.45; the 'life-giving spirit' is the Spirit of God.

55. See further my *Theology of Paul* 263, 594-98.

'It is God who establishes us with you in Christ and has anointed (or we may say, has "christed") us, by sealing us and giving us the *arrabōn* of the Spirit in our hearts' (2 Cor. 1.21-22). For Paul, the Spirit that anointed Jesus at the Jordan is the same Spirit that anointed believers and was shaping them into the image of Christ. The very language implies that Paul was well aware that Jesus had been anointed by the Spirit and that the continuum between Jesus' anointing and the gift of the Spirit to those who believed was firm and unbroken.

3. The Love Command

A third feature which allows a line to be drawn directly between Jesus and Paul is their shared attitude to the law and their shared insistence that the law was summed up in the command to love one's neighbour as oneself.

3.1. Jesus and the Law

One of the most depressing features of the quest for the historical Jesus has been the attempt by a succession of questers to set Jesus apart from his Jewish context. A classic expression of this was Ernest Renan's *Life of Jesus,* in which we find the following claim: 'Fundamentally there was nothing Jewish about Jesus'; after visiting Jerusalem, Jesus 'appears no more as a Jewish reformer, but as a destroyer of Judaism . . . Jesus was no longer a Jew'.[56] The key issue was Jesus' attitude to the law. Here it was easy to build on Jesus' controversies with various Pharisees, particularly on the Sabbath and on purity,[57] and to draw out the inference that Jesus in effect did away with the law. So it has been argued: the law and the prophets were until John the Baptist, but now, for Jesus, they belonged to the past.[58]

Part of the attraction of this argument was that it allowed a clear line to be drawn from Jesus to Paul. For Paul has traditionally been seen as the one who above all broke with the law and rendered it totally irrelevant for Christianity. My near neighbour in Durham, Charles Cranfield, for example, did not hesitate to draw a direct line between Jesus and Paul in claiming that Jesus

---

56. E. Renan, *The Life of Jesus* (London: Truebner, 1863; ET 1864), cited by S. Heschel, *Abraham Geiger and the Jewish Jesus* (Chicago: University of Chicago Press, 1998) 156-57.

57. Mark 2.23–3.5; 7.1-23.

58. J. Becker, *Jesus of Nazareth* (Berlin: De Gruyter, 1998) 227.

knew himself to be the *telos nomou*, 'the end of the law' of which Paul speaks in Rom. 10.4.[59]

But this simply will not do. For a start, it consigns Matthew's portrayal of Jesus and the law to a later attempt to re-Judaize Jesus. Matthew has Jesus saying:

> Do not think I have come to abolish the law or the prophets; I have not come to abolish but to fulfil. For truly I tell you, until heaven and earth pass away, not one letter, not one stroke of a letter, will pass from the law until all is accomplished. Therefore, whoever breaks one of the least of these commandments, and teaches others to do the same, will be called least in the kingdom of heaven; but whoever does them and teaches them will be called great in the kingdom of heaven. (Matt. 5.17-19)

So we are bound to ask whether Jesus' teaching on the law was quite so negative and dismissive as many of the questers for the historical Jesus have maintained. Has Matthew perverted the teaching of Jesus? Or was Jesus more ambiguous, or more subtle in his teaching on the law? Did he use the law to penetrate to what was of primary importance in the relationship between God and his people? Did he think of the law more as an icon than an idol — a window through which one could look to see what God really wants of his people, rather than an object on which to focus attention as the goal in itself? Is it possible to keep together veneration of the Torah as God's enduring gift for his people and at the same time a reprioritisation of the function of the law when and where God's kingdom is at hand?[60]

The answer begins to become clearer when we look at the other Gospel traditions on the subject. The Sabbath disputes show Jesus not ignoring or disputing the sanctity of the Sabbath, but rather asking how that sanctity is best maintained and celebrated. So, the Sabbath does not rule out what was otherwise a quite acceptable way of relieving hunger. And the Sabbath does not rule out doing good or saving life, but gives opportunity to do just that (Mark 2.23–3.5). And Matthew's version of the dispute about purity raises the question whether Jesus actually dismissed all laws of ritual purity or rather reminded

---

59. C. E. B. Cranfield, *St. Mark* (Cambridge: Cambridge University Press, 1959) 244.

60. For such an understanding of the Torah, see R. Deines, *Die Gerechtigkeit der Tora im Reich des Messias: Mt 5,13-20 als Schlüsseltext der matthäischen Theologie* (WUNT 177; Tübingen: Mohr Siebeck 2004); see also his 'Not the Law but the Messiah: Law and Righteousness in the Gospel of Matthew — an Ongoing Debate', in D. M. Gurtner and J. Nolland, eds., *Built upon the Rock: Studies in the Gospel of Matthew* [Grand Rapids: Eerdmans, 2008] 53-84).

his critics that the purity of the heart was much more important than the purity of the hands (Matt. 15.16-20). Again, in the Sermon on the Mount, what does Jesus do with commandments like those against murder and adultery? He does not disown them; he deepens them. The commandment against murder is intended to rule out not simply murder, but also the unjustified anger or insult. The commandment against adultery is intended to rule out not simply adultery, but also the lustful look and desire (Matt. 5.21-22, 27-28).[61]

Most striking of all is the way Jesus was prepared to sum up the law in just two commandments, the greatest commandments.

> The first is this, 'Hear, O Israel, you shall love the Lord your God with all your heart, and with all your soul, and with all your mind and with all your strength'. The second is this, 'You shall love your neighbour as yourself'. (Mark 12.29-31)

To be noted here is that Jesus did not refuse to sum up God's covenant obligations on his people in commandments. The first of his two commandments, of course, was Israel's own creedal confession, the Shema: 'Hear, O Israel, the LORD is our God, the LORD is one. You shall love the LORD your God . . ' (Deut. 6.4-5). So Jesus' fellow Jews would have had no difficulty in recognising that as the top priority. But the second was a complete surprise: 'You shall love your neighbour as yourself'. For this is also a commandment from the Torah (Lev. 19.18b). But it comes in a sequence of disparate rulings in Lev. 19. Jesus evidently extracted this particular commandment from these rulings and gave it a key role in interpreting the law. We should not miss the fact that Jesus seems to have had no precedent for doing so. Explicit references to Lev. 19.18 are lacking in Jewish literature prior to Jesus. And such allusions as there are give it no particular prominence, though subsequently the opinion is later attributed to Rabbi Akiba (early second century) that Lev. 19.18 is 'the greatest general principle in the Torah' (*Sifra* on Lev. 19.18). Almost certainly, then, it was Jesus himself who extracted Lev. 19.18 and gave it this preeminent status within the law.[62] And quite possibly Rabbi Akiba was influenced by Jesus, knowingly or unknowingly, in giving Lev. 19.18 a similar key role in interpreting the Torah.

This helps explain Jesus' attitude to the Sabbath and his attitude in the other disputes with various Pharisees, including, as we have seen earlier, his openness to sinners. It was because Jesus himself lived by the love command. For Jesus it was not possible to love God with all one's heart unless one also

---

61. See further my *Jesus Remembered* #14.4.
62. See further my *Jesus Remembered* #14.5.

loved one's neighbour as oneself. Just as, no doubt, Jesus would have maintained that it was not possible fully to love one's neighbour as oneself unless one first loved God fully.

3.2. Paul and the Law

The same problem has largely dominated scholarship's appreciation of Paul and the law. Lutheran scholarship has traditionally set gospel and law in sharp antithesis and attributed the antithesis wholly to Paul. The law and gospel are polar opposites; where the law is there can be no gospel. And it is true that Paul does speak negatively of the law on several occasions. The law multiplied sin, aroused sinful passions (Rom. 5.20; 7.5). The written law represented a ministry of condemnation and death (2 Cor. 3.7, 9). Paul himself had died to the law (Gal. 2.19). But once again there is more to it. In both Romans and Galatians Paul seems to build up a damning indictment of the law, only to reject that indictment. 'Is the law sin?' Paul asks in Romans (7.7). No, of course not, he replies. The law as such is holy and just and good (7.12). The blame lies in the power of sin which abuses the law (7.7-25). 'Is the law opposed to the promises of God?' Paul asks in Galatians (3.21). Certainly not, he replies. The law in its role as Israel's guardian was passé (3.21-26), but there is more to the story than that. Perhaps, then, Paul was reacting not so much against the law as such as against *one function* of the law, as I believe to be the case but have not time to develop here.[63]

What seems to have been ignored, or too much played down, is the very *positive* attitude Paul shows to the law. When the law is read with the eyes of faith, then its relevance and continuing validity are sustained. 'Do we nullify the law through faith?' Paul asks in Rom. 3.31, and immediately answers, 'Not at all, we establish the law'. He goes on to show how Abraham expressed his faith in his reliance upon God (4.16-22) and later defines sin not as breach of the law, but as conduct 'which is not of faith' (14.23). It is by living out of faith (trust and reliance on God) that one does the will of God. In Rom. 8.4 Paul can even say that the whole point of God sending his Son to deal with sin was 'in order that the requirement of the law might be fulfilled in us who walk not in accordance with the flesh but in accordance with the Spirit'. And in 1 Cor. 7.19 he can make the astonishing assertion that 'Circumcision is nothing, and uncircumcision is nothing; but obeying the commandments of God is everything'. The assertion is astonishing because, of course, circumcision is one of

---

63. See my *Theology of Paul* ##6, 14, 23; and *New Perspective on Paul* ch. 1.

God's commandments in the Old Testament. Here it becomes obvious that Paul was able to *differentiate* within the law. He maintains that some laws, here the law of circumcision, no longer counted for anything. But in the same breath he reasserts the importance of keeping the laws of God.

Does this not remind us of Jesus? For Paul emphasises, in effect, that the law can be understood in a too-surface way and be applied in a too superficial way — what he refers to as *gramma,* the visible, outward letter.[64] What he had in mind was the contrast with the Spirit working in the heart.[65] Paul evidently was alluding to the promises of Jeremiah and Ezekiel, for the law to be written in the heart, and no longer merely on tablets of stone (Jer. 31.33), for the Spirit to be given to enable the law to be kept properly.[66] This is an emphasis which echoes, does it not, Jesus' teaching on the commandments against murder and adultery and the real causes of impurity. And was Paul unaware of that aspect of Jesus' teaching? I doubt it.

The most striking evidence of the influence of Jesus' teaching on Paul is Paul's reference to the love command. In both Romans and Galatians he makes the same point — the same point that Jesus made! All the commandments are 'summed up in this word, in the command, "You shall love your neighbour as yourself"' (Rom. 13.9). 'The whole law is fulfilled in one word, in the well-known "You shall love your neighbour as yourself"' (Gal. 5.14).[67] Where did Paul get this from? We have already noted that no other teacher known to us in Second Temple Judaism had extracted this commandment from the sequence of rulings in Lev. 19. So how was it 'well known'? Paul can only be referring to the fact that Jesus' teaching on the love command was well known among the Christian communities. *Paul drew his attitude to the law from Jesus.* No other explanation makes such sense of the evidence available to us. It was Jesus' teaching and example which showed him that 'In Christ neither circumcision counts for anything nor uncircumcision, but faith operating effectively through love' (Gal. 5.6). And it was no doubt this teaching and that example which Paul had in mind when he spoke of 'the law of Christ' (Gal. 6.2).

In short, *nowhere is the line of continuity and influence from Jesus to Paul clearer than in the love command.* In summary, we may say, Jesus taught that the love command is the second-greatest commandment of the law, and he lived by that command in his mission. So Paul followed in his train and

64. Rom. 2.28; 2 Cor. 3.6-7.
65. Rom. 2.29; 2 Cor. 3.3, 6, 8.
66. Ezek. 11.19-20; 36.26-27.
67. Literally 'in the "You shall love your neighbour as yourself"', so the reference is clearly to something familiar, as in Rom. 13.8-9, written to a church Paul had never previously visited.

summed up the whole law in that same command and, like Jesus, used the criterion it gave him to discern the commandments that really mattered in directing the relationship between God and his people and between the individual members of his people.

Conclusion

Should we then speak of a gulf between Jesus and Paul? No! Should we deduce that Paul departed from or corrupted the good news which Jesus brought? No! Should we conclude that Paul transformed Jesus' message into something Jesus himself would not have recognised? No!

Of course, there is much more to be discussed than we can deal with in one lecture. But enough has been said, I hope, to show that those who have answered yes to such questions as these were too hasty, ignored too much that was of relevance, assumed too quickly that traditional perspectives gave a view of the whole.

In fact, however, Jesus' good news of God's kingly rule as active in and through his ministry was a close antecedent of Paul's message of grace for the ungodly here and now. Jesus' good news for sinners in Israel was the direct precedent and perhaps the direct inspiration for Paul's gospel for Gentile sinners. Jesus' good news for the poor was reflected in the same priority which Paul gave to his churches' care for the poor.

So too Paul's maintenance of the uncomfortable tension between the already and the not yet in the process of salvation is a fairly clear mirror of Jesus' maintenance of the tension between God's kingdom already in action in the present and God's kingdom still to come. And Paul's understanding of the Spirit as both the sign of fulfilled hope and as the first instalment of the still richer inheritance yet to come equally mirrors, if less clearly, Jesus' own claim to have been anointed by the Spirit for his mission.

And not least, Jesus' discriminating attitude to the law and his selection of the love command as the primary rule to govern human relationships are a clear precedent to Paul's similarly discriminating attitude to the law and his similar insistence that the whole law is best summed up and fulfilled by loving one's neighbour as oneself.

Paul, who may never have heard or seen Jesus for himself, nevertheless can be characterised as *one of the truest disciples of Jesus* — not simply of the exalted Lord Jesus Christ, but also of Jesus of Nazareth.

PART THREE

THE BIMILLENNIAL PAUL

CHAPTER 6

Who Did Paul Think He Was?

The Second Founder of Christianity?

There were three absolutely crucial figures in the first generation of Christianity — Peter, Paul and James the brother of Jesus.[1] Of these, Paul probably played the most significant role in shaping Christianity. Prior to Paul what we now call 'Christianity' was no more than a messianic sect within first-century Judaism, or better, within Second Temple Judaism — 'the sect of the Nazarenes' (Acts 24.5), the followers of 'the Way' (that is, presumably, the way shown by Jesus).[2] Without Paul this messianic sect might have remained a renewal movement within Second Temple Judaism and never become anything more than that. Almost certainly that is how James would have preferred the new movement to remain. Peter may have been more ambivalent — somewhere in between James and Paul, a bridge figure perhaps, a *pontifex* indeed. But it was Paul who transformed this new Jewish sect which believed Jesus to be Messiah into something more. Paul's mission *was the single most important*

---

1. In my *Christianity in the Making*, vol. 2, *Beginning from Jerusalem* (Grand Rapids: Eerdmans, 2009), I focus attention especially on these central figures of first-generation Christianity. I draw heavily on this volume particularly in chs. 6 and 7. For this chapter, see also my earlier 'Who Did Paul Think He Was? A Study of Jewish Christian Identity', *NTS* 45 (1999) 174-93. And in addition to the relevant bibliography in *Beginning from Jerusalem*, see particularly J. Frey, 'Paul's Jewish Identity', in J. Frey, D. R. Schwartz and St. Gripentrog, eds., *Jewish Identity in the Greco-Roman World — Jüdische Identität in der griechisch-römischen Welt* (Leiden: Brill, 2007) 285-321.

2. Acts 9.2; 19.9, 23; 22.4; 24.14, 22.

development in the first decades of Christianity's history. Paul's mission and the teaching transmitted through his letters did more than anything else to transform embryonic Christianity from a messianic sect, quite at home within Second Temple Judaism, into a religion hospitable to Greeks, increasingly Gentile in composition, and less and less comfortable with the kind of Judaism which was to survive the ruinous failure of the two Jewish revolts against Rome (66-73, 132-135 CE).

The crucial impact of Paul's work was made during his mission in the Aegean, recounted in Acts 16–20. For one thing, it marked a decisive shift *westwards*. This development alone was sufficient to shift the centre of gravity in earliest Christianity from Jerusalem and the eastern seaboard of the Mediterranean towards the metropolitan centres of Asia Minor and Greece, and then Rome. For another, the churches founded by Paul were increasingly *Gentile*, non-Jewish, in membership. These two factors alone might have been sufficient to ensure the transformation of a Jewish sect into a predominantly Gentile religion. But in the longer term the third reason was even more decisive. For *it was during his Aegean mission that Paul wrote most of his letters* — almost certainly his most important letters, but possibly *all* the letters which can be attributed to Paul himself.[3] Paul's letters are the only Christian writings which can assuredly be dated to the first generation (thirty-five years) of Christianity. And it is these letters which ensured that Paul's legacy would continue to influence and indeed give Christianity so much of its definitive character.

In other words, the eight or so years of Paul's Aegean mission stand alongside the three years of Jesus' own mission, the first two or three years of the Jerusalem church's existence and the initial expansion of the new sect led by the Hellenists.[4] Like these earlier periods, the period of Paul's mission was absolutely crucial for Christianity's existence and enduring character. And it is Paul's Aegean mission and its lasting outcome, in terms of both churches established and letters composed and circulated, which make appropriate the title sometimes accorded to Paul — 'the second founder of Christianity'. As already noted, this title was first given to Paul at the beginning of the twentieth century, initially with some degree of disparagement: 'the second founder of Christianity' who has 'exercised beyond all doubt the stronger — not the better — influence' than the first (Jesus).[5] But it has been revived more re-

---

3. Certainly 1 and 2 Corinthians, Romans, 1 (and 2) Thessalonians, probably Galatians, and possibly Philippians, Colossians and Philemon are all to be dated to Paul's Aegean mission.

4. Acts 6–8; 11.19-26.

5. See above, ch. 5 n. 13.

cently as a way of giving proper recognition of the debt which Christianity owes to Paul.[6] And as a title it is deserved not because Paul was the first to preach the gospel to Gentiles, or the first to preach Christ in Rome, or the first to break out from the matrix of Second Temple Judaism; but because *it was Paul's mission which made it impossible for Gentile believers to be retained within the traditional forms of Judaism,* and because *his writings became the most influential reinterpretations of the original traditions and forms of the new movement.*

Precisely because Paul stands at the fulcrum or transition point, where a Jewish messianic sect began to become something more, he is a controversial figure. For most Jews interested in Christianity's origins, Paul is one who abandoned his past and sold his birthright. He is a traitor to his people, an apostate from Israel, now a Christian and no longer a Jew. So we start by asking, Who did *Paul* think he was? How did he see his own role? How would Paul have thought of himself? How would Paul have introduced himself to a stranger?

In a number of passages in his letters Paul speaks in explicitly autobiographical terms. Apart from the self-introduction of his letters, where he describes himself most often as 'Paul, an apostle of Jesus Christ', the most relevant are:

- Rom. 11.1 — 'I am an Israelite, of the seed of Abraham, of the tribe of Benjamin'.
- Rom. 11.13 — 'I am apostle to the Gentiles'.
- Rom. 15.16 — 'a minister of Christ Jesus for the Gentiles, serving the gospel of Christ as a priest'.
- 1 Cor. 9.1-2 — 'Am I not an apostle? Have I not seen our Lord? . . . If to others I am not an apostle, at least I am to you'.
- 1 Cor. 9.20-21 — 'To the Jews I became as a Jew, in order that I might win Jews; to those under the law I became as one under the law (though not myself actually under the law) in order that I might win those under the law; to those outside the law I became as one outside the law (though not actually outside the law of God but in-lawed to Christ) in order that I might win those outside the law'.
- 1 Cor. 15.9-10 — 'I am the least of the apostles, not worthy to be called an apostle . . . but by the grace of God I am what I am'.
- 2 Cor. 11.22-23 — 'Are they Hebrews? So am I. Are they Israelites? So am

---

6. M. Hengel and A. M. Schwemer, *Paul between Damascus and Antioch* (London: SCM, 1997) 309.

I. Are they seed of Abraham? So am I. Are they ministers of Christ? . . . I more'.

- Gal. 1.13-14 — 'You have heard of my way of life previously in Judaism, that in excessive measure I persecuted the church of God and tried to destroy it, and that I progressed in Judaism beyond many of my contemporaries among my people, being exceedingly zealous for my ancestral traditions'.
- Gal. 2.19-20 — 'I through the law died to the law. . . . No longer I live, but Christ lives in me'.
- Phil. 3.5-8 — 'circumcised the eighth day, of the people of Israel, of the tribe of Benjamin, a Hebrew of the Hebrews, as to the law a Pharisee, as to zeal a persecutor of the church, as to righteousness which is in the law, blameless. But what was gain to me, these things I have come to regard as loss on account of the Christ. More than that, I regard everything as loss on account of the surpassing value of knowing Christ Jesus my Lord'.

Four striking aspects of Paul's self-identity come to vivid expression in these passages.

No Longer 'in Judaism'

Gal. 1.13-14 — 'You have heard of my way of life *previously in Judaism,* that in excessive measure I persecuted the church of God and tried to destroy it, and that I progressed *in Judaism* beyond many of my contemporaries among my people, being exceedingly zealous for my ancestral traditions'.

It is clear from Gal. 1.13-14 that Paul regarded his 'way of life within Judaism' as something past. As a Christian, he would no longer describe himself as 'in Judaism'. However, it is important to appreciate that the 'Judaism' referred to in Gal. 1.13-14 is *not* to be confused with what we today denote by the term 'Judaism' or describe as 'Second Temple Judaism'. The historical term ('Judaism') was coined in the second century BCE to describe the Judeans' spirited religio-nationalistic resistance to their Syrian rulers.[7] It will be remembered that the regional Syrian superpower was attempting to enforce an empire-wide homogeneity of religion by suppressing the distinctives of Israel's religion, particularly Torah, circumcision, and laws of clean and unclean. The

7. 2 Macc. 2.21; 8.1; 14.38.

Maccabean revolt resisted this to the death.[8] And 'Judaism' was the term which emerged to denote this resistance. So 2 Macc. 2.21 describes the Maccabean rebels as 'those who fought bravely *for Judaism*'. 8.1 describes their supporters as 'those who had continued *in Judaism*'. And 14.38 describes the martyr Razis as one who had formerly been accused of *Judaism* and who had eagerly risked body and life *'on behalf of Judaism'*. Reflecting the same traditions, 4 Macc. 4.26 describes the attempt of the Syrian overlord Antiochus Epiphanes 'to compel each member of the nation to eat defiling foods and to renounce *Judaism*'. So *Ioudaismos* was the term coined in the Maccabean period to denote the unyielding resistance which the Maccabees maintained against *hellēnismos* (Hellenism) and *allophylismos* (foreignness).[9]

Gal. 1.13-14 confirms that Paul used the term 'Judaism' with this same sense: the 'way of life' he described as 'in Judaism' was his life as a zealous Pharisee; the 'way of life' was marked by a readiness to persecute, even to destroy fellow religionists who (as we shall see) were considered to pose a threat to the holiness and distinctiveness of this 'Judaism'. The same point emerges from Paul's other look backwards — Phil. 3.5-7.

> Phil. 3.5-7 — 'circumcised the eighth day, of the people of Israel, of the tribe of Benjamin, a Hebrew of the Hebrews, as to the law a Pharisee, as to zeal a persecutor of the church, as to righteousness which is in the law, blameless. But what was gain to me, these things I have come to regard as loss *(skybala)* on account of the Christ'.

Here too it is clear that what Paul had turned his back on and now regarded as so much 'garbage' *(skybala)* was particularly the same Pharisaic zeal and righteousness.[10]

So, the 'Judaism' Paul converted from was his zealous Pharisaism. Previously he had been as 'zealous' as Phinehas in Num. 25 and as the Maccabees. That is, he had dedicated himself to safeguarding Israel's holiness. Like them, he had been willing to take violent action (persecution) against those who threatened Israel's set-apartness to God. We will go into this in more detail in chapter 8 below.

It was this 'zeal', then, from which Paul had been converted, turned away from, by his encounter with the risen Christ on the Damascus road. So

---

8. See e.g. E. Schürer, *The History of the Jewish People in the Age of Jesus Christ* (rev. and ed. G. Vermes and F. Millar; 4 vols.; Edinburgh: T. & T. Clark, 1973-87) vol. 1, pt. 1, 'The Maccabean Rising and the Age of Independence'.

9. 2 Macc. 4.13; 6.24.

10. *Ta skybala* can denote 'excrement' (BDAG 932).

we can certainly say that as a result of his conversion and commission to serve as an 'apostle of Jesus Christ', as 'apostle to the Gentiles', Paul no longer thought of himself as belonging to 'Judaism'. But in so saying, Paul was thinking only in terms of *Pharisaic* Judaism, that is, of the Pharisaic understanding of Israel's heritage, or in particular, of the zealous faction of what we today call Second Temple Judaism.

But can or should we say more? Had Paul, for example, ceased to think of himself as a Jew?

Paul the Jew?

If Paul no longer thought of himself as being 'in Judaism', does it not also follow that he no longer thought of himself as a *Jew?* For it is difficult to avoid an ethnic sense in the term 'Jew' *(Yehudi, Ioudaios).* The term, after all, derives from the region or territory known as 'Judea' *(Yehudah, Ioudaia).* And Paul remained ethnically Judean in origin, even though he had initially been brought up as a Judean living in the diaspora. It is true that for more than a century *Ioudaios* had been gaining a more religious connotation (not dependent on ethnic origin) — better translated as 'Jew' rather than 'Judean'.[11] But recent discussions have concluded that ethnicity remained at the core of Jewish identity.[12] So the question stands: How could Paul have left 'Judaism' behind without leaving behind his religious (or ethnic, or cultural) identity as a 'Jew'?

Something of the ambiguity in which Paul's identity was caught is indicated by two references in his letters. In Rom. 2 Paul addresses his interlocu-

---

11. S. J. D. Cohen, *The Beginnings of Jewishness: Boundaries, Varieties, Uncertainties* (Berkeley: University of California Press, 1999), concludes that prior to the Hasmonean period *Ioudaios* should always be translated 'Judean' and never as 'Jew' (70-71, 82-106); the shift from a purely ethno-geographical term to one of religious significance is first evident in 2 Macc. 6.6 and 9.17, where for the first time *Ioudaios* can properly be translated 'Jew'; and in Greco-Roman writers, the first use of *Ioudaios* as a religious term appears at the end of the first century CE (90-96, 127, 133-36).

12. J. M. G. Barclay, *Jews in the Mediterranean Diaspora from Alexander to Trajan (323 BCE–117 CE)* (Edinburgh: T. & T. Clark, 1996) 404. P. M. Casey, *From Jewish Prophet to Gentile God: The Origin and Development of New Testament Christology* (Cambridge: James Clarke, 1991), similarly concludes his discussion on 'identity factors', that ethnicity outweighs all the rest (especially 14). Note also the observation of L. H. Schiffman, *Who Was a Jew?* (Hoboken, NJ: Ktav, 1985), that 'Judaism is centred on the Jewish people, a group whose membership is fundamentally determined by heredity', and his argument that even heretics did not lose their 'Jewish status' (38, 49, 61).

tor as one who calls himself a 'Jew': 'you call yourself a Jew and rely on the law and boast of your relation to God' (2.17). But Paul then goes on to indicate his disapproval of the attitudes and conduct which he attributes to the interlocutor: 'If you call yourself a Jew . . . (why) do you dishonour God by breaking the law?' (2.17-24). Here he seems to distance himself from the 'Jew'. Yet in Gal. 2 Paul represents his rebuke to Peter at Antioch, and continues by appealing to Peter, 'We [two, you and I] are Jews by nature and not Gentile sinners' (2.15). In this case Paul's continuing identity as a 'Jew' was precisely the basis of his exhortation to Peter.

More striking is the fact that a few sentences later in Rom. 2, Paul offers a definition of 'Jew' which removes the defining factor of Jewishness from what is outward and visible in the flesh (presumably ethnic characteristics as well as circumcision itself). This is what he says: 'For the Jew [we might translate "the true Jew", or "the Jew properly speaking"] is not the one visibly so, nor is circumcision that which is visibly performed in the flesh; but (the Jew) is one who is so in a hidden way, and circumcision is of the heart, in Spirit not in letter.[13] His praise comes not from men but from God' (2.28-29).[14] We should not conclude that Paul thereby disowned his Jewish identity. For in fact he was using the term 'Jew' in a positive way. Indeed, he immediately proceeds to affirm 'the advantage' of 'the Jew' in the very next sentence: 'What advantage has the Jew? . . . Much, in every way' (3.1-2). Moreover, the contrast between outward appearance and inward reality had been long familiar in the religion of Israel[15] and more widely.[16] At the same time, however, by switching the emphasis away from the outward and visible, Paul in effect was playing down the role of the term 'Jew' as an ethnic identifier. 'Jew' as a term denoting distinctiveness from the (other) nations was no longer relevant. On the contrary, the positive mark of 'the Jew' was nothing observable by others but was determined primarily by relationship with God.[17] So a degree of ambiguity remains.

---

13. For detail see my *Romans* (WBC 34A; Dallas: Word, 1988) 123-24. The seer of Revelation uses similar language — Rev. 2.9 and 3.9.

14. Note how Paul retains the wordplay from Gen. 29.35 and 49.8: in Hebrew, 'Jew' = *Yehudi*, and 'praise' = *hodah*. 'In popular etymology it [the patriarchal name Judah *(Yehudah)*] was often explained as the passive of *hodah* "(someone) praised"' (J. A. Fitzmyer, *Romans* [AB 33; New York: Doubleday, 1993] 323). The pun, of course, would probably be lost on Paul's Greek-speaking audiences.

15. Cf. particularly Isa. 29.13 and Jer. 9.25-26.

16. See especially A. Fridrichsen, 'Der wahre Jude und sein Lob: Röm. 2.28f.,' *Symbolae Arctoae* 1 (1927) 39-49.

17. Note the similar argument regarding circumcision in Phil. 3.3: circumcision is reaffirmed, but redefined in terms of the work of the Spirit in the heart; see my 'Philippians 3.2-14 and the New Perspective on Paul', in *The New Perspective on Paul* (WUNT 185; Tübingen: Mohr

Even more striking is 1 Cor. 9.20-21, already cited.

> To the Jews I became as a Jew, in order that I might win Jews; to those under
> the law I became as one under the law (though not myself actually under
> the law) in order that I might win those under the law; to those outside the
> law I became as one outside the law (though not actually outside the law of
> God but in-lawed to Christ) in order that I might win those outside the law.

The striking feature in this case is that Paul, even though himself ethnically a
Jew, could speak of *becoming* 'as a Jew'. Here, 'to become as a Jew' is obviously
to follow the patterns of conduct distinctive of Jews, to 'Judaize'.[18] In other
words, Paul speaks here as one who did not acknowledge 'Jew' as his own
identity, or as an identity inalienable from his person as an ethnic Jew. Instead
he treats 'Jew' almost as a *role* which he might assume or discard. The term
denotes not so much an actual identity, an identity integral to him as a person, but rather an identity which could be taken on or put off as needs or circumstances demanded.[19] Here again, therefore, it is clear that Paul wanted to
disentangle the term 'Jew' from the narrower constraints of ethnicity, and to
treat it more as denoting a code of conduct or a manner of living.[20]

In short, whereas Paul seems to have been willing to regard his time 'in
Judaism' as past, *he was nevertheless unwilling to abandon the term 'Jew' as a
self-referential term.* As a term marking off 'Jew' ethnically from 'Gentile', or
'Jew' culturally from 'Greek', it still had a functional role.[21] As a term denoting
an inner reality and relationship with God in which non-Jews could partici-
pate, it still had meaning to be cherished. But as a term giving the distinction
between Jew and non-Jew any continuing religious validity, or as signifying a
divine partiality towards the 'Jew', its role was at an end.[22]

Siebeck, 2005; rev. ed., Grand Rapids: Eerdmans, 2007) ch. 22 (465-67). The recognition of the
need for the *heart* to be circumcised (and not just the flesh) is a repeated theme in Jewish writing (Deut. 10.16; Jer. 4.4; 9.25-26; Ezek. 44.9; 1QpHab 11.13; 1QS 5.5; 1QH 10.18; 21.5; Philo, *On the
Special Laws* 1.305).

18. The meaning of 'Judaize' should not be confused by the nineteenth- and twentieth-
century use of 'Judaizer' to refer to Paul's Jewish opponents = Jews who wanted Gentile converts
to become Jewish proselytes. The term was used at the time of Paul to denote the action of non-
Jews living like Jews. See my *Beginning from Jerusalem* #27 n. 255.

19. C. K. Barrett, *1 Corinthians* (BNTC; London: A. & C. Black, 1968) 211.

20. Cassius Dio comments on the name 'Jews': 'I do not know how this title came to be
given them, but it applies to all the rest of mankind, although of alien race, who affect [better
"emulate" — *zēlousi*] their customs' (37.17.1 — *GLAJJ* #406 = 2.349, 351).

21. Hence Paul's frequent use of the pairs, Jews/Greeks, Jews/Gentiles — Rom. 1.16; 2.9-
10; 3.9, 29; 9.24; 1 Cor. 1.22-24; 10.32; 12.13; Gal. 2.15.

22. Hence Rom. 2.6-11; Gal. 3.28.

'I Am an Israelite'

Apart from Gal. 2.15, Paul never called himself a Jew; and even there he uses the term only as a way of claiming common ground with Peter.[23] Paul shows similar ambivalence with regard to other terms usually understood to denote national or cultural identity. In Phil. 3.5 *'Hebrew'* is a status he seems to consign to the rubbish bin — 'a Hebrew of the Hebrews. . . . But what was gain to me, these things I have come to regard as loss/garbage on account of the Christ' (3.7-8). Yet in 2 Cor. 11 Paul affirms his continuing identity as a 'Hebrew' in vigorous rejoinder to those who were operating in opposition to him in Corinth: 'Are they Hebrews?' he asks, and quickly affirms, 'So am I' (11.22). Evidently, there was something important about himself and his missionary role which could still be expressed by the term 'Hebrew', however foolish he thought it to continue investing too much significance in the term (11.21).

Membership of *'the tribe of Benjamin'* and descent from Abraham are caught in much the same ambivalence. The former seems also to be something once valued but now discarded as of lasting importance. Being of the tribe of Benjamin, once counted as 'gain', now is regarded 'as loss on account of the Christ' (Phil. 3.5). Yet in Rom. 11 the status is affirmed without disclaimer: 'I am an Israelite, of the seed of Abraham, of the tribe of Benjamin' (11.1). And *descent from Abraham* ('of the seed of Abraham') is again strongly affirmed, albeit polemically in 2 Cor. 11.22, and similarly without qualification in Rom. 11.1. In the same polemical context Paul's identity as an *'Israelite'* is also asserted alongside his being a 'Hebrew' and 'of the seed of Abraham' (2 Cor. 11.22). And belonging to the race of Israel is part of the heritage discounted in Phil. 3.5-7. But again 'I am an Israelite' is affirmed as self-identification *ex anima* and without qualification in Rom. 11.1.[24]

What is striking about the Rom. 11.1 references is that the verse comes after Paul has attempted to redefine both who can be counted as 'Abraham's seed' (ch. 4; also Gal. 3) and what constitutes Israel as Israel (Rom. 9). The identity of Israel is not defined or determined by physical descent. For the promise came through Isaac alone, and not through Ishmael, even though Ishmael too was a child of Abraham (9.7-9). Nor is it defined or determined by doing what the law requires, living like a Jew. For it was Jacob who was called, not Esau (9.10-13). No, *the identity of Israel is defined and determined*

---

23. Only in Acts does Paul declare, 'I am a Jew' (Acts 21.39; 22.3).

24. Note also Rom. 9.4: Paul's kindred according to the flesh 'are [still] Israelites' — 'are', not 'were'; the covenant blessings (9.4-5) now enjoyed by believing Gentiles remain *Israel's* blessings.

solely by the call of God; 'the purpose of God in election operates not in terms of keeping the law but from him who calls' (9.11-12). And that calling includes Gentiles as well as Jews — all 'whom God calls' (9.24-26).[25] In so arguing, we should recognise that Paul was attempting a redefinition of 'Abraham's seed' and of 'Israel' which transcends (or, we should say, absorbs) the ethno-religious distinction indicated by the contrast Jew/Gentile.[26] The significance of Paul's self-identifying confession, 'I am an Israelite' (Rom. 11.1), therefore becomes clear. That it includes an ethnic identification is not to be disputed. In the context of Paul's exposition in Rom. 9-11 the point is hardly deniable. For he insists that in the end 'all *Israel* will be saved' (11.26), where 'Israel' must be the same Israel, the ethnic Jews, the great majority of whom were rejecting the gospel of Jesus Messiah (11.7-12, 25). Ethnic Israel continues to be 'beloved'; 'the gifts and the calling of God are irrevocable' (11.28-29).

So when Paul confesses, 'I am an Israelite', he is confessing an identity primarily and precisely as *determined by God*. It is a different kind of identity from the term 'Jew', where identity is expressed by making a distinction from other nations — Jew and not Gentile. And it is a different kind of identity from one determined by conformity to *halakhic* principles, as was to become the emphasis in rabbinic Judaism.[27] Rather, *Paul's whole concern was to reassert Israel's identity as primarily determined by God and in relation to God, and thus as transcending ethnic and social distinctions and as absorbing ethnic and social diversity.*

'In Christ'

Probably, however, we should allow our appreciation of how Paul thought of himself to be determined primarily by *frequency of usage,* rather than the few explicit self-references thus far reviewed. That directs us at once to Paul's pervasive use of the phrases 'in Christ' and 'in the Lord' in his letters. The phrase identifies by self-location, by indicating where one sets oneself, where one be-

25. See my *Romans* 537; also my work *The Theology of Paul the Apostle* (Grand Rapids: Eerdmans; Edinburgh: T. & T. Clark, 1998) 510-11.

26. Note that in the climax of his argument in Romans (Rom. 9-11), Paul switches from the predominant Jew/Greek, Jew/Gentile usage ('Jew' appears nine times in Rom. 1-3) to predominant talk of 'Israel' (in Rom. 9-11, 'Israel' eleven times; 'Jew' twice); and that in Rom. 9-11 the topic is not 'Israel and the church', as so often asserted, but solely 'Israel', that is, his people viewed from God's perspective (see my *Romans* 520; *Theology of Paul* 507-8).

27. See C. T. R. Hayward, *Interpretations of the Name Israel in Ancient Judaism and Some Early Christian Writings* (Oxford: Oxford University Press, 2005) 355.

longs. As such, it is Paul's primary reference point for understanding himself as well as his converts. The phrase 'in Christ' appears some eighty-three times in the Pauline corpus (sixty-one if we exclude Ephesians and the Pastorals). Similarly, 'in the Lord' is used forty-seven times in the Pauline corpus (thirty-nine if we exclude Ephesians). And we should not forget the many more 'in him/whom' phrases with the same referent.[28] The term 'Christian' had recently been invented as a new word, a neologism to denote those deemed to be followers of the one known as '(the) Christ' (Acts 11.26). Paul never uses the term. But the phrase 'in Christ' at times does serve in its place, and is often translated as 'Christian' in modern translations.[29] Its co-referent in corporate terms is the less frequently used, but obviously important, 'body of Christ' (particularly Rom. 12.4-8 and 1 Cor. 12).[30]

The importance of the self-understanding thereby encapsulated is indicated by two of the passages quoted earlier:

Gal. 2.19-20 — 'I through the law died to the law. . . . No longer I live, but Christ lives in me'.

Phil. 3.5-8 — 'circumcised the eighth day, of the people of Israel, of the tribe of Benjamin, a Hebrew of the Hebrews, as to the law a Pharisee, as to zeal a persecutor of the church, as to righteousness which is in the law, blameless. But what was gain to me, these things I have come to regard as loss on account of the Christ. More than that, I regard everything as loss on account of the surpassing value of knowing Christ Jesus my Lord'.

In both cases we see a shift in identity, or in what constitutes self-identity for Paul. He has 'died to the law' (Gal. 2.19), a phrase which epitomises Paul's conversion. As a result of his conversion he had abandoned what he had previously valued about and for himself (Phil. 3.4-6) — his ethnic identity, his righteousness as a Pharisee, his zealous defence of Israel's covenant prerogatives, his faithful observance of the law. As a consequence of his encounter with Christ, he counted all that as so much 'garbage' (3.8) in comparison with what now really mattered to him.[31] And what really mattered now was to

28. Full details in my *Theology of Paul* #15.2 (with bibliography). See also C. J. Hodge, 'Apostle to the Gentiles: Constructions of Paul's Identity', *BibInt* 13 (2005) 270-88.

29. BDAG 327-28 gives various instances where the phrases can be treated as periphrases for 'Christian' (328); see further *Theology of Paul* 399 n. 48.

30. *Theology of Paul* 405-6, but noting the variation in usage (n. 76). See further below, ch. 9.

31. See more fully my 'Philippians 3.2-14 and the New Perspective on Paul': 'The sharpness of the contrast is not so much to denigrate what he had previously counted as gain, as to en-

'gain Christ', to 'be found in Christ' (3.8-9), to 'know Christ' (3.8, 10), to become like Christ in death as well as resurrection (3.10-11). Alternatively expressed, 'Christ in him' was now the determining and defining character of his living (Gal. 2.20). Similarly in Rom. 8.9-11 Paul comes as close as he ever does to providing a definition of a Christian, of what determines whether a person 'belongs to Christ' — 'If anyone does not have the Spirit of Christ, that person does not belong to him' (8.9). The indwelling Spirit, or alternatively, 'Christ in you' (8.10), is what determines Christian status.[32] That was what now determined Paul as a person, his values, his objectives, and his identity. The other identifiers need not and should not be entirely discounted and devalued. But in comparison with being 'in Christ', nothing else really counted for anything very much at all.

One indicator of the shift in Paul's self-understanding is given by the transition from Romans chapter 11 to chapter 12. For in Rom. 9–11, as already noted, the concern was exclusively with Israel, including his hopes for ethnic Israel. But in Rom. 12 the first social context within which Paul wanted his readers/hearers to recognise and affirm themselves was *the body of Christ* (12.3-8).[33] We will return to this in chapter 9. Here we need simply to note that for Paul a community called out and constituted by Christ was to be the primary reference by which Christians' identity and mode of living were determined. Paul would hardly have thought otherwise about himself, as his 'in Christ/Lord' language clearly indicates.

A Changing Identity

'Identity' is a much used term today in attempts to achieve satisfactory self-definition. The problem is that it is a more slippery term than we often care to admit. Is a person's identity defined or determined by his or her parents? By physical appearance? By place of birth and upbringing? By DNA? By memories? By education? By career? By likes and dislikes? By friends or family? The same person will have many identities — a son or daughter, a brother or sister or cousin, a father or mother, a colleague, a friend, and so on. So when we talk of Paul's identity, we could speak of his multiple identity — a Jew, an Israelite,

---

hance to the highest degree the value he now attributes to Christ, to the knowledge of Christ, and to the prospect of gaining Christ' (*New Perspective on Paul* 475).

32. See also A. du Toit, '"In Christ", "In the Spirit" and Related Prepositional Phrases: Their Relevance for a Discussion on Pauline Mysticism', in *Focusing on Paul: Persuasion and Theological Design in Romans and Galatians* (BZNW 151; Berlin: De Gruyter, 2007) 129-45.

33. See further my *Romans* 703; *Theology of Paul* 534-35, 548.

a believer in Jesus Messiah, and more. Does one disqualify the other, make it any less true?

What we can speak of is Paul's *changing* identity. He no longer thought of himself as 'in Judaism'. He was now 'in Christ'. His self-understandings as a Hebrew, as of the tribe of Benjamin, as a Jew, were more ambivalent, not valued by him as he had previously valued them. His identity as one of the seed of Abraham, as an Israelite, was still highly valued but had been redefined.

And when we ask the question, 'Who did Paul think he was?' the simplest answer is the phrase he used evidently of himself in 2 Cor. 12.2 — 'a person in Christ'.[34] He had not ceased to be an ethnic Jew, but no longer counted that as definitive of his relation to God, and therefore of his identity. The key factor for Paul himself was that his identity was primarily determined by his relationship to Christ, even though that did not entirely deny the value of his other identities (particularly as a circumcised Jew). Gal. 3.28 sums up Paul's position clearly: 'There is neither Jew nor Greek; there is neither slave nor free; there is no male and female; for you are all one in Christ Jesus'.

All this is of continuing relevance not only for a better understanding of Paul, but also for a better understanding of Christian identity. For Paul did more to define the identity of *Christianity* than any other contributor to the New Testament. Indeed, Paul himself embodies and expresses Christian identity as no one else does. For Christianity and Christians generally must never be allowed to forget:

- that Christianity came out of the religion of Israel — that within the purposes of God Christians belong with Israel;
- that Jesus is only Jesus Christ as Israel's Messiah;
- that all the first Christians were Jews;
- that two-thirds or three-quarters of the Christian Bible is Israel's scriptures; and
- that for Paul the saving promise of God fulfilled in and through Christ is the promise God made to Abraham.

So Christians can only understand *themselves* in the terms given them by the Hebrew Bible, by the Jewish scriptures — that is, in Jewish terms. *The Jewishness of Christianity is integral to Christianity.* And it is Paul who wrestles most effectively with the tensions and questions which Christianity's Jewishness continues to raise for Christians, but also for Jews concerned about

---

34. That Paul intended a self-reference at this point is almost universally agreed among commentators.

the overlap between Judaism and Christianity. As Paul wrestled with what it meant to be a Jew who believed in Jesus Messiah, so Christians today must wrestle with what it means to be a Gentile who believes in the Messiah of Israel. As Paul wrestled with the issue of what is central in Israel's heritage and what continued to be the Word of God for him, so Christian (and Jew) cannot escape the same issue. And as Paul resolved these issues, so far as he did resolve them, by making the key defining factor the purpose of God and the relationship with Christ, so today's Christians may learn to resolve the issues which plague them by the same priorities. For Paul, it was not tradition, not church, not even Scripture, which was the primary test of Christian identity, of belonging to Christ, but only being 'in Christ'.

CHAPTER 7

Apostle or Apostate?

Paul the Apostle

In 1990 Alan Segal, a prominent Jewish scholar of early Christian and Jewish literature, wrote a book entitled *Paul the Convert: The Apostolate and Apostasy of Saul the Pharisee.*[1] The title nicely sums up the ambiguity and contested character of Paul's identity and lasting significance — apostle *and* apostate? apostle *or* apostate? As already observed, Jews who take any note of Paul have little doubt that he was an apostate — a traitor to the Torah, an apostate from Israel. And Christians equally have little doubt that he was an apostle, even if not one of the Twelve. But both remind us of Paul's changing identity, and both titles have greater problems and carry a greater weight of implication than most Jews and Christians realise.

We start once again with Paul's own estimate of who and what he was. In the previous survey of Paul's autobiographical claims I omitted one which was of first importance for Paul himself — his self-claimed title 'apostle'. It is clear from the way he introduces himself in most of his letters that this was how Paul wanted to be heard and known.

- Rom. 1.1, 4-5 — 'Paul, a slave of Jesus Christ, called to be an apostle, set apart for the gospel of God . . . Jesus Christ our Lord, through whom we received grace and apostleship with a view to the obedience of faith among all the nations for the sake of his name'.

1. New Haven: Yale University Press, 1990.

- 1 Cor. 1.1 — 'Paul, called to be an apostle of Christ Jesus by the will of God'.
- 2 Cor. 1.1 — 'Paul, apostle of Christ Jesus by the will of God'.
- Gal. 1.1 — 'Paul, apostle, not from human beings nor through a human being, but through Jesus Christ and God the Father'.
- Col. 1.1 — 'Paul, apostle of Christ Jesus by the will of God'.[2]

For convenience I repeat the relevant references from chapter 6 —

- Rom. 11.13 — 'I am apostle to the Gentiles'.
- Rom. 15.16 — 'a minister of Christ Jesus for the Gentiles, serving the gospel of Christ as a priest'.
- 1 Cor. 9.1-2 — 'Am I not an apostle? Have I not seen our Lord? . . . If to others I am not an apostle, at least I am to you'.
- 1 Cor. 15.8-10 — 'Last of all, as to an abortion, he appeared also to me. For I am the least of the apostles, not worthy to be called an apostle . . . but by the grace of God I am what I am'.

Here we have the answer to the earlier question, 'How would Paul have introduced himself?' 'Apostle of Messiah Jesus/Jesus Christ' was his chosen self-designation, what he would have printed on his 'calling card', and how he in fact did introduce himself in his letters.

There are two important implications of at least several of these references. One is that Paul thought it *necessary* to lay claim to this title ('apostle'). And the other is that his claim to this title was *contested* by some, indeed by a significant group within earliest Christianity. The unusual opening of Paul's letter to the Galatians is itself quite remarkable. Paul does not even begin his letter with the usual (and his usual) courtesies of such a letter — reference to his thanksgivings and prayers on their behalf.[3] Instead he swings at once, abruptly and discourteously, into a sequence of denials/affirmations — 'an apostle not from human beings nor through a human being, but through Jesus Christ and God the Father' (Gal. 1.1). And throughout the first two chapters of Galatians it is clear that Paul was very much aware that his status as an apostle, independent of Jerusalem, was being questioned, at least by those 'causing trouble' in Galatia (Gal. 5.12). He asks, 'Am I now seeking human approval . . . ?' (1.10). He insists, 'The gospel that was

---

2. Similarly Eph. 1.1; 1 Tim. 1.1; 2 Tim. 1.1; Titus 1.1; if these letters are post-Pauline, the openings indicate how established the usage and status had become.

3. Rom. 1.8-10; 1 Cor. 1.4; Phil. 1.3-5; Col. 1.3-10; 1 Thess. 1.2-3; 2 Thess. 1.3, 11; Phlm. 4-6.

proclaimed by me is not of human origin; for I did not receive it from a human source, nor was I taught it' (1.11-12). He objects that after his conversion, 'I did not confer with any human being, nor did I go up to Jerusalem to those who were already apostles before me' (1.16-17). Clearly there were those who claimed that apostleship belonged to the Jerusalem leadership, and that only if Paul had gone up to Jerusalem and been inducted there could he claim apostolic authority for the gospel he preached. So he protests with an oath, 'I did not see any other apostle except James. . . . In what I am writing to you, before God, I do not lie!' (1.19-20). Clearly the apostolic authority behind Paul's preaching to non-Jews was under serious question from the more traditionalist Jewish believers. This is no doubt why Paul was so relieved that at the Jerusalem council his commission and 'engracement' for that mission to the uncircumcised were recognised and affirmed by the Jerusalem leaders, the 'pillar apostles' (2.1-10).

In the same connection, we should also note that *Paul did not meet the conditions for recognition/election of an 'apostle' as indicated by Luke.* It should be recalled that, according to Acts 1.21-22, when Judas's place as an apostle, one of the Twelve, was filled, the qualifications for apostleship were clearly defined. Candidates for the position vacated by Judas should have been with Jesus from the time of his baptism by John until Jesus' ascension; and they should have been witnesses of Jesus' resurrection — that is, according to Luke, a witness of the resurrection appearances which lasted for forty days before Jesus' ascension (Acts 1.3). Paul, of course, would not qualify as an 'apostle' under such criteria. This probably means that Luke intended his later description of Paul and Barnabas as 'apostles' (Acts 14.4, 14) to be understood as denoting their function as 'apostles or representatives of the church of Antioch', missionaries sent out by the church of Antioch.[4] Paul also knew of (as we might say) lesser 'apostleship' — 'apostles or delegates of the churches' (2 Cor. 8.23); Epaphroditus, the apostle or messenger from the church of Philippi (Phil. 2.25). But his consistent insistence that he was apostle by appointment of God indicates Paul's unyielding refusal to be regarded as 'apostle' in any lesser sense than 'those who were apostles before me' (Gal. 1.17).

What, then, did Paul's claim to apostleship and the title 'apostle' signify to Paul?[5]

---

4. See also e.g. C. K. Barrett, *The Acts of the Apostles* (2 vols.; ICC; Edinburgh: T. & T. Clark, 1994, 1998) 1.666-67, 671-72.

5. The bibliography on 'apostle' is extensive; see e.g. the reviews by H. D. Betz, 'Apostle', *ABD* 1.309-11; J. A. Bühner, '*apostolos*', *EDNT* 1.142-46; P. W. Barnett, 'Apostle', *DPL* 1.45-51.

Apostle of Christ

The basic sense of 'apostle *(apostolos)*' was 'one sent out', so 'delegate, envoy, messenger, authorized emissary'.[6] What gave it the weight which Paul obviously saw in it, and claimed by using it in self-reference, was the fact that the commissioning authority was *Christ*, 'by the will of God'. It was as *an emissary of Christ*, in accordance with God's will, that he was an apostle, and as such his appointment carried the full weight of that authority behind it. This was what he was insisting on so emphatically in the opening of Galatians.

The act of authorising appointment was still more restricted. Paul had not simply been appointed by Christ (a status and role which could legitimately be claimed for many pioneering evangelists in subsequent centuries). He had been *appointed by the risen Christ in the course of his resurrection appearances*. This is the claim that Paul explicitly makes twice in 1 Corinthians: 'Am I not an apostle? Have I not seen our Lord?' (9.1); 'Last of all, as to an abortion, he appeared also to me' (15.8). In the latter passage Paul makes a threefold assertion and implication:

- the appearance to himself was of the same order and significance as the appearances to Peter, the Twelve and 'all the apostles' (15.5-7);[7]
- the appearance to himself was 'last of all', the almost explicit inference being that after Paul nobody else had been granted an appearance of the risen Christ; and
- his description of his conversion as an 'abortion' is equally significant. An abortion is an unnaturally early birth. So the implication of the jibe is that Paul's birth (as a believer) had to be unnaturally hastened in order to ensure his inclusion within the circle of apostles before that circle finally closed.[8]

---

6. BDAG 122.

7. 'All the apostles' seems to have included Barnabas (Gal. 2.9; 1 Cor. 9.5-6) and Andronicus and Junia (Rom. 16.7); see also W. Reinbold, *Propaganda und Mission im ältesten Christentum: Eine Untersuchung zu den Modalitäten der Ausbreitung der frühen Kirche* (Göttingen: Vandenhoeck & Ruprecht, 2000) 37-39, 40-41. Is the plural in 1 Thess. 2.1-12 'so personal to Paul that Silas and Timothy could not be included' in 2.6-7 (an 'epistolary plural'), as A. J. Malherbe, *The Letters to the Thessalonians* (AB 32B; New York: Doubleday, 2000) 144, argues (similarly Reinbold 39-40)? And given Apollos's relatively late appearance on the scene, it is less likely that he would have been numbered among 'the apostles' referred to in 1 Cor. 15.7, though he may be included in the 'apostles' of 1 Cor. 4.9.

8. On 'abortion' see my *The Theology of Paul the Apostle* (Grand Rapids: Eerdmans; Edinburgh: T. & T. Clark, 1998) 331 n. 87.

On the first two points, we should note, Paul was in agreement with Luke. For Luke too, the qualification to be an apostle was a resurrection appearance, because the essential role of an apostle was to bear witness to Jesus' resurrection (Acts 1.22). And the resurrection appearances as such continued only for a limited period — forty days (1.1-3); consequently after the end of the appearances there would be no grounds for the appointment of other apostolic witnesses.

Paul's claim, therefore, was to *a unique status and authority.* That was no doubt one of the reasons why Paul's claim to the status was questioned by some, although we have already noted that his claim was in effect acknowledged by the Jerusalem leadership, though possibly with qualifications.[9] But probably the greater question mark was put against Paul's *understanding* of his apostolic commissioning.

Servant of the Gospel

Equally worthy of note is the degree to which Paul understood 'apostle' and 'gospel' as in a mutually reinforcing symbiotic relationship:

- in Rom. 1.1 the two self-introductory phrases, 'called to be an apostle' and 'set apart for the gospel of God', are coterminous;
- as 'a minister of Christ Jesus' his function was to 'serve the gospel of Christ as a priest' (Rom. 15.16);
- as apostle his role was to proclaim the gospel (1 Cor. 15.11);
- Paul's insistence that he was an apostle, 'not from human beings nor through a human being, but through Jesus Christ and God the Father' (Gal. 1.1), is mirrored in his equally vehement insistence a few sentences later that his gospel was 'not of human origin; for it was not from a human being that I received it, neither was I taught it, but through a revelation of Jesus Christ' (1.11-12).

As has been pointed out by others, Paul's agitation in Gal. 1–2 was not so much in *self*-defence as in defence of his *gospel,* because he feared that 'the

---

9. In Gal. 2.7-9 some hesitancy on the part of the Jerusalem leadership may be indicated by the fact that whereas Peter's mission is designated as 'the apostleship *(apostolēn)* of the circumcision', Paul's is described only as 'for the Gentiles' *(apostolēn* is not repeated) (2.8). 'The agreement must have recognized Peter's apostleship, but left Paul without a specific title' — H. D. Betz, *Galatians* (Hermeneia; Philadelphia: Fortress, 1979) 82, 98; '. . . unmistakably failing to grant formal apostolicity to Paul's labors' — J. L. Martyn, *Galatians* (AB 33A; New York: Doubleday, 1997) 203.

truth of the gospel' (2.5, 14) was being endangered by the attacks on his evangelistic success as falling short of what God demanded.[10]

The authority which Paul claimed as an *apostle,* therefore, was the authority of the *gospel.* In fact, 'the truth of the gospel' was his *first* concern; his own apostolic status was secondary to and in service of the gospel. Which explains:

- why Paul was willing to acknowledge the prior status and authority of 'those who were apostles before me' (Gal. 1.17),
- why the thought that the Jerusalem apostles might not approve his gospel caused him such anxiety, and
- why in trumpeting the agreement achieved in Jerusalem, Paul in effect acknowledged the right of the pillar apostles to approve his preaching (2.2).

It was more important that the *same* message should be preached by *all* the apostles. So Paul ends his reference back to the gospel by which the Corinthians were being saved (1 Cor. 15.2) with the joyful affirmation, 'Whether then it was *I or they,* so we proclaim and so you have come to believe' (15.11). Just as later, when Paul was in prison, it was more important that Christ was being proclaimed, even if some of the proclamation was intended to increase Paul's suffering in imprisonment (Phil. 1.17-18).

In short, *it was more important for Paul that his preaching of the gospel should be affirmed by the Jerusalem apostles (Gal. 2.6-9), than that his apostleship should be formally acknowledged.* For the apostle was ever subservient to 'the truth of the gospel'. Which brings us to the really sensitive issue.

Apostle to the Gentiles

It would appear that Paul saw his commissioning, apparently from the first, as *a commissioning to take the gospel to the Gentiles.* We can never be sure when the full significance of Paul's conversion came home to him. But so far as our evidence goes, Paul never saw himself simply as 'apostle', with some roving

---

10. 'Apostolic authority was conditional upon the gospel and subject to the norm of the gospel' (Dunn, *Theology of Paul* 572; with bibliography in n. 35); 'apostleship and the gospel were inseparable for Paul' — P. Stuhlmacher, *Biblische Theologie des Neuen Testaments* (2 vols.; Göttingen: Vandenhoeck & Ruprecht, 1992, 1999) 1.249.

commission. He had been specifically commissioned to preach the gospel *among the nations:*[11]

- he had 'received grace and apostleship with a view to the obedience of faith among all the nations for the sake of his name' (Rom. 1.5);
- in his major treatment of 'Israel' he does not hesitate to assert simply, 'I am apostle to the Gentiles' (Rom. 11.13);
- he was 'a minister of Christ Jesus for the Gentiles' (Rom 15.16);
- God chose to reveal his Son in Paul, in order that Paul might preach his Son 'among the Gentiles' (Gal. 1.16);
- the later letter to the Ephesians emphasises that 'the mystery of Christ' had been especially revealed to Paul, and that he had been specially commissioned to enact the mystery. This mystery was that 'the Gentiles have become fellow heirs, members of the same body, and sharers in the promise in Christ Jesus through the gospel' (Eph. 3.2-6).

It is sufficiently clear from Gal. 1–2 that this was where 'the shoe began to pinch' for Paul, where the problems arose, when his role as apostle and servant of the gospel came to be evaluated by others. The point is too important for our appreciation both of Paul's self-understanding and of how he carried out his commission to be passed over. For one thing, it was precisely this commission which Paul claimed to have received, to take the good news of Jesus to non-Jews, which proved so controversial in the beginnings of Christianity. So controversial was it, indeed, that it caused a schism in the early Jesus movement, a schism which stretched into the next three centuries in the hostile relations between what became the mainstream of Christianity and the so-called Jewish-Christian heretical sects. And for another, it was precisely this commission which caused Paul to formulate 'the truth of the gospel' so clearly and definitively — as an offer of God's acceptance to *all* who believe, without further qualification, 'justified through faith in Jesus Christ and not by works of the law' (Gal. 2.16). In these words Paul crystallised the heart of the Christian gospel in effect for all time. We return to this theme so central to Paul's apostleship in chapter 8.

It was this understanding of his commission, apostle = missionary = evangelist, which gave the Christian concept of 'apostle' its distinctive sense. And not only distinctive, but groundbreaking sense. For while the concept of

---

11. The Greek *ethnē* can be translated equally 'nations' or 'Gentiles', 'the Gentiles' being one way of describing all the (other) nations (other than Israel). See also D. J.-S. Chae, *Paul as Apostle to the Gentiles* (Carlisle, UK: Paternoster, 1997); Reinbold, *Propaganda* 164-81.

'apostle' = 'messenger, emissary' was self-evident (*apostolos* from *apostellō*, 'send'), and while *apostolos* was familiar in that sense, the sense of 'apostle' as *one commissioned to win adherents to one's faith, to convert others,* was new. We know of Jewish apologists, concerned to help their fellow Jews to take a proper pride in their religion and to explain its peculiarities to others. We know of wandering philosophers who sought to persuade others of the wisdom of their views. To be sure, the model provided by Jesus, of a summons to radical trust in God in the light of the coming kingdom, had already broken old moulds, and was resumed by the first believers in the risen Jesus in their initial preaching in Jerusalem and Judea. But it was this sense of commission *to convert others,* to win adherents to the new movement *from well beyond the boundaries of Second Temple Judaism* by summoning them to faith in Israel's Christ, which gave the Christian understanding of 'apostle' its distinctive character.[12]

Here we should recall that Judaism was not a missionary religion.[13] Pharisees and Essenes were more naturally concerned to win fellow Jews to a stricter devotion to their covenant obligations;[14] but they were not in the business of trying to win *non*-Jews to adopt their praxis.[15] Judaism was, after all, the national religion of the Jews; it was not a matter of going out to convert non-Jews to a nonethnic religion. Israel was very welcoming of Godfearers and proselytes, and looked for an influx of the nations to Zion as part of the eschatological homecoming of the diaspora; but an outgoing to persuade Gentiles to come in was not part of the script. So what Paul believed he was called to do was exceptional and mind-blowing and established Christianity's character as essentially a missionary religion.

---

12. Cf. E. J. Schnabel, *Early Christian Mission,* vol. 1, *Jesus and the Twelve;* vol. 2, *Paul and the Early Church* (Downers Grove, IL: InterVarsity, 2004) 1:536-45; C. Roetzel, *Paul: The Man and the Myth* (Edinburgh: T. & T. Clark, 1999) ch. 2.

13. See particularly S. McKnight, *A Light among the Gentiles: Jewish Missionary Activity in the Second Temple Period* (Minneapolis: Fortress, 1991); M. Goodman, *Mission and Conversion: Proselytizing in the Religious History of the Roman Empire* (Oxford: Clarendon, 1994); R. Riesner, 'A Pre-Christian Jewish Mission?', in J. Ådna and H. Kvalbein, eds., *The Mission of the Early Church to Jews and Gentiles* (WUNT 127; Tübingen: Mohr Siebeck, 2000) 211-50; L. J. L. Peerbolte, *Paul the Missionary* (Leuven: Peeters, 2003) ch. 1; Schnabel, *Mission,* vol. 1, ch. 6.

14. This is probably where Matt. 23.15 comes in. The readiness of 'scribes and Pharisees' to 'cross sea and land to make a single proselyte' probably refers to the zeal of an Eleazar to ensure that would-be converts to Judaism, like Izates, king of Adiabene, were converted all the way (Josephus, *Antiquities* 20.38-46).

15. As noted above in ch. 5, 4QMMT can now be seen as a classic example, written with the explicit hope of persuading fellow Jews to accept and follow the rulings listed in the letter (C26-32).

Apostle of Israel

Less explicit but, we may judge, equally important for Paul was the conviction that his commission as 'apostle to the Gentiles' was not only in accordance with the will of God, but was also *an extension of Israel's own commission from God*. This inference is clearest, once again, in Galatians.

Gal. 1.15-16 contains clear echoes of Jer. 1.5 and Isa. 49.1-6 in Paul's description of his conversion/calling.

- Gal. 1.15-16 — '. . . the one who set me apart *(aphorisas) from my mother's womb,* and called me through his grace . . . in order that I might preach him *among the Gentiles'.*
- Jer. 1.5 LXX — Jeremiah expresses his sense of call: 'Before I formed you *in the womb* I knew you, and before you were born I consecrated you; I appointed you a prophet *to the nations'.*
- Isa. 49.1-6 LXX — the Servant of Yahweh = Israel (49.3) speaks: '*From my mother's womb* he called my name. . . . Behold I have set you for a covenant of the people, to be for *a light of the nations/Gentiles,* for salvation to the end of the earth'.

There can be little doubt, therefore, that Paul saw his conversion as a prophetic commissioning — a prophetic commissioning like that of Jeremiah in Jer. 1.5 ('appointed a prophet to the nations');[16] and more specifically in terms used for Israel, the Servant of Second Isaiah (to be given 'as a light to the nations' — Isa. 49.6). This continuity between his own vocation and that of Israel (identified as the Servant of Yahweh in Isa. 49.3) was evidently an important part of Paul's self-understanding. What happened on the Damascus road *was* a conversion, a conversion *from* Saul's previous understanding of how God's will and purpose for Israel were to be carried forward. But Paul saw it as a conversion *to* a better, a more correct understanding of that will and purpose for Israel. Apostle to the Gentiles, yes; but not thereby an *apostate from* Israel; rather an *apostle of* Israel, commissioned to carry forward Israel's destiny as 'a light to the nations'.[17]

Equally striking is Paul's handling of the original promise made to Abra-

---

16. See further K. O. Sandnes, *Paul — One of the Prophets?* (WUNT 2.43; Tübingen: Mohr Siebeck, 1991) ch. 5 (but he fails to bring out the 'to the nations' dimension integral to the call). The *aphorisas* (set me apart) of Gal. 1.15 may also be a deliberate play on the word which gave the Pharisees their nickname (= 'separated ones'): his 'separatism' as a Pharisee in service of the law was replaced by his 'separation' to be an apostle in service of the gospel.

17. See further my 'Paul: Apostate or Apostle of Israel?' *ZNW* 89 (1998) 256-71.

ham in Gen. 12.2-3 and repeated to Abraham and to the patriarchs regularly thereafter. The two most prominent strands of the promise were the promise of seed for Abraham, descendants from Abraham,[18] and of land, the promised land, so prominent once again in the politics of modern Israel.[19] Paul takes up both strands, in the slightly curious argument of Gal. 3 that the promise of 'seed' is fulfilled in and through Christ (Gal. 3.16), and in the parallel argument of Rom. 4, where the promise of land is also expanded to the promise that Abraham 'would inherit the world' (Rom. 4.13).[20] But here our interest is particularly in the way Paul takes up the *third* strand of the promise to Abraham, the covenant promise that 'In you shall all the nations be blessed'.[21] This third strand is not much mused upon in Israel's scriptures, though implied in the commissions of Jeremiah and the Servant to go to the nations, and in the story of the prophet Jonah.[22] But Paul goes much further. Indeed, he describes the promise that the Gentiles will be blessed in Abraham as 'the gospel preached beforehand' (Gal. 3.8). Here it is clear that Paul identified the *gospel* as the good news of God's covenant grace *extending to the Gentiles*. This he no doubt saw as an integral part of Israel's commission. And clearly, from what Paul says in Gal. 3, he understood his own role as carrying forward precisely that agenda, God's own agenda for *Israel,* the gospel for Gentiles as well as Jews.

The same point follows from what Paul says about his role as 'apostle to the Gentiles' in Rom. 9–11. For there he is clear that his role vis-à-vis the nations/Gentiles was part of God's great scheme — the 'mystery' of the divine purpose — to extend mercy to *all,* not least, including Israel (11.13-15, 25-32).[23]

In short, Paul would have strongly resisted the charge that historic Judaism has laid against him, that he was an '*apostate* from Israel'. To the contrary, Paul's claim is in effect that he was not only an apostle of Christ Jesus, but also an 'apostle *of Israel*'.[24] Sad to say, this self-claim, and claim for his apostleship

18. Gen. 13.16; 15.5; 17.2-4, 19; 18.18; 22.17; 26.4.

19. Gen. 12.7; 13.14-17; 15.18-21; 17.8; 26.3.

20. Cf. Sir. 44.21; 2 *Bar.* 14.13; 51.3; see further my *Romans* (WBC 34A; Dallas: Word, 1988) 213.

21. Gen. 12.3; 18.18; 22.18; 26.4. The Genesis texts can be variously understood (see e.g. G. J. Wenham, *Genesis* [WBC 1; Waco: Word, 1987] 277-78), but Paul's interpretation is clear.

22. See further J. R. Wisdom, *Blessing for the Nations and the Curse of the Law: Paul's Citation of Genesis and Deuteronomy in Gal. 2.8-10* (WUNT 2.133; Tübingen: Mohr Siebeck, 2001) 36-42.

23. See also A. J. Hultgren, 'The Scriptural Foundations for Paul's Mission to the Gentiles', in S. E. Porter, ed., *Paul and His Theology* (Leiden: Brill, 2006) 21-44.

24. The case was pressed earlier, particularly by J. Munck, *Paul and the Salvation of Mankind* (London: SCM, 1959), and J. Jervell, *The Unknown Paul: Essays on Luke-Acts and Early Christian History* (Minneapolis: Augsburg, 1984) chs. 3-4.

and gospel, has not been adequately appreciated within historic Christianity and ignored within historic Judaism. On this point at least, Paul needs to be listened to afresh, and in his own terms.[25]

Eschatological Apostle

If we are to understand the first generation of Christianity adequately, it is of crucial importance that we take into account the eschatological temper and perspective of the first believers. For they believed that in Jesus Messiah the new age had dawned — not just *a* new age, but the final age, the *eschaton* (= last) in which the ultimate promises of God and hopes for Israel would be realised. This conviction focused on two features:

- Jesus' resurrection as the beginning of the general/final resurrection;[26]
- the soon-coming return of Jesus as manifestly Messiah and Lord (Acts 3.19-21).

Luke does not make much at all of this emphasis — presumably because Luke chose not to highlight the eschatological motivation, which we may assume to have been a factor in that expansion, beyond the echoes in old traditional forms that he took over (Acts 2.17; 3.19-21).

With Paul, however, we can see how this eschatological perspective shaped his understanding of his calling as an apostle — again, not from what Luke tells us of Paul, but from his own letters.

- He recalls how the Thessalonian believers had 'turned to God from idols to serve the living and true God and to await his Son from the heavens' (1 Thess. 1.9-10; as in Acts 3.19-21).
- He seems to have believed that he would still be alive when Jesus returned: 'we who are alive, who are left until the coming *(parousia)* of the Lord' (1 Thess. 4.15); similarly, 1 Cor. 15.51: 'we will not all die, but we will all be changed'.
- Christ's resurrection was the 'first fruits of those who have died', that is, the beginning of the (general/final) resurrection (1 Cor. 15.20, 23).

25. See further my 'Paul: Apostate or Apostle of Israel?'; also 'The Jew Paul and His Meaning for Israel', in U. Schnelle and T. Söding, eds., *Paulinische Christologie: Exegetische Beiträge*, H. Hübner FS (Göttingen: Vandenhoeck & Ruprecht, 2000) 32-46; reprinted in T. Linafelt, ed., *A Shadow of Glory: Reading the New Testament after the Holocaust* (New York: Routledge, 2002) 201-15.

26. Rom. 1.4; 1 Cor. 15.20, 23.

- He encouraged his converts in Corinth to refrain from marriage, because 'the time is short', 'the form of this world is passing away' (1 Cor. 7.29, 31).
- He believed that 'the night is nearly over, and the day (of complete salvation) is near' (Rom. 13.12).

That this perspective shaped Paul's understanding of his apostleship[27] is clearest from three passages in particular.

(1) 1 Cor. 4.9:

it seems to me that God has put us apostles on display as the grand finale [*eschatous apedeixen*], as those doomed to die [*epithanatious*], because we have been made a spectacle [*theatron*] in the eyes of the world, of angels, and of humankind. (Thiselton)

Here Paul takes up 'the metaphor of a great pageant, in which criminals, prisoners, or professional gladiators process to the gladiatorial ring, with the apostles bringing up the rear as those who must fight to the death'.[28] In other words, he conceives of the whole sweep of history, or of God's programme for the world, as climaxing in the acts of the apostles. The apostles constitute the last act on the stage of cosmic history (watched also by angels). The imagery is somewhat vainglorious, though the imagery is hardly of a 'stage triumph'. In the terms of the metaphor, they have been 'condemned to death' *(epithanatios)* in the eyes of the watching cosmos; their public execution would 'bring the curtain down' on the pageant of history.

(2) Rom. 11.13-15:

I am speaking to you Gentiles. So then, inasmuch as I am apostle to the Gentiles, I magnify my ministry, in the hope that I might provoke my kindred to jealousy, and might save some of them. For if their rejection means reconciliation for the world, what shall their acceptance mean other than life from the dead?

27. My interest in this aspect of Paul's self-understanding goes back to A. Fridrichsen, *The Apostle and His Message* (Uppsala: Lundequistska, 1947) — 'this idea that an *apostolate* is to stand in the centre of the eschatologic development between the resurrection and return of the Messiah' (4); O. Cullmann, *Christ and Time* (London: SCM, ³1962) 157-66; and Munck, *Paul* 36-55, though their interpretation was too heavily dependent on a very disputable interpretation of 2 Thess. 2.6-7.

28. A. C. Thiselton, *1 Corinthians* (NIGTC; Grand Rapids: Eerdmans, 2000) 359; see further W. Schrage, *1 Korinther* (EKK VII/4; Düsseldorf: Benziger, 2001) 1.340-42.

The point to note here is Paul's hope and expectation for his apostolic ministry. He pressed forward with his mission to the Gentiles, not because he believed his own people had been cast off by God, and therefore had turned to the Gentiles in despair of his own people. Rather, his hope was that his success as apostle to the Gentiles would 'provoke his kindred to jealousy' and bring them to the faith which he preached. In Paul's perspective that 'acceptance' by and of his own people would mean something still more wonderful than 'reconciliation for the world'. In fact, it would mean nothing less 'than life from the dead', that is, the final resurrection at the end of the age/history.[29] In other words, Paul hoped that his own mission would trigger the end events, including the coming of the deliverer out of Zion (11.26). That was why his mission had such overwhelming priority for him.

(3) Col. 1.24:

> Now I rejoice in my sufferings for your sake and I fill up what is lacking of the afflictions of the Christ in my flesh for the sake of his body, which is the church.

Here Paul, or his co-writer, probably takes up the imagery of Christ's sufferings and death as the eschatological tribulation (commonly referred to as 'the messianic woes') expected as a crucial antecedent to the age to come.[30] Paul himself had no qualms about the thought of sharing Christ's sufferings,[31] or indeed of himself in some measure fulfilling the role of the Servant of Yahweh. The logic of a suffering still being shared, of course, is of a suffering not yet ended, an incomplete suffering. The writer of Colossians, however, is bold enough to regard Paul's apostolic sufferings as actually completing, 'filling up' this *hysterēma* ('lack' or 'deficiency'), with the corollary that the work of redemption/salvation would then be complete.[32] Here again the claim

---

29. 'The eschatological force here is put beyond dispute by the *ek nekrōn*, which elsewhere always denotes resurrection. [And] the rhetorical structure demands that the final phrase should describe something which outstrips the earlier . . . ; here "life from the dead" presented as something more wonderful still than "reconciliation of the world"' (Dunn, *Romans* 658, where I also note that most commentators agree that final resurrection is in view here); see further D. J. Moo, *The Epistle to the Romans* (Grand Rapids: Eerdmans, 1996) 694-96; B. Witherington, *Paul's Letter to the Romans* (Grand Rapids: Eerdmans, 2004) 269.

30. For details see my *Christianity in the Making*, vol. 1, *Jesus Remembered* (Grand Rapids: Eerdmans, 2003) #11.4c and 395.

31. Particularly Rom. 8.17; 2 Cor. 4.10-12; Phil. 3.10-12; see further my *Theology of Paul* #18.5.

32. See further my *The Epistles to the Colossians and to Philemon* (NIGTC; Grand Rapids: Eerdmans, 1996) 114-16; H. Stettler, 'An Interpretation of Colossians 1:24 in the Framework of

smacks of a vainglorious exaltation of Paul's role.[33] But it is simply the most striking expression of Paul's conviction regarding the importance of his apostolic mission. It was this last apostolic act on the stage of cosmic history which would complete God's purpose in history and trigger 'the consummation of all things'.

It is difficult for us who read such language nearly twenty centuries later — especially when neither the end of history nor the coming of Christ has taken place! It is difficult for us to enter with much sympathy into such a conception of Paul's apostolic role. But we need to make the attempt, since it presumably provided much of the motivation and energy which brought about such major results and such lasting effects. Paul's eschatology was integral to his sense of apostolic mission. At the same time, it should always be recalled that the decisive eschatological consideration for Paul was not what was still to happen, but what God had *already* done in and through Christ, particularly in raising him from the dead. That was the eschatological act which determined all else. 'Paul's gospel was eschatological not because of what he still hoped would happen, but because of what he believed had already happened'.[34]

Apostate or Apostle?

So our question about the status of Paul, 'apostate or apostle', can be answered so far as Paul's (and Christianity's) relation to Judaism (or Second Temple Judaism) is concerned. As Paul understood his mission, he was no apostate from Israel. On the contrary, he was engaged in endeavouring to fulfil Israel's own apostolic mission — to be a light to the nations, to proclaim the good news of God's covenant love and, as we shall see, of God's saving righteousness to Gentiles as well as Jews. As such he is an *authentically Jewish* voice, drawing his inspiration and motivation in large part from Israel's own scriptures. He is a Jewish contributor to a Jewish debate — as to how Israel can remain true to its gifts and calling. His voice has been almost wholly ignored within that debate. He is still predominantly regarded as an apostate from Israel. But in fact he is one of numerous other voices from Second Temple Judaism — also in that debate, also disputing among themselves and with one an-

Paul's Mission Theology', in Ådna and Kvalbein, *Mission of the Early Church* 185-208; J. L. Sumney, '"I Fill Up What Is Lacking in the Afflictions of Christ": Paul's Vicarious Suffering in Colossians', *CBQ* 68 (2006) 664-80.

33. 'A theologically untenable glorification of the apostle by one of his followers' (H. Hübner, *EDNT* 3.110); others in my *Colossians* 116.

34. Dunn, *Theology of Paul* 465.

other. Paul deserves to be brought back into that debate and his voice heeded — argued with, no doubt, but not ignored.

But the question 'apostate or apostle' also has to be asked and answered within *Christianity*. For Paul seems to have moved on well beyond Jesus' own message.[35] He was an awkward voice within earliest Christianity, calling in question the mother church's understanding of the gospel. In opening the door to the wider world he began a process of transforming an eschatological messianic sect into a predominantly non-Jewish religion. He was not one of Jesus' own immediate circle of disciples, and his status as apostle was questioned from within infant Christianity itself. His claim to apostleship direct from Christ and independent from the mother church of Christianity sets *an uncomfortable precedent* for similar claims in later years. Indeed, it is arguable that Paul was only retained within the New Testament because it is the milder, more eirenic Paul of the Acts and the Pastoral Epistles who was canonised, whereas the Paul of the earlier epistles alone was too controversial, too demanding for the church's peace of mind. If truth be told, *Paul is an awkward and somewhat uncomfortable member of the New Testament canon.* It is little wonder that many Christian traditions effectively ignore him. The Gospels provide all the material for homilies that Christians could ever want, don't they? A homily on an early epistle of Paul is too demanding to contemplate, is it not?

And yet, what do Christians thereby miss? What do they miss by reading Paul only canonically, an ecclesiasticised Paul — that is, softening his awkwardness by reading him only through Acts and the Pastorals? Israel, I claim, by dismissing Paul as an apostate, may be missing those emphases of their own scriptures and tradition which inspired Paul. So today, in a similar way, by largely ignoring Paul, Christians may be ignoring the voice of the Spirit who inspired Paul. The diversity and tensions within the New Testament canon are what help to prevent Christians falling asleep and remaining content with the old ways, even when they are demonstrably failing to give effective voice to the gospel, even when they no longer express the vitality of mission. And here is where Christians need to listen again to Paul with new ears, to ask why his gospel was so effective, his mission so vital, and whether his gospel and mission can point the way forward for the church of the twenty-first century. In the bimillennial year of Paul, the rediscovery of Paul — or is it actually the *discovery* of Paul? — is long overdue!

---

35. But see ch. 5 above.

CHAPTER 8

The Gospel — for All Who Believe

What Made the Difference?

In the light of what we have so far seen, we can and have to say that Paul changed. He changed from being a traditionalist Jew to become a Jew 'in Christ'. He changed from being a Pharisee to become, at least in his own eyes, an apostle, indeed, the apostle to the Gentiles. What made the difference? To answer this question we have to consider first of all the change which took place in Paul, that is, what is called by common consent Paul's *conversion*. So our question, What made the difference? becomes a twofold question: What was he converted *from?* And what was he converted *to?* We have already considered a large part of the answer to the second question. He was converted to become an apostle to the Gentiles. But we have still to plumb the depths of the question. We have to explore the way the two questions tie in to each other, the way in which the answer to the question, What was Paul converted *to?* depends on the answer to the prior question, What was he converted *from?*

Paul's Previous Conviction

The most striking feature of Paul's pre-Christian past as he himself recalled it was his role as a *persecutor* of the church, that is, of his fellow Jews who believed Jesus to be Messiah. He refers to this pre-Christian past several times: 'I persecuted the church of God' (1 Cor. 15.9); 'I persecuted the church of God in excessive measure and tried to destroy it' (Gal. 1.13); 'as to zeal, a persecutor of the church' (Phil. 3.6). In Gal. 1.23 he recalls that he was commonly known among the Judean churches as 'he who persecutes us', 'the persecutor'.

Why did Paul take on the role of persecutor? The answer he himself gives has just been mentioned: he did so as an expression of his 'zeal' — 'as to zeal, a persecutor of the church' (Phil. 3.6). The account of Paul in Acts agrees. According to Acts, Paul testified that he had been trained as a Pharisee 'at the feet of Gamaliel, educated strictly according to our ancestral law, being a zealot for God. And I persecuted this Way to the point of death' (Acts 22.3-4). Why did Paul's 'being a zealot for God' cause him to persecute the followers of the Way, the sect of the Nazarene? Why did zeal motivate him to persecute those he subsequently identified as 'the church of God'? Somewhat surprisingly, this answer to our question, Why did Paul persecute his fellow Jews? has not been given the attention it deserves, even though it is actually Paul's own answer to the question. So it requires more attention than it has been given.

a). *A Pharisee.* The answer lies partly in Paul's training as a Pharisee, as indeed a Pharisee who progressed in Judaism beyond many of his contemporaries, being so exceptionally zealous for his ancestral traditions (Gal. 1.14). Now we know that the name 'Pharisees' was probably something of a nickname — the *perushim,* the 'separated ones' (from the Hebrew *parash,* 'to separate').[1] This indicates the conviction of the Pharisees that, to maintain their level of purity, or holiness, they had to maintain a high degree of separation from the sources of impurity and defilement. Since for the Pharisees these sources were other people who did not maintain such a strict level of law observance, that meant separation from other Jews. So Pharisees were notable for their practice of eating their meals among themselves, separate from other Jews, probably maintaining the level of purity required for priests while in service in the Temple.[2] We see indications of this in the criticism of Jesus' ta-

1. See above, ch. 5 n. 25.
2. See above, ch. 5 n. 26; and further e.g. A. J. Saldarini, *Pharisees, Scribes, and Sadducees in Palestinian Society* (Edinburgh: T. & T. Clark, 1988) 212-16, 233-34, 285-87, 290-91; M. Hengel and R. Deines, 'E. P. Sanders' "Common Judaism", Jesus, and the Pharisees', *JTS* 46 (1995) 1-70 (here 41-51); H. K. Harrington, 'Did the Pharisees Eat Ordinary Food in a State of Ritual Purity?' *JSJ* 26 (1995) 42-54; J. Schaper, 'Pharisees', in W. Horbury et al., eds., *Judaism,* vol. 3, *The Early Roman Period* (Cambridge: Cambridge University Press, 1999) 402-27 (here 420-21). The old view that the Pharisees sought to extend the holiness of the Temple throughout the land of Israel, on the basis of Exod. 19.5-6, is probably still warranted (E. Schürer, *The History of the Jewish People in the Age of Jesus Christ* [rev. and ed. G. Vermes and F. Millar; 4 vols.; Edinburgh: T. & T. Clark, 1973-87] 2.396-400; A. F. Segal, *Rebecca's Children: Judaism and Christianity in the Roman World* [Cambridge: Harvard University Press, 1986] 124-28).

ble fellowship with tax collectors and sinners which the Gospels attribute to Pharisees.[3] 'Sinners' were those who broke the law. So for Pharisees, who interpreted the law with scrupulous accuracy and exactness *(akribeia)*,[4] in order to observe it more faithfully, other Jews who did not share or follow the Pharisees' interpretation, their *halakhoth,* were lawbreakers, 'sinners'.[5]

Since Paul was such a zealous Pharisee, we may assume that the same reasoning determined his own conduct. In his pre-Christian state he would have counted it as of first importance to maintain his separation from sin, and from 'sinners'. He would have conducted himself as one who saw it as a priority to observe the patriarchal traditions (Gal. 1.14). He would almost certainly have condemned and looked down on other Jews who did not share that priority. This was what 'righteousness which is in the law' demanded, and Paul could claim that in terms of this righteousness he had been 'blameless' (Phil. 3.6). He was not saying he had never sinned, but that he had lived completely within the terms of the law, including faithfulness to its requirements and atonement for his failures.

But there is more to it. The language of 'zeal' takes us more deeply.

b). *A zealot.* The theology of zeal within the religion and traditions of Israel is not hard to trace. Integral to the concept of 'zeal' or 'jealousy' (it is the same word, Hebrew *qn'*) was the fundamental conviction that YHWH is a jealous/zealous God. YHWH's zeal was expressed in his insistence that Israel must not worship any other gods but remain dedicated to him alone. 'You shall not bow down to them or worship them; for I the LORD your God am a jealous God' (Exod. 20.5).[6] E. Reuter notes that the relationship between YHWH and his worshippers 'is characterized by an intolerant demand for exclusivity: it is Yahweh's will "to be the only God for Israel, and . . . he is not disposed to share his claim for worship and love with any other divine power"'.[7] In the LXX God himself is described as a 'zealot'.[8]

It was this 'zeal' of YHWH which was seen as requiring and providing the pattern for Israel's own 'zeal' — a 'zeal' for holiness, as YHWH is holy

3. Matt. 11.19/Luke 7.34; Mark 2.16-17; Luke 15.2.
4. Josephus, *War* 1.110; 2.162; *Antiquities* 17.41; *Life* 191; Acts 22.3; 26.5; see particularly A. I. Baumgarten, 'The Name of the Pharisees', *JBL* 102 (1983) 413-17.
5. See also ch. 5 above.
6. So too Exod. 34.14; Deut. 4.23-24; 5.9; 6.14-15; 32.21; 11QT 2.12-13.
7. E. Reuter, *qn'*, *TDOT* 13.54, citing G. von Rad, *Old Testament Theology* (2 vols.; Edinburgh: Oliver and Boyd, 1962) 1.208. Paul's plea to the Corinthians, 'I am jealous for you with the jealousy of God' (2 Cor. 11.2), is a direct echo of this divine zeal/jealousy.
8. Exod. 20.5; 34.14; Deut. 4.24; 5.9; 6.15.

(Lev. 19.2). Holiness was understood here as being set apart to God alone. But it was taken for granted that so to be set apart *for* God unavoidably meant also being set apart *from* the other nations. Consequently, 'zeal' was a burning concern to maintain Israel's identity as a people set apart to God, a passionate concern to protect Israel's holiness over against other nations. This gives us the clue as to why Paul's zeal caused him to persecute his fellow Jews.

The most famous of Israel's 'heroes of zeal' was Phinehas, who, when an Israelite brought a Midianite woman into his tent (into the congregation of YHWH), forthwith slew them both, 'because he was zealous for God' (Num. 25.6-13). In Num. 25.11 Phinehas's zeal is understood as a direct reflection of YHWH's zeal.[9] For this single deed he was often recalled and his zeal praised,[10] and he became the model and inspiration for the later Zealots who led Israel's revolt against Rome.[11]

Other examples in Israel's roll call of heroes of zeal are easily catalogued:

- Simeon and Levi, who 'burned with zeal' and avenged the seduction of their sister Dinah, 'the pollution of their blood' (Jdt. 9.2-4), by slaughtering the villagers where she had been seduced (Gen. 34).
- The Maccabean revolt against their Syrian overlords was sparked by Mattathias of Modein, when, 'burning with zeal', 'with zeal for the law', just like Phinehas's, he executed the Syrian officer and the fellow Jew who was made to apostatise by offering forbidden sacrifice (1 Macc. 2.23-26). Mattathias rallied the rebellion by crying out, 'Let everyone who is zealous for the law and supports the covenant come with me' (2.27; Josephus, *Antiquities* 12.271), and his deathbed testimony is a paean in praise of the zeal displayed by the heroes of Israel (1 Macc. 2.51-60).
- Philo bears witness to the same attitude when, writing possibly only a decade or so before Paul's role as a persecutor, he warned that 'there are thousands . . . who are zealots for the law, strictest guardians of the ancestral customs, merciless to those who do anything to subvert them' (*On the Special Laws* 2.253).

9. 'Like Joshua's zeal on behalf of Moses (Nu. 11:29), Phinehas's zeal on behalf of Yahweh realizes Yahweh's own jealousy . . . which otherwise would have consumed all Israel' (Reuter, *qn'*, *TDOT* 13.56). As A. Stumpff observed (*TDNT* 2.879), the term ('zeal') is linked with 'anger' (Deut. 29.20) and 'wrath' (Num. 25.11; Ezek. 16.38, 42; 36.6; 38.19); see also 1QH 17[= 9].3; 4Q400 1.1.18; 4Q504 frag. 1-2 3.10-11; 5.5; similarly M. Hengel, *The Zealots* (1961, ²1976; ET Edinburgh, T. & T. Clark 1989) 146-47.

10. Ps. 106.28-31 (the deed was 'reckoned to him as righteousness'); Sir. 45.23-24 ('third in glory for being zealous in the fear of the Lord'); 1 Macc. 2.26, 54 ('Phinehas our ancestor, because he was deeply zealous, received the covenant of everlasting priesthood'); 4 Macc. 18.12.

11. Hengel, *The Zealots* ch. 4.

- In the same spirit are the rulings preserved in the Mishnah: 'If a man . . . made an Aramean woman his paramour, the zealots may fall upon him. If a priest served (at the altar) in a state of uncleanness his brethren the priests did not bring him to the court, but the young men among the priests took him outside the Temple court and split open his brain with clubs' (m. Sanhedrin 9.6).

In the light of this evidence, we can see that the tradition of 'zeal for the Lord/Torah' was marked by three features in particular:

1. It was sparked by the sight of fellow Jews disregarding the law, particularly when it meant that *Israel's set-apartness to God and from the defilement of other nations and their gods was being threatened or compromised.*
2. It could be *directed against fellow (compromising) Jews* as much as against the foreign 'others' whose involvement marked the breach of Israel's boundaries.[12]
3. It regularly *involved violence and bloodshed,* as necessitated (in the view of the zealots) by the severity of the danger to Israel's exclusive set-apartness to and holiness before God.

All this, of course, explains why 'Zealots' was the name used for those who led the revolt against Rome in the 60s. Their revolt was the ultimate attempt of Second Temple Judaism to maintain its loyalty to God alone, and to retain its set-apartness to God and from other nations.

What is immediately striking for us, of course, is that the three features provide a remarkably accurate description of Paul's persecution of the Jews who believed in Messiah Jesus. For Paul's persecution was directed against fellow Jews (the Hellenists) and was evidently as fierce as the tradition of zeal documented — 'I persecuted the church of God in excessive measure and tried to destroy it' (Gal. 1.13). Since the latter two of the three characteristics of Israel's tradition of zeal match Paul's own persecuting zeal *(violence,* directed against *fellow Jews),* it suggests that the first characteristic was true of Paul's zeal too. That is, Paul probably persecuted the first Christians because he regarded the Hellenists, those identified with the views of Stephen, as some

---

12. 'Sinners and lawless men' in 1 Macc. 1.34 and 2.44, 48 certainly included those whom the Maccabees regarded as apostate Jews, Israelites who had abandoned the law; see further my 'Pharisees, Sinners and Jesus', in *Jesus, Paul, and the Law* (London: SPCK; Louisville: Westminster John Knox, 1990) 61-86 (here 74).

kind of *threat to Israel's set-apartness to God*. For reasons we cannot fully explain, Paul seems to have regarded the attitudes and actions of some (representative) Hellenists as endangering Israel's holiness and separateness. Presumably Paul saw the threat posed by the Hellenists as potentially breaching the protective boundaries formed by the law and maintained by doing the law. That could also be described as 'zeal for the law'; but in this case it was the law in its role as a bulwark against the corruptions and the defilements of other nations. This understanding of the role of the law is classically expressed in the *Letter of Aristeas* 139-142:

> In his wisdom the legislator [i.e. Moses] . . . surrounded us with unbroken palisades and iron walls to prevent our mixing with any of the other peoples in any matter, being thus kept pure in body and soul. . . . To prevent our being perverted by contact with others or by mixing with bad influences, he hedged us in on all sides with strict observances connected with meat and drink and touch and hearing and sight, after the manner of the Law. (Charlesworth)

If this function of the law, if Paul's concern to shelter behind the protective boundary of the law, and his zeal to maintain Israel's holiness in separation from the Gentiles explain what Paul was converted from, then what was he converted to?

To What Was Paul Converted?

a). One answer must be that Paul came to the conclusion that Jesus was indeed God's Messiah. In fact, that belief in Jesus as Messiah does not seem to have motivated sustained persecuting zeal against the Jerusalem Jews. But certainly Paul 'the persecutor' would have been convinced that Jesus was *not* Israel's Messiah. As a crucified criminal, Jesus was under God's curse (Gal. 3.13). A crucified Messiah made no sense, a 'stumbling block' indeed to Jews generally (1 Cor. 1.23). But on the Damascus road Paul encountered Christ, saw Christ alive and exalted to heaven (1 Cor. 9.1; 15.8). In Gal. 1.15-16 he describes his conversion as God revealing his Son 'in me'. And in Phil. 3.7-11 it is clear that it was the wonder of gaining Christ, and the hope of being found in him and of sharing fully in his death and resurrection, which transformed everything he had previously counted upon into mere rubbish. According to Acts, the heavenly Christ confronted Paul, struck down on the Damascus road: 'Saul, Saul, why do you persecute me? . . . I am Jesus whom you are persecuting'.[13] Whatever the detail of the event itself, it must have been a shattering blow to Paul, and must have convinced him that he had been totally wrong about Jesus. He was converted to what he had previously denied.

b). Bound up with this would be the revelatory realisation that those he had been persecuting were *right after all.* He had persecuted them for their readiness to set aside Israel's previous policy of maintaining separateness from Gentiles, for the threat of their being more open to Gentiles than the law allowed. So presumably Paul's conversion also included a conversion to such openness. This indeed is what Paul expressly states in Gal. 1.15-16, that God had revealed his Son in him 'in order that I might preach the good news of him among the Gentiles'. This is why several scholars have argued that what happened on the Damascus road was more of a *commissioning* than a *conversion.* It is hardly necessary to regard the two aspects as mutually exclusive. We have seen clearly enough that Paul's conversion was indeed a turning from. But it is very striking that Paul emphasised the commissioning character of his conversion so strongly. This is what was at stake for Paul in his insistence that he was an apostle (Gal. 1.1, 11-12). He was an apostle because he had seen the Lord (1 Cor. 9.1). His apostleship was as 'apostle to the Gentiles' (Rom. 11.13) — a commission which the leading Jerusalem apostles had readily conceded when they met in Jerusalem (Gal. 2.7-9). And it is also worth noting that here too Acts accords with the Pauline letters. Each of the three accounts of Paul's conversion in Acts includes the element of Paul's commissioning to take the gospel to the nations.[14] In other words, it was *Paul the convert who took up the very tendencies which he had so violently opposed and transformed them into active mission;* the openness of the Hellenists to the Gentiles became the Gentile mission of Paul the apostle.

c). As we have seen in chapter 7, Paul regarded this not as a betrayal of his Jewish heritage. Quite the contrary, as an apostle of Jesus Christ, he was also an apostle of Israel, not an apostate from Israel. His commission was towards the fulfilment of Israel's commission to be a light to the Gentiles. His claim is elsewhere reinforced by Paul's exposition of Israel's own fundamental creed to make the point. Thus in Rom. 3.29-30 he presses this very point: if God is one, as he is indeed (Deut. 6.4), then he is not simply God of the Jews but also God of the Gentiles. And as such he will justify the uncircumcised through faith just as he justifies the circumcised through faith.

13. Acts 9.4-5; 22.7-8; 26.14-15.
14. Acts 9.15; 22.15, 21; 26.16-18.

The same basic logic of Paul's gospel is indicated in his use of the key motif 'the righteousness of God'. This phrase, we recall, is at the centre of the thematic statement of Paul's principal theological writing, his letter to Rome:

> I am not ashamed of the gospel, since it is the power of God for salvation, to all who believe, Jew first but also Gentile. For the righteousness of God is being revealed in it from faith to faith — as it is written, 'He who is righteous by faith shall live'. (Rom. 1.16-17)

No one with knowledge of Israel's scriptures could fail to recognise here a major motif of Israel's theology and understanding of how God conducts his dealings with his creation and his chosen people (Israel). For 'righteousness' in Hebrew thought refers to the *meeting of obligations* which arise out of a relationship. So the phrase 'the righteousness of God' refers to *God's enactment of the obligation he had accepted in so creating the world and in so choosing Israel to be his people*.[15] His righteousness was the obligation he had taken upon himself to sustain and save both creation and people. For Jews the phrase had an inescapably covenant connotation: it denoted God's *saving* righteousness — which is why the Hebrew term *tsedhaqah* (righteousness) is often better translated 'deliverance' or 'vindication', as we see in modern translations.[16] Since God's righteousness was revealed by the gospel, 'the power of God for *salvation*', Paul had surely done enough to ensure that the recipients of his letter would understand this 'righteousness' as *saving* righteousness. It was Martin Luther's realisation that this is what Paul had in mind — 'God's righteousness' as saving righteousness ('the righteousness by which through grace and sheer mercy God justifies us through faith'), and *not* God's righteousness as his 'justice' ('that justice whereby God is just and deals justly in punishing the unjust')[17] — which gave birth to the Reformation and to the key Reformation doctrine of 'justification by faith'.

---

15. For 'righteousness' as a relational term, denoting that which meets the obligations laid upon the individual by the relationship of which he/she is part, see my *The Theology of Paul the Apostle* (Grand Rapids: Eerdmans; Edinburgh: T. & T. Clark, 1998) 341-44 and the bibliography there. I also note that the relational character of God's righteousness undercuts the traditional debates of post-Reformation theology as to whether 'the righteousness of God' is a subjective or objective genitive, 'an activity of God' or 'a gift bestowed by God' — a case of unnecessary and unjustified either-or exegesis (344).

16. E.g. Pss. 51.14; 65.5; 71.15; Isa. 46.13; 51.5-8; 62.1-2; Mic. 6.5; 7.9.

17. *Luther's Works* (ed. J. Pelikan; St Louis: Concordia, 1960) 34.336-37, as cited by R. Bainton, *Here I Stand* (London: Hodder and Stoughton, 1951) 65; full quotation in my *New Perspective on Paul: Collected Essays* (Tübingen: Mohr Siebeck, 2005; 2nd ed., Grand Rapids: Eerdmans, 2008) 187. See also E. Lohse, 'Martin Luther und die Römerbrief des Apostels Paulus — Biblische Entdeckungen', *KD* 52 (2006) 106-25.

For Paul, of course, the key point was that this gospel is *'to all who believe, Jew first but also Gentile'*. This is not a simple statement of (naive) universalism ('to all who believe'). The 'all' Paul had in mind, here as elsewhere in Romans,[18] was the 'all' that transcends and breaks down the barrier between Jew and Greek,[19] between Jews and Gentiles.[20] So, for Paul, the gospel which he had been commissioned to proclaim was precisely the good news of God's saving righteousness, of God's covenant grace, now extending beyond Jew to embrace also Gentile. That was what Paul had been convinced of by his Damascus road conversion. That was at the heart of the gospel for Paul — Israel's good news for Jew and Greek, for Gentile as well as Jew.

The Confirmation of God's Spirit/Grace

Without in any way diminishing the importance of Paul's conversion in transforming his understanding of God's saving purpose for humankind, another factor must also be noted. This is the fact that the conviction which came to Paul, regarding the openness of God's saving grace to Gentiles, *was confirmed by the actuality of that grace bestowed on Gentiles.* This includes the fact that the same grace was bestowed on Gentiles solely on the basis of their believing the gospel of Jesus Christ, and without their being circumcised. The point came home with decisive force at two points in the earliest Christian mission.

Acts 10–11

The first, according to Acts, was Peter's mission to the Roman centurion Cornelius, living in Caesarea (Acts 10–11). One of the most striking features of this account is that before Cornelius could be converted, *Peter himself had to be converted,* that is, to change his mind on the acceptability of Gentiles. The episode is vividly told, and referred to no less than three times by Luke,

---

18. 'In all the nations' (1.5); 'to all who believe' (1.16); 'to all who believe' (3.22); 'father of all who believe' (4.11); 'to all the seed' (4.16); 'to all' (5.18); 'gave his Son for us all' (8.32); 'to all who believe' (10.4); 'all who believe' (10.11); 'he is Lord of all, rich towards all who call upon him' (10.12); 'everyone who calls upon the name of the Lord' (10.13); 'God has confined all in disobedience in order that he might have mercy on all' (11.32); 'all the nations, all the peoples' (15.11); echoed in the 'all's' of 1.18, 29; 2.1, 9, 10; 3.9, 12, 19, 20, 23; 5.12.

19. Rom. 1.16; 2.9-10; 3.9; 10.12.

20. Rom. 3.29; 9.24.

since evidently it had been so important in determining the development and transformation of earliest Christianity.

The conversion of Peter was on the issue of *the inherent uncleanness of Gentiles*. It was this conviction of Gentile uncleanness which lay behind Israel's need to keep themselves separate from the other nations and which lay at the root of Paul's persecuting zeal. What is less well understood is that the Torah laws of clean and unclean foods were an expression of the *same* conviction. The laws of clean and unclean were based on the premise of Gentile uncleanness and reinforced the separation required of Israel. This is nowhere more clear than in Lev. 20.23-26:

> You shall not follow the practices of the nations that I am driving out before you. Because they did all these things, I abhorred them. . . . I am the LORD your God; *I have separated you from the peoples.* You shall *therefore* make a distinction between the clean animal and the unclean, and between the unclean bird and the clean; you shall not bring abomination on yourselves by animal or by bird or by anything with which the ground teems, which I have set apart for you to hold unclean. *You shall be holy to me; for I the LORD am holy, and I have separated you from the other peoples to be mine.*

In other words, *the laws of clean and unclean were important because they indicated the importance of Israel's separation from the uncleanness of other nations.*

To recognise this helps us to understand Peter's reaction when, on the rooftop in Joppa, he was given a vision. The vision was of a large sheet let down from heaven and crowded with clean and unclean animals. When the heavenly voice told Peter to 'kill and eat', Peter's immediate reaction was to refuse: 'By no means, Lord, for I have never eaten anything that is profane or unclean' (Acts 10.13-14). Peter is presented as a loyal Jewish traditionalist, who had never breached the laws of clean and unclean. But the heavenly voice immediately rebukes this attitude: 'What God has made clean, you must not call profane' (10.15). This happened three times, says Luke. And what did Peter learn from this? When the messengers from Cornelius invite him to go to Cornelius, he goes with them without question, to this Gentile's house. And when he arrives, what is the first thing he says? Not that God had shown him that it was all right for him to eat unclean food, to share table fellowship with his Gentile host. No, what he says is, 'God has shown me that I should not call any *person* profane or unclean' (10.28). This, we may say, was fully the equivalent of Paul's conversion. As *Paul* had been changed from one who regarded openness to the Gentiles as a threat to Israel's holiness, so *Peter* had been changed from one who regarded Gentiles as such as unclean and a threat to Israel's purity.

But the story is not complete. For as it began with the conversion of Peter, so it climaxes with the conversion of Cornelius. Following his welcome by Cornelius, Peter had been preaching the gospel to Cornelius and his friends. And he had hardly begun to speak, so Acts narrates (11.15), when the Spirit fell upon his audience in a visible and indisputable way (10.44; 11.15). What happened to Cornelius was just so similar to what had happened to Peter and the first disciples at Pentecost, that they simply could not fail to recognise that God had accepted Cornelius and his friends — and had done so without any expectation that they would have first to be circumcised or to be circumcised as a consequence.[21] *Here was a case where God's Spirit had acted in disregard for the sacred traditions which had hitherto governed Jewish faith and praxis.* The Spirit had rendered one of Israel's most defining *scriptures* null and void. So much so that even the more traditional Jewish believers, both those who had accompanied Peter and those to whom he reported in Jerusalem, could not gainsay what had happened or its significance.[22]

Gal. 2.6-9

In the account of Acts it is this episode which proves decisive when the first Christians meet in council in Jerusalem to decide whether circumcision should be required of Gentile believers (Acts 15.5-29). The equivalent crucial decision is recalled somewhat differently by Paul. In Gal. 2.1-10 he tells how, in what was probably the same Jerusalem meeting,[23] some 'false brothers' had tried to insist that Titus, the Gentile believer accompanying Paul and Barnabas, should be circumcised. Paul recalls how he had vigorously resisted this. The issue was essentially the same as in the Acts account: whether Gentiles who had believed the gospel must be circumcised before they could be regarded as full members of the Jewish sect of Jesus messianists. And the outcome was essentially the same. For the assembled Christians, says Paul, were so impressed by Paul's account of the mission success of Paul and Barnabas that they had little choice but to accept the conclusions which Paul drew. *They recognised the grace* which had so evidently been given to and through Paul and Barnabas. They recognised that God was manifestly working through the mission to the uncircumcised just as he was working through Peter's mission

21. Acts 10.47; 11.15-17; 15.8-9.
22. Acts 10.45-48; 11.18; 15.14.
23. Though the point is disputed; see my *Christianity in the Making*, vol. 2, *Beginning from Jerusalem* (Grand Rapids: Eerdmans, 2009) #27.3.

to the circumcised (Gal. 2.7-9). Since Paul saw 'grace' and 'Spirit' as overlapping terms,[24] presumably he was thinking of God's grace manifested to Paul's converts in the terms he uses a few verses later, when he reminds the Galatians of their reception of the Spirit (3.2-5).

This is a very important point to take on board: that *the development of Christianity was shifted on to a new track by the manifest work of the Spirit.* Christianity might have remained a Jewish messianic sect had it not been for *the unexpected and scripture-breaking, tradition-breaking initiative of the Spirit.* The Spirit opened up a whole new vista for the first Christians, and they were brave and bold enough to follow where the Spirit showed the way. If we are to fully appreciate Paul the apostle, Paul the theologian, Paul the church founder, we must take full account of this vital aspect of his gospel. Having been converted by the Christ to recognise that God's saving righteousness reached out to embrace Gentile as well as Jew, Paul was also quick to recognise that God's Spirit was breaking away from the old patterns established by scripture and sanctified by tradition. *This is why Christians need to rediscover Paul and to let him provide a fresh challenge to our own traditions where they no longer express the life of the Spirit, and to restore to us a fresh vision of how the initiative of the Spirit may once again be taking us in unexpected directions.*

The Double Dimension of Justification

One of the corollaries which comes home forcibly from all this is that there is a *social* dimension to the gospel which is integral and fundamental to the gospel.

a). As we all know, Paul's doctrine of justification by faith was at the heart of the Western Reformation. But typically within Reformed theology the doctrine of justification has been understood in very individualistic terms: how the individual is accepted by God; how the individual can find peace with God. As part of this, Paul's slogan, 'a person is justified not by works of the law but through faith in Jesus Christ' (Gal. 2.16), has been traditionally understood in terms of an antithesis between faith and good works. The individual cannot earn his way to heaven by performing good works; justification before God cannot be attained by merit and self-achievement.

This is all true, and Paul clearly affirms that God 'justifies the ungodly' (Rom. 4.5), that God operates by grace (11.6). But the typical Reformed expo-

---

24. See my *Theology of Paul* 322 and n. 28.

sition of justification has left to one side an important dimension of Paul's teaching on justification, a dimension which was actually central to Paul's own gospel and teaching.[25] For when Paul spoke of 'works of the law', he was not thinking primarily of 'good works'. He was thinking of doing what the law demands. By 'works of the law' he was thinking primarily of the obligations Jews had taken on — to do what the Torah lays down, to live in accordance with the law. This is why the issue for Paul was whether *Gentiles* should be expected to observe works of the law. This was why his great statement in Gal. 2.16 is the climax of his rejection of Peter's attempt in effect to compel the Gentile believers in Antioch to 'Judaize', that is, to live like Jews (2.15). To do the works of the law is to Judaize, to live like a Jew. This was why the whole issue arose out of the two episodes recalled in Gal. 2: the attempt in Jerusalem to require Gentile believers to be circumcised; and the attempt in Antioch to require Gentile believers to observe the laws of clean and unclean. These were the works of the law that the false brothers and Peter had attempted to impose on the Gentile believers. And it was these attempts to compromise and constrict the gospel that Paul resisted so forcefully.[26]

The point for Paul, then, was, as we have seen, that the gospel of Jesus Christ is good news for *all* who believe, for Gentile as well as Jew. Alternatively expressed, the gospel is the fulfilment of God's purpose to bring Jew and Gentile to worship God together. The point is made most explicitly in two other passages in the Pauline corpus.

b). In the conclusion to his great letter to Rome (Rom. 15.7-12), Paul sums up and rounds off what this great letter is all about, and what he regards as the central passion of his own life and mission. Christ, he reminds his Roman audiences, had 'become servant of the circumcised' (15.8). Why? 'For the sake of the *truth* of God' — that is, for the sake of the reliability and integrity of God and of the constancy of his purpose.[27] This purpose of God is and, Paul

25. For my understanding of Paul's theology of justification, see my *Theology of Paul* #14.

26. I discuss all the issues involved in this exegesis in my *New Perspective on Paul*. The older disputes and misunderstandings between Catholics and Protestants have been almost entirely removed by the *Joint Declaration on the Doctrine of Justification* by the Lutheran World Federation and the Roman Catholic Church (Grand Rapids: Eerdmans, 2000). See e.g. D. E. Aune, ed., *Reading Paul Together: Protestant and Catholic Perspectives on Justification* (Grand Rapids: Baker Academic, 2006).

27. It is helpful and important to appreciate that here, as in Rom. 3.4 and 7, Paul plays upon the Hebrew *'ĕmunah* and *'ĕmeth* (both denoting 'reliability', and so also 'faith' and 'faithfulness'); see my *Romans* (WBC 34A; Dallas: Word, 1988) 133, 135-36, 847; and further, *NIDB* 2 (2007) 407-23.

would say, always has been twofold (15.8-9). One purpose is to confirm the promises of the fathers; as in 11.29, Paul reaffirms the irrevocable nature of God's calling of Israel. And second, that 'the Gentiles should give praise to God for his mercy' ('mercy', that key term in both Israel's and Paul's understanding of God's purpose).[28] Here not least is confirmation, if confirmation were needed, that *central to Paul's gospel and the primary motivation of his apostleship and mission, was precisely the realisation of that vision: the fulfilment of God's promises to Israel, and Gentiles praising God for his mercy.* Here, as the climax of this letter, the letter in which he laid out most carefully and most completely his understanding of the gospel and of God's saving righteousness, Paul sums up his hope and prayer in scriptures drawn from all sections of the Tanak, from the law (Deut. 32.43), prophets (Isa. 11.10) and psalms (Pss. 18.49; 117.1). Paul's supreme goal and sublime hope were that Jews and Gentiles would rejoice together and together praise God (Rom. 15.9-11); and that Isaiah's vision of the Messiah's rule embracing the nations (Gentiles) and of the Gentiles finding their hope in him (Isa. 11.10) would now, finally, be realised (Rom. 15.12).

c). The other passage is the clarification that the letter to the Ephesians brings to the mission and theology of Paul. For it insists that *Christ's saving mission was all about bringing in the Gentiles.* They had been 'without Christ, aliens from the commonwealth of Israel, strangers to the covenants of promise, having no hope and without God in the world. But now in Christ Jesus those who once were far off have been brought near by the blood of Christ' (Eph. 2.12-13). In his flesh Christ had made both groups into one and had broken down the dividing wall of hostility between Jew and Gentile, the partition which in Jerusalem's Temple prevented Gentiles from entering nearer to the divine presence (2.14). Christ had abolished the law, the law which demanded and maintained the separation between Jew and Gentile, 'that he might create in himself one new humanity in place of the two, thus making peace, and might reconcile both groups to God in one body through the cross, thus putting to death that hostility through him' (2.15-16). Consequently, Gentile believers were 'no longer strangers and aliens, but citizens with the saints and also members of the household of God', growing into 'a holy temple in the Lord', 'built together in the Spirit into a dwelling place for God' (2.19-22). In the following chapter Paul's own

28. Exod. 34.6-7, a theological insight and assertion frequently echoed in Israel's scriptures (see my *Romans* 552). The theme is prominent in Rom. 9–11: Rom. 9.15, 18; 11.30-32 (*eleeō*); 9.23; 11.31; 15.9 (*eleos*).

role in this great enterprise is underlined. The mystery of God's purpose to include Gentiles among his people had been specially revealed to Paul, and he had been specially commissioned to bring this gospel of God's riches in Christ to the Gentiles (3.1-10).

Implications for Jewish/Christian Dialogue, and for the Social and Ecumenical Dimensions of the Gospel

To conclude, it is well worth reflecting on the implications of Paul's understanding of the gospel/good news. And not just well worth doing, but essential if the challenge of Paul's understanding of the gospel, as the fulfilment of God's ages-old purpose for humankind, is not lost to sight. I focus on three dimensions.

a). *The Jewish/Christian dialogue.* To his *Jewish readers* who did not accept Jesus to be Messiah, Paul still posed a challenge, and continues to impose a challenge. When holiness is understood as requiring separateness from others, perhaps even from the Godfearer and righteous Gentile, is the emphasis not becoming misplaced? When zeal for God is understood as requiring force to enforce it, is not something going wrong? Or again, can the circumcised sufficiently recognise circumcision of the heart in the gift of the Spirit to the uncircumcised? How exclusive to Israel is the call of God, is the outreach of God's saving righteousness? Or again, how may or should Israel be bringing into action the promise that Abraham would be a blessing to the nations? And is it possible that the good news concerning and through Jesus might be one of the ways in which that blessing has come about?

At the same time, such readers might well put questions back to Paul, questions he never fully answered, and perhaps was unable to answer satisfactorily. How can Paul claim that God's election of Israel was 'irrevocable' (Rom. 11.29) while maintaining that God calls Gentile equally with Jew (9.24)? Could Paul really expect Jew and Gentile to form one community when the laws of kashrut and purity were not fully respected and honoured, that is, when Jewish identity was so casually treated as to be dispensed with when deemed inappropriate? Is there not a vital difference between prioritising within Torah and dispensing with Torah? Has Paul made more of Jesus than Jesus himself would have approved? Any Jewish/Christian dialogue which reintroduces Paul to the dialogue must expect not a few hard and uncomfortable questions, on and from both sides. But maybe that is reason enough to bring Paul back into the dialogue.

b). *The social dimension of Paul's gospel.* The above emphasis on *Paul's apostleship for the Gentiles* is not just an incidental add-on to what else can be said about his apostleship. It is not a case of describing Paul's role and status as an apostle, and then adding, 'Oh yes, and he was also apostle to the Gentiles'. No, this was *central* to Paul's apostleship. This is what Paul's apostleship had been all about. This was why he was prepared to allow a breach with James the brother of Jesus to grow. This was why he was prepared to rebuke Peter in public. This was what he directed all his energies and his very life to accomplish.

Alternatively expressed, Christians today should not be content to say that for Paul the gospel was about how individuals are accepted by God — by faith. And only then to add, 'Oh yes, and that also meant that Jew and Gentile could come together in the same community, could eat together, and be fully accepted by each other'. For that was at the *heart* of the gospel for Paul. It was *not* gospel unless it meant that Jew and Gentile could worship together, could sit at the same table, together form the one body, the one worshipping congregation.

Another way of putting it is that for Paul the gospel had both a vertical dimension and a social dimension. It could not function on the one dimension unless it also functioned on the other dimension. Paul did not work with a facile distinction between the gospel as a purely *spiritual* phenomenon, opening people to the grace of God and bringing the grace of God to them, and the *social* corollaries of that gospel as something quite different. For too long evangelical Christians, whose name is a reminder that their position is determined by the gospel, operated with a distinction between the (true) gospel and the social gospel — the assumption being that the social gospel was a departure from and corruption of the true gospel. But Paul would never have agreed. For Paul, *if the gospel did not have a social effect, a breaking down of racial and national antagonism and disharmony, it was not the gospel.* If the gospel did not bring together different races and nations and classes in the one worship, round the one table, then it was not the gospel. If it did not express itself in believers truly loving their neighbours as themselves, it was not the gospel. It simply is impossible for me to be accepted by God if I do not welcome and fully respect those who are also accepted by God.

In a word, Paul teaches Christians that if they forget the horizontal dimension of the gospel, they lose the gospel for which Paul gave his life.

c). *The ecumenical dimension of Paul's gospel.* What continuing weight should Christians give to one of the most fundamental of Paul's statements: that 'no human being is justified by the works of the law, but only through faith in Jesus Christ' (Gal. 2.16)? It seems straightforward enough: that faith in Christ is the *one* thing that matters, indeed, is the *only* thing that matters to God; that to require *anything more* than faith, some legal requirement or ritual obligation or claim of tradition, is to undermine the gospel, to destroy what Paul calls 'the truth of the gospel'. The issue had come home to Paul in all its sensitivity and sharpness in the incident at Antioch. There Peter and the other Jewish Christians had withdrawn from table fellowship, no doubt including eucharistic fellowship, with the Gentile Christians. In effect, Paul says, they were trying to compel the Gentile believers to live like Jews, to observe Israel's sacred laws of clean and unclean. In effect, they were trying to add works of the law to the gospel's invitation to faith alone.

How does Paul's gospel speak to the Christian ecumenical scene today? For Christians today are all in one degree or another in a position similar to that of Peter and the other Jewish Christians. They say to fellow believers, in effect, 'We cannot sit at the same table as you; there are certain things we cannot do with you, because you do not recognise traditions and rituals which we hold as central to our own identity as Christians'. And in effect they make their traditions and distinctive beliefs *as important as the gospel itself*, as important as belief in Christ, as important as being in Christ. They deny Paul to his face: they affirm by their actions that a person is *not* justified by faith alone, but must also observe certain works of tradition. They take the side of Peter and, like Peter, they abuse and forsake the truth of the gospel. Do they really think that Paul would commend them for their unwillingness to sit at the same table as their fellow Christians, at the table of our Lord, at *his* table? I think not. I think rather that he would say with John Wesley: 'If your heart beats with mine in love for our common Lord, then give me your hand', and let us sit and eat together, let us stand and worship together, let us go forth together and together spread the good news of Jesus Christ.

CHAPTER 9

The Church — Paul's Trinitarian Ecclesiology

When we turn to Paul's understanding of the church, much of what we have already been looking at becomes still more relevant. Not least of importance, what we have already seen prepares us for what might be called the Trinitarian character of Paul's understanding of the church. So I look first at the very concept of 'church' as 'the church of *God*'. This will include a parenthesis on what we can say of the historical actuality of the Pauline churches in the first century. Then I turn to Paul's other principal way of speaking of the church as 'the body of *Christ*'. This will include an attempt to clarify Paul's concept of apostles as church founders. Finally I turn to church as 'the fellowship of the *Spirit*', or shared experience of the Spirit. This will inevitably include further clarification of Paul's concept of the body of Christ as a charismatic community.

The Church of God

If there is a single term in the NT writings which denotes the existence and character of the embryonic Christian movement in various centres where it became established, that term is *ekklēsia*, 'church'. The word occurs 114 times in the NT; 23 in Acts; 62 in the Pauline corpus; and 20 in Revelation.[1] The choice of the term *ekklēsia* is interesting in itself. In common usage it denoted

---

1. E.g. Matt. 18.17; Acts 5.11; 8.1, 3; etc.; Rom. 16.1, 4-5, 16, 23; 1 Cor. 1.2; 4.17; etc.; James 5.14; Rev. 2–3; *1 Clement* inscr.; Ignatius, *To the Ephesians* inscr.; *Didache* 4.14; *Shepherd of Hermas, Vision* 2.4.3.

simply an 'assembly or gathering' of people for some shared purpose. It occurs in this sense twice in Luke's account of the city assembly in Ephesus (Acts 19.32, 41). It has also been found occasionally in reference to some associations or the business meetings of some clubs *(collegia)*.[2] But its predominant usage was to the regularly summoned citizen body in legislative assembly.[3] So the earliest Christian usage could have been simply to denote the 'meeting' which their coming together constituted. The alternative term, *synagōgē,* was equally capable of signifying a 'gathering or coming together', but it probably had already become too much identified as the 'assembly of Jews, the synagogue'.[4] It is not very likely, however, that Paul used the term to imply that the Christians in a Mediterranean city saw themselves as an alternative to or in competition with the assembly of citizens. The fact that Paul can speak both of *ekklēsiai* (plural) in a region[5] and of individual *ekklēsiai* (house churches, probably more than one) which met in the same city[6] suggests that the common sense of 'gathering, meeting' was in mind, and was so understood by others who heard it being used.

The determining factor for Paul's usage, however, was almost certainly the LXX use of the term *ekklēsia* to translate the 'assembly of YHWH/Israel' *(qahal YHWH/Israel).* This is indicated by Paul's frequent reference to 'the church of God' or 'the churches of God'.[7] To be noted is the fact that this usage also indicates a background in the Aramaic-speaking congregations, and that *ekklēsia* probably emerged as the translation of *qahal,* again in preference to *synagōgē.*[8] The point, of course, is that the inspiration for the use of the term *ekklēsia* was almost certainly more *theological* than political.[9] Paul's usage was

2. Examples of *ekklēsia* used for voluntary associations and their meetings are provided by J. S. Kloppenborg, 'Edwin Hatch, Churches and Collegia', in B. H. McLean, ed., *Origins and Method,* J. C. Hurd FS (JSNTS 86; Sheffield: JSOT, 1993) 212-38 (here 215-16 n. 13, 231 n. 65).

3. LSJ 509; K. L. Schmidt, *TDNT* 3.513-14.

4. Cf. LSJ 1692 with BDAG 963; see further E. Schürer, *The History of the Jewish People in the Age of Jesus Christ* (rev. and ed. G. Vermes and F. Millar; 4 vols.; Edinburgh: T. & T. Clark, 1973-87) 3.90-91, 95-98.

5. 1 Cor. 16.1 (the churches of Galatia); 16.19 (the churches of Asia); 2 Cor. 8.1 (the churches of Macedonia); Gal. 1.22 (the churches of Judea).

6. Rom. 16.5; 1 Cor. 16.19; Col. 4.15; Phlm. 2. There is wide agreement that the greetings of Rom. 16.14-15 have in view other house churches in addition to the meeting in the house of Prisca and Aquila (16.5).

7. 'The church of God' — 1 Cor. 1.2; 10.32; 11.22; 15.9; 2 Cor. 1.1; Gal. 1.13. 'The churches of God' — 1 Cor. 11.16; 1 Thess. 2.14; 2 Thess. 1.4.

8. In LXX *qahal* is translated by *ekklēsia* sixty-eight times and by *synagōgē* thirty-six times; see H.-J. Fabry, *TDOT* 12.546-61 (here 561); details in Hatch & Redpath 433 and 1309-10. Note Acts 7.38.

9. See also J. Roloff, *ekklēsia, EDNT* 1.412.

not original to him or to his mission, as his reference to 'the churches of Judea' (Gal. 1.22) also implies. It embodied not so much a claim to be a new political entity as a claim to be *in direct continuity with Israel,* the Israel that God called out *(ek-kalein)* to be his people in the world. To be 'the church of God' meant to be in line with God's purpose for his people from the time he first called them out to be his people. Here again the regularity of Paul's use of the plural ('churches') is worth noting: Paul evidently thought of separate gatherings, in houses or cities, several in a city or region, as individually 'churches'. The thought of 'the church' as a national or universal entity had not yet come to expression.[10] Wherever a group of believers in Jesus as Lord came together *(syn-agomai),* there was 'the church of God'.

The richer vision of the universal church which we find in the later Paulines we should certainly not ignore. Particularly striking is the way the letters to the Colossians and the Ephesians envisage the church as the place of reconciliation, where reconciliation between different nations and warring parties takes place (Eph. 2.13-22; Col. 1.18-20). But here I wish to focus more on the house churches so typical of Paul's mission, since we need to be aware of the historical realities Paul had in mind when he spoke about church and about its functioning and organisation.

House Churches

It is probably unnecessary to point out that when Paul speaks of the Corinthian believers 'coming together in church' (1 Cor. 11.18), the thought was not of 'church' as place ('in a building'). Rather it was of *the individuals themselves coming together* to be church, *as* church. 'Church' denoted *people,* not place. In view of the later connotations which have become attached to 'church' (= 'building'), it might be less confusing to use terms like 'congregation', 'gathering', 'meeting', 'assembly'. That said, of course, an important question is, Where did the first believers come together in the cities of the Aegean mission? What accommodation did they use for their comings-together? This involves something of a parenthesis, but one which I hope will be worthwhile.

---

10. See further my *The Theology of Paul the Apostle* (Grand Rapids: Eerdmans; Edinburgh: T. & T. Clark, 1998) 537-40.

The Archaeological Evidence

Since the Pauline mission almost certainly began in one or another of the synagogues in the city entered,[11] it is useful to begin by noting what we know of first-century synagogues in the western diaspora. Archaeology has uncovered several synagogue buildings which were almost certainly already established in the first century in Italy, Greece and Asia Minor — for example, at Ostia, Rome's port; at Stobi, in Macedonia; on the Aegean island of Delos; and at Priene, between Ephesus and Miletus.[12] In many, probably most, cases, however, the Jewish community had to make *private houses* serve as synagogues, wherever there was a significant Jewish community.[13]

What then of the meeting places of the first believers, when the latter moved out of the immediate synagogue context? Archaeology has uncovered no structure which can be both identified as a 'church' and confidently dated earlier than a century or more later than Paul. So we have to assume that these meetings took place either in private homes or in larger premises rented for the occasion. Nothing in our sources indicates that the latter (larger premises) was realistic in the great majority of cases. The cost of regular bookings would probably have been beyond the means of the first small groups, and in any case local associations would hardly welcome competing societies to their premises. And temple property would hardly be conducive to a Christian gathering. The only obvious conclusion is that the first believers met as 'church' *in each other's houses,* with the wealthiest member and the largest house providing a regular venue for 'the whole church' in different centres. This deduction is strengthened by the various references to house churches in Paul's letters, and by Paul's reference to Gaius as 'host to the whole church' at the end of his letter to Rome (Rom. 16.23), which was written from Corinth. Paul likewise speaks of 'the whole church' in Corinth coming together for worship (1 Cor. 14.23), so presumably in both cases he was think-

---

11. Acts 13.14; 14.1; 16.13; 17.1, 10, 17; 18.4, 19; 19.8; 28.17, 23. See further my *Christianity in the Making,* vol. 2, *Beginning from Jerusalem* (Grand Rapids: Eerdmans, 2009) #29.5b.

12. Details in C. Claussen, *Versammlung, Gemeinde, Synagoge: das hellenistisch-jüdisch Umfeld der frühchristlichen Gemeinden* (Göttingen: Vandenhoeck & Ruprecht, 2002) 191-206.

13. L. M. White, 'Synagogue and Society in Imperial Ostia: Archaeological and Epigraphic Evidence', in K. P. Donfried and P. Richardson, eds., *Judaism and Christianity in First-Century Rome* (Grand Rapids: Eerdmans, 1998) 30-68: 'The evidence indicates that most, if not all, of the earliest synagogues were renovated from existing buildings, usually houses' (34); see further his *Social Origins of Christian Architecture* (2 vols.; Harvard Theological Studies 42; Harrisburg, PA: Trinity, 1996-97) 1.60-101. The synagogue buildings at Priene, Stobi and Dura Europos were originally private houses (Schürer, *History* 3.24, 67; Claussen, *Versammlung* 208).

ing of those occasions when all the local believers could meet together, as distinct from the several (and more frequent?) smaller gatherings in smaller homes.

What then does archaeology tell us about such homes in the larger cities fringing the Aegean? Some sites are no help whatever. For example, Thessalonica in Macedonia and Smyrna in Asia Minor, as indeed also Rome, have been so built over that little remains open to view. Fortunately, however, the changing geography and economic fortunes of places like Ostia, Corinth and Ephesus have left substantial remains which are still being worked on and from which we can gain a good grasp of the range of housing stock in such cities during or around our period. Attention has usually been caught by the more substantial properties, occupying most of a small block within a network of streets. But in places the ruins extend above the first-floor level (Ostia in particular) and give us a better idea of what must have been one-room or small apartments in tenement blocks.

In his article in the *The Oxford Classical Dictionary*, Nicholas Purcell sums up the situation well:

> By the imperial period, multi-storey tenement blocks, which are usually known as *insulae,* housed all but a tiny fraction of the population of Rome and other big cities. Not all this accommodation was of low quality; some was sited in attractive areas, some *cenacula* (apartments) were sufficiently large, those on the lower floors were not inconvenient . . . and many people of quite high status could afford no better.[14]

Juvenal, in his *Satires* 3.193-202, gives a vivid picture of the shoddy buildings which during the second half of the first century must often have been built too hastily and too high by landlords anxious to maximise their rental income:

> We live in a city shored up for the most part with gimcrack stays and props: that's how our landlords arrest the collapse of their property, papering over great cracks in the ramshackle fabric, reassuring the tenants they can sleep secure, when all the time the building is poised like a house of cards. I prefer to live where fires and midnight panics are not quite such common events. By the time the smoke's got up to your third-floor apartment (and you still asleep), your heroic downstairs neighbour is roaring for water and shifting his bits and pieces to safety. If the alarm goes at ground level, the last to fry will be the attic tenant, way up among

---

14. *OCD* 731-32.

the nesting pigeons with nothing but the tiles between himself and the weather.[15]

The Size of First-Century Churches

What deductions can we make concerning the churches which met within the range of property which literature and archaeology have revealed to us? Given that the majority of any group of converts in any city was likely to be illiterate, lacking in influence and lowborn (1 Cor. 1.26), we certainly have to assume that their accommodation would have been at the lower end of the scale. That is to say, if Purcell is correct, most would have lived in multistorey tenement blocks, perhaps several stories above the ground. Presumably some gatherings at least took place in such apartments, or at least the larger ones nearer street level. A church in such a 'house' would consist of only a small group, of, say, up to twelve. Though since the word 'house' inevitably carries connotations of a larger property, such cell groups would probably be better referred to as 'tenement churches'.[16] Again, if Purcell is correct, even the relatively prosperous Aquila and Priscilla could almost certainly have been able to afford no more than a larger ground-floor apartment of a more substantial tenement property, so that the churches which met in their houses (Rom. 16.5; 1 Cor. 16.19) might only have been fifteen or twenty-five strong.

However, it is sufficiently clear that most city groups of early disciples would have included at least some higher-status members. And the probability is that these latter would have invited the local believers to meet as church in their larger property. Gaius has already been mentioned as hosting 'the whole church' in Corinth (Rom. 16.23), making it possible for 'the whole congregation' to come together *(synerchesthai)* 'at the same place *(epi to auto)*' (1 Cor. 11.20; 14.23). And Philemon's house in Colossae could accommodate both several guests[17] and some slaves.[18] If, then, we should envisage Christians coming together as churches in more substantial houses, houses with an

15. As quoted by S. Goodenough, *Citizens of Rome* (London: Hamlyn, 1979) 62.

16. R. Jewett has for some years insisted on the more realistic term 'tenement churches' rather than the potentially misleading 'house churches' (with reference to villas uncovered in places like Pompeii and Corinth); see his 'Tenement Churches and Communal Meals in the Early Church', *BR* 38 (1993) 23-43; now also R. Jewett, *Romans* (Hermeneia; Minneapolis: Fortress, 2007) 53-55, 64-66.

17. Phlm. 22: 'Prepare a guest room for me'; not *'the* guest room'.

18. There is no suggestion that Onesimus, the subject of the letter to Philemon, was the latter's only slave.

atrium and a dining room (triclinium), we can certainly assume that larger gatherings were accommodated. How much larger is a matter of some dispute. The best estimates run up to fifty,[19] though quite how such a large group could meet as a single, coherent meeting is less than clear. Were they divided among two or more rooms? When the church met for the common meal, not all, presumably, could have been accommodated in the triclinium, a fact which probably helps to make sense of the unsatisfactory arrangements for the only church about whose gatherings Paul speaks (Corinth).[20] Certainly numbers able to be accommodated should not be calculated on the bare data of square feet or square metres, since space would presumably be taken up with furnishings and possibly also statues or ornaments.

The basic point which emerges is that the earliest house churches, in most cases, must have been fairly small, a dozen or twenty people in all. And even when 'the whole church' in a city or section of a city could meet as church in one place, we may very well be talking of only forty or fifty people, and not necessarily gathered in a single room. The dynamics of church life, of the shared life of believers in most cities, must have been dependent on and to some extent determined by the physical space in which they were able to function as church. We, of course, are accustomed to visualising huge church buildings and congregations which can be numbered in the hundreds or even thousands. So it is important for us to remember that *the typical church of the first century or more of Christian history was the gathering of a small cell* comprising twenty or so, and less regularly up to about fifty. This is important, since we are now well aware that the social dynamics of small groups is very different from that of large groups. And the accompanying theology needs to take such factors more into account than is usually the case. In many cases our concern should be not that our churches are too small but that they are too large!

The same applies when we turn to the second aspect of Paul's Trinitarian ecclesiology — the body of Christ.

The Body of Christ

In chapters 6 and 7 I emphasised the strong continuity between Paul and his Jewish heritage. In Rom. 9–11 in particular Paul insisted that God remained

---

19. R. J. Banks, *Paul's Idea of Community* (Exeter, UK: Paternoster, 1980) 40-42; J. Murphy-O'Connor, *St. Paul's Corinth* (Wilmington, DE: Michael Glazier, 1983) 153-58.
20. 1 Cor. 11.17-22.

faithful to his covenant with and promises to Israel. This strong sense of continuity is underlined by his use of *ekklēsia* to denote the gatherings of believers in Messiah Jesus — Christians gathering as the *qahal YHWH*. It is notable, however, that when Paul turned from the subject of Israel and its future, in Romans 12, he reached for a different image or metaphor for the assembly of Christians — the body of Christ. In chapter 6 I also emphasised that the principal identity factor for Paul himself was not so much his status as an Israelite, but his being 'in Christ'. Here the point which needs to be emphasised is that the communal equivalent to the individual believer 'in Christ', the corporate equivalent to being 'in Christ', is 'the *body* of Christ'. 'We are all one body in Christ' (Rom. 12.5). 'Just as the body is one and has many members . . . so also is Christ' (1 Cor. 12.12). 'You [Corinthians] are Christ's body and individually members' (12.27). To be 'in Christ' is to be a member of 'the body of Christ'. Why this image?

One Body, Many Members

Much the most plausible source of the imagery is the use of the metaphor of the body as a vital expression of the *unity* of a community despite the *diversity* of its members. The image of the city or state as a body (we still use it in speaking of 'the body politic') was already familiar in political philosophy. The famous fable of Menenius Agrippa, narrated by Livy and Epictetus, is the best-known example.[21] The point being made by Menenius Agrippa was that plebs and patricians could not cease to cooperate with each other. It would be like the limbs of the body refusing to cooperate with the bodily organs, with disastrous results for the body. Paul's exposition in 1 Cor. 12.14-26 closely echoes the concerns of the fable: that the unity and well-being of the state depended on the *mutual interdependence* of its diverse members, the trade guilds and national groupings, being fully recognised and lived out in mutually beneficial interaction. Paul seems to have adapted this familiar metaphor of community and drew from it the same implications for mutual recognition and cooperation. The Christian assembly is a body, like the body politic. It functions as a unity *only* by the different members acting in harmonious interdependence. However, it is different from the body politic precisely because its distinctive and identifying feature is that it is the body *of Christ*.

The significance of this should be pondered. For Paul in effect shifts the corporate image of the Christian community from that of the nation-state (his-

---

21. Livy, *History* 2.32; Epictetus 2.10.4-5.

torical Israel) to that of the citizen assembly. That is, he shifts the image from a community identified by ethnic and traditional boundary markers to one whose members are drawn from different nationalities and social strata, and whose prosperity depends on their mutual cooperation and their working harmoniously together. The identity of the *Christian* assembly as 'body', however, is not given by geographical location or political allegiance, or by race, social status or gender. It is given by their common allegiance to Christ, visibly expressed not least in baptism in his name and in the sacramental sharing of his body. The implication is clear. Only when that common allegiance is given primacy in mutual relations can the potential factional differences be transformed into the necessary mutual cooperation for the common good. *It is the common commitment to Christ, being 'in Christ', which determines Christians' communal character as the body of Christ.* Anything which diminishes or obscures that central fact diminishes and obscures the reality of the body of Christ. And if Christ is present on earth in his body, through his body, as his body, then Christian failure to embody that central fact actually hinders and prevents Christ's presence and ministry for the world. That is a sobering corollary to have to draw. For Paul, the term 'Jew' had to be redefined not by circumcision but as one praised by God (Rom. 2.28-29). And the term 'Israel' had to be redefined not in ethnic or national terms but as those 'called by God' (Rom. 9.6-12). So Christians too should try to ensure that the definition of the body of Christ is not confused by political status or traditional ritual but remains determined *first and always by the attachment of each of its members to Christ.*

The Apostolic Church

When we look at the ministries in Paul's understanding of the church as the body of Christ, the most prominent is that of apostle: 'God has appointed in the church first apostles' (1 Cor. 12.28). This enables us to tie in Paul's concept of his role as apostle with his understanding of the apostolic church. For one of the fundamental aspects of Paul's apostolic mission was to found (or plant) churches. For Paul, an apostle was commissioned, sent forth, *to found churches.* This is clearest in 1 Cor. 9.1-2: 'Am I not an apostle? Have I not seen our Lord? . . . If to others I am not an apostle, at least I am to you; for you are the seal of my apostleship in the Lord'. Here the authority of the 'apostle' is very much tied to the apostle's role in establishing a church: Paul was *not* apostle to others, because he had not converted them, had not founded their churches; but he *was* to the Corinthians, because it was through his evangelism that the church of Corinth had come into existence. In other passages in the Corinthian letters Paul's conviction that he had been commissioned as a church-planting missionary comes to repeated expression:

- 1 Cor. 3.5-15 — 'like a skilled master builder' he laid the foundation.
- 1 Cor. 15.10-11 — he worked harder than the other apostles to bring his audiences to faith.
- 2 Cor. 5.20 — he saw his role as an 'ambassador for Christ'.

This ties in to the agreement to which Paul was party in Jerusalem: that he (and Barnabas) would be responsible for the Gentiles (Gentile believers) and for mission to the Gentiles (Gal. 2.9). It is important to note that *Paul did not regard his apostolic commission as something very general, apostle to all believers.* Rather, it was specific — to the *Gentiles.* So it was to that extent limited, limited to the churches for which he was responsible, and Paul seems to have accepted that it was so limited. This is why he became so angry when others encroached on his territory and was so hesitant about overstepping the limitations of his own commission (2 Cor. 10.13-16).[22] Here we should note the symbiotic relation between apostle and church which Paul thus worked with. So when he says that 'God appointed in the church first apostles' (1 Cor. 12.28), he was most likely *not* thinking of the *universal* church and of apostles with universal authority.[23] Rather he was most likely thinking of 'the church' in the sense that the Corinthian believers came together to be the church in Corinth (11.18; 12.27). The 'apostles' of 12.28 were *the apostles who had established the Corinthians as believers,* brought them together to be the body of Christ in Corinth. The apostles appointed to the church in Corinth were, in the first place, Paul himself, and possibly also Apollos (4.9). We can probably draw similar conclusions from Paul's description of Andronicus and (his wife?) Junia as 'outstanding among the apostles' (Rom. 16.7). Here we should note that Andronicus and Junia are the only apostles Paul mentions in regard to the Roman Christians. So the most likely explanation is that Andronicus and Junia were the apostles who founded (one or more of) the house church(es) in Rome.[24] Should we be embarrassed at the thought that one of

---

22. See further my *Beginning from Jerusalem* #29.4b.

23. See also particularly J. Hainz, *Ekklesia: Strukturen paulinischer Gemeinde-Theologie und Gemeinde-Ordnung* (Regensburg: Pustet, 1972) 252-55.

24. On Junia as a female name — so Andronicus and Junia possibly the only husband and wife among 'all the apostles' of 1 Cor. 15.7 — see now particularly E. J. Epp, *Junia: The First Woman Apostle* (Minneapolis: Fortress, 2005), with extensive bibliography. For the phrase *episēmoi en tois apostolois* as meaning 'outstanding among the apostles' rather than 'well known to the apostles', see Epp 72-78 and Jewett, *Romans* 963.

the founding apostles of the church in Rome was a woman? If so, why, since Paul himself seems to relish Junia's apostolic role?

So the second Trinitarian feature of Paul's ecclesiology is his understanding of the church as the body of Christ. What of the third feature?

The Fellowship of the Spirit

Paul brought two other words into play in his references to the church. One was *koinōnia;* the other was *charisma.* Each calls for attention.

The Shared Experience of the Spirit

The key phrase comes in the parting benediction of 2 Corinthians: 'The grace of the Lord Jesus Christ, the love of God, and the *koinōnia* of the Holy Spirit be with you all' (2 Cor. 13.13). The phrase is usually translated 'the fellowship of the Spirit'. This is misleading, because it is usually taken as referring to the community formed or created by the Spirit — as in 'The Women's Fellowship', an organisation within a church. But repeated studies have made it clear that the basic meaning of the phrase is better given in a translation like *'participation in the Spirit'.*[25] That is to say, what is in view is not a physical entity, like a congregation, but the *subjective experience* of the Spirit as something shared, mutually participated in. The point is, then, that *what draws and keeps believers together for Paul* was not simply a common membership of a congregation, but *the common experience of the Spirit.* It was believers' awareness that their experience of the Spirit was one which others had also shared which provided the bond of mutual understanding and sympathy.

As we saw earlier, it was precisely this recognition, that uncircumcised Gentiles were experiencing the Spirit of God just as those at Pentecost had experienced the Spirit, the same Spirit, the same experience of being baptised in the Spirit (Acts 10.47; 11.15-17; 15.8), which ensured that the Gentile believers would be accepted as full members of the church without their being circumcised. The unity was the direct outcome of the *koinōnia* of the Spirit, the shared experience of the Spirit. Paul drove home the same point in

---

25. J. Y. Campbell, '*KOINŌNIA* and Its Cognates in the New Testament', *JBL* 51 (1932), reprinted in *Three New Testament Studies* (Leiden: Brill, 1965) 1-28 (especially 25-27); F. Hauck, *TDNT* 3.804-8; J. Hainz, *EDNT* 2.203-5, drawing on his larger study, *KOINŌNIA: 'Kirche' als Gemeinschaft bei Paulus* (BU 16; Regensburg: Pustet, 1982).

1 Cor. 12.13: it was their common experience of being baptised in *one* Spirit which constituted them as *one* body; it was their common experience of being drenched with *one* Spirit which rendered irrelevant their differences of nationality and social status. And in Eph. 4.3-4 the same point is reinforced. The unity of the church is understood as the direct outworking of the unity of the Spirit. The choice of verb is instructive: 'make every effort to preserve *(tērein)* the unity of the Spirit in the bond of peace'. The unity of the Spirit was something given, the basis of unity, not something they could create or contrive. All that believers could do, bound together as they were by their shared experience of the Spirit, was either to preserve that unity or to destroy it.

The Charismatic Community

Perhaps the most striking feature of Paul's understanding of the body of Christ is that in each of the passages in which Paul expounds the concept at some length he envisages the body of Christ as a *charismatic* community.

> Just as in one body we have many members, and all the members do not have the same function, so we all are one body in Christ . . . having charisms which differ according to the grace given to us. (Rom. 12.4-6)

> There are diversities of charisms, but the same Spirit. There are diversities of service, and the same Lord. There are diversities of activities, but the same God, who effects all things in everyone. [Note again the Trinitarian ecclesiology.] To each is given the manifestation of the Spirit for the common good. . . . One and the same Spirit distributes to each as he wills. For just as the body is one and has many members and all the members of the body, though many, are one body, so also is Christ. For in one Spirit we were all baptised into one body, whether Jews or Greeks, whether slaves or free, and all watered with the one Spirit. For the body does not have one member but many. (1 Cor. 12.4-7, 11-14)

> To each of us has been given grace in accordance with the measure of the gift of Christ. . . . 'He gave gifts to humans'. . . . And he gave some as apostles, some as prophets. . . . (Eph. 4.7, 8, 11)

The key word in the Romans and 1 Corinthians passages is *charisma*, 'charism'. It is a word whose status in Christian theology we owe almost entirely to Paul. It had little significance before he took it up. And in the NT there is only one occurrence of the word outside the Pauline corpus.[26] Obviously *charisma* is formed from *charis*, 'grace', and can be described in shorthand terms as the result or effect or expression of grace. *Charisma* for Paul is *that which brings grace to expression, to concrete reality.* Here again we should recall that it was such clear evidence of grace in the lives of Paul's converts which convinced the Jerusalem leadership, not just that God was working through Paul on behalf of Gentiles, but also that such Gentile converts had to be fully accepted as part of the church of God, without requiring any further works of the law. So for Paul, a charism is *divine grace coming to effect and expression in word or deed* — as clearly in the lists of charisms in Rom. 12.6-8 and 1 Cor. 12.8-10, and in 1 Pet. 4.11.[27] Conscious of the imagery of the body, Paul defines a charism as the 'function' *(praxis)* of an organ or limb of the body. And conscious of the point of the body metaphor, Paul is quick to insist that the charism is not for personal use or benefit, but as a function of the body, and so 'for the common good' (1 Cor. 12.7), for the benefit of others, for the benefit of the whole.

To gain a proper grasp of Paul's concept of the body of Christ as charismatic community, we need to observe a number of other points.

First, Paul conceives of a rich diversity of charisms. The lists he offers in the three passages just referred to were certainly not intended as comprehensive or complete lists. The fact that several of the charisms he includes in these lists are rather vague or overlap makes the point — for example, prophecy and exhortation, sharing, caring and acts of mercy in the list in Romans. The list in 1 Cor. 12 obviously had in view the particular experiences and fascinations of the Corinthian assembly, particularly speaking in tongues, and experiences of inspiration, healings and miracles. The point is that for Paul, a word or action *was a charism whenever it brought grace to expression.* One corollary which follows is worth noting immediately: that we should beware of limiting the concept of 'means of grace' to the sacraments or the preaching of the Word. For Paul, any word or action through which God's grace comes to expression for the benefit of others is a charism, a means of grace.

Second, Paul did not think of charisms as limited to few, to a special order within the body of Christ. In his fuller exposition of the body of Christ in 1 Cor. 12 he makes a special point of denying that the functioning of the body could be limited to the gifts or ministry of one individual. In effect he draws a cartoon to show how ridiculous that thought could be. He draws, as it were, a large eye, with a little head, arms and legs, or a large ear, with a little head,

---

26. Rom. 1.11; 5.15, 16; 6.23; 11.29; 12.6; 1 Cor. 1.7; 7.7; 12.4, 9, 28, 30, 31; 2 Cor. 1.11; 1 Tim. 4.14; 2 Tim. 1.6; 1 Pet. 4.10.

27. See further my *Theology of Paul* #20.5, on which I draw in what follows.

arms and legs. Is that a body? Could that single individual, that single ministry, function as a whole body? 'If all were a single member, where would the body be?' (1 Cor. 12.19). Where indeed? A church so dependent historically on its order of priests, each individual congregation historically so dependent on its priest or minister, needs to take Paul's question with more seriousness than has been the case hitherto. Christians as a whole have hardly begun to appreciate what 'the ministry of the whole people of God' involves or requires. When ministry is limited to the few, the result is a grotesque parody of the body, a body 80 or 90 percent paralysed, with only a few organs functioning, and functioning to little effect, since the effectiveness of the body depends on its diversity functioning in unity.

Third, the lists of charisms Paul provides include not just the eye-catching prophecy, speaking in tongues, or miracles. Also charisms are 'helpful deeds', 'giving guidance' (1 Cor. 12.28), sharing and doing acts of mercy (Rom. 12.8). In his fuller exposition in 1 Cor. 12.14-26 Paul makes a point of insisting that no charism, however modest or humble it may seem to be, is to be looked down upon or regarded as dispensable. Once again, the ministry of the whole people of God needs to be paid more than the lip service which it has so often been given. Paul did not split his concept of the body of Christ into those who ministered and those who were ministered to. To *each* was given the manifestation of the Spirit. The variety of ministries, of charismatic function, extended to *all* members.

Fourth, Paul also makes a point of noting that the charisms include a system of checks and balances. The charism of speaking in tongues should always be checked and in a sense controlled by the charism of interpretation of tongues (1 Cor. 14.13-19, 27-28). The charism of prophecy should always be evaluated (1 Cor. 14.29; 1 Thess. 5.20-22), checked by the charism of 'discernment of spirits' (1 Cor. 12.10). And, not least, all charisms are to be regarded as of less importance than the manifestations of love (1 Cor. 13).

A final aspect of Paul's concept of assembled believers as the body of Christ, as charismatic community, should not be overlooked. This is Paul's understanding of what we might call the balance of authority in the congregation. Of course, there were the authoritative ministries of apostle, prophet and teacher. And Paul did not hesitate to exercise his own authority when he deemed it necessary, as in 1 Cor. 11.16 and 14.37-38. But he also recognised the *responsibility and authority of the congregation* itself. On several occasions he exhorted *all* members of different churches to teach, admonish, judge and comfort.[28] In exhorting the Corinthians he never seems to envisage a recog-

---

28. Rom. 15.14; 1 Cor. 5.4-5; 2 Cor. 2.7; Col. 3.16; 1 Thess. 5.14.

nised leadership group, overseers or elders, to whom he could appeal to maintain better order in the shared meals and worship gatherings. His hope was rather that when they came together as church someone would be given a word of wisdom to lead them (1 Cor. 6.5). As Stephanas and his household had 'appointed themselves' to a ministry for the saints which they saw was lacking (1 Cor. 16.15), so he presumably hoped that others would respond to the prompting of the Spirit to speak or act. So too the congregation was responsible to recognise such charisms when they were displayed (16.18; 1 Thess. 5.12). And not just the prophets were responsible to evaluate particular prophecies (1 Cor. 14.29), but the whole congregation, all the members of the body, were responsible to 'test everything' (1 Thess. 5.21).[29]

For those who think of the church functioning primarily or even solely by orders of ministry, by ecclesial hierarchy, it is a sobering thought to reckon with that *Paul thought of the body of Christ functioning charismatically,* that is, by the function of the different charisms in harmonious interaction. But this seems to be what Paul had in mind — an interplay of authority, of apostle, prophet and teacher on the one hand, and of the charismatic community on the other. Hans von Campenhausen's summary description of Paul's 'vision of the structure of the community as one of free fellowship, developing through the living interplay of spiritual gifts and ministries, without the benefit of official authority or responsible "elders"' still seems to be closer to the reality envisaged in Paul's letters than most other formulations.[30]

What is important here is the full recognition of the third dimension of Paul's Trinitarian ecclesiology. 'We believe in the Holy Spirit' does not mean, cannot surely mean, belief in the Spirit given only through the sacraments, in the Spirit shut up in the Bible, in the Spirit in effect subordinated to the hierarchy. The Spirit of Pentecost, the Spirit who broke through the boundaries round Israel to open the grace of God to Gentile as well as Jew, is not, cannot be, so bound. As Hans Küng warned forty years ago, 'In a Church or community where only ecclesiastical officials rather than all the members of the community are active, there is grave reason to wonder whether the Spirit has not been sacrificed along with the spiritual gifts'.[31]

---

29. As I note in *Theology of Paul* 594 n. 144, *Lumen Gentium* #12 at this point is exegetically at fault, since it limits the responsibility envisaged in 1 Thess. 5.19-21 to 'the men who are over the Church', whereas 1 Thess. 5.12-22 is clearly addressed to the Thessalonian congregation as a whole.

30. H. von Campenhausen, *Ecclesiastical Authority and Spiritual Power in the Church of the First Three Centuries* (1953; London: A & C Black, 1969) 70-71.

31. H. Küng, *The Church* (London: Burns and Oates, 1967) 187.

Conclusion

In sum, then, if Christians could recapture the full sweep of Paul's Trinitarian ecclesiology, it would save them from many of their traditional failings. As *the church of God,* the church stands in full continuity with the *qahal YHWH;* recognition of that fact might well have saved Christianity from its hateful tradition of anti-Judaism. So too the church as the place where reconciliation happens between God and humankind, between Jew and Gentile, between races and cultures might have been much more of a reality than it has been. As *the body of Christ,* the church is Christ's bodily presence still in the world today. But Christian failure to recognise that *all* 'in Christ' *are* the body of Christ has surely disabled and crippled Christ's bodily presence in the world for far too long. As *the fellowship of the Spirit,* the church should function as charismatic community, the body functioning by the grace bestowed by the Spirit. But Christians have fled from God's Spirit for too long; they have hidden themselves from the Spirit. And when the life of the Spirit bubbles up in charismatic excess without learning the lessons which history teaches, without drawing on the wisdom of tradition, they don't really know what to do. But one thing which would help is if Christians were fully to recover Paul's Trinitarian teaching on the church. The challenge posed by the bimillennial Paul, here as in other matters, is one which Christians generally have ignored for too long!

Bibliography

Suggestions for further reading

Jesus and the Gospels

Bockmuehl, M., ed. *The Cambridge Companion to Jesus*. Cambridge: Cambridge University Press, 2001.

Brown, R. E. *An Introduction to the New Testament*. New York: Doubleday, 1997.

Burridge, R. A. *What Are the Gospels? A Comparison with Graeco-Roman Biography*. 2nd ed. Grand Rapids: Eerdmans, 2004.

―――. *Four Gospels, One Jesus: A Symbolic Reading*. 2nd ed. London: SPCK, 2005.

Dunn, J. D. G., and S. McKnight. *The Historical Jesus in Recent Research*. Sources for Biblical and Theological Study, vol. 10. Winona Lake, IN: Eisenbrauns, 2005.

Evans, C. A. *Fabricating Jesus: How Modern Scholars Distort the Gospels*. Downers Grove, IL: InterVarsity, 2006.

Fortna, R. T., and T. Thatcher, eds. *Jesus in Johannine Tradition*. Louisville: Westminster John Knox, 2001.

Gerhardsson, B. *The Reliability of the Gospel Tradition*. Peabody, MA: Hendrickson, 2001.

Gooder, P. *Searching for Meaning: An Introducton to Interpreting the New Testament*. London: SPCK, 2008.

Hengel, M. *The Four Gospels and the One Gospel of Jesus Christ*. London: SCM, 2000.

Hengel, M., and A. M. Schwemer. *Jesus und das Judentum*. Tübingen: Mohr Siebeck, 2007.

Keener, C. S. *The Historical Jesus of the Gospels*. Grand Rapids: Eerdmans, 2009.

Kloppenborg, J. S. *Q, the Earliest Gospel: An Introduction to the Original Stories and Sayings of Jesus*. Louisville: Westminster John Knox, 2008.

Kysar, R. *Voyages with John: Charting the Fourth Gospel.* Waco, TX: Baylor University Press, 2005.

Lachs, S. T. *A Rabbinic Commentary on the New Testament: The Gospels of Matthew, Mark, and Luke.* Hoboken, NJ: Ktav, 1987.

Powell, M. A. *Jesus as a Figure in History: How Modern Historians View the Man from Galilee.* Louisville: Westminster John Knox, 1998.

Riches, J., W. R. Telford, and C. M. Tuckett. *The Synoptic Gospels.* Sheffield: Sheffield Academic Press, 2001.

Sanders, E. P. *Jesus and Judaism.* London: SCM, 1985.

Sanders, E. P., and M. Davies. *Studying the Synoptic Gospels.* London: SCM, 1989.

Schnelle, U. *The History and Theology of the New Testament Writings.* London: SCM, 1998.

Smith, D. M. *John among the Gospels: The Relationship in Twentieth-Century Research.* Minneapolis: Fortress, 1992.

Stanton, G. *The Gospels and Jesus.* 2nd ed. Oxford: Oxford University Press, 2002.

Stuhlmacher, P., ed. *The Gospel and the Gospels.* Grand Rapids: Eerdmans, 1991.

Thatcher, T., ed. *Jesus, the Voice and the Text.* Waco, TX: Baylor University Press, 2008.

Theissen, G., and A. Merz. *The Historical Jesus: A Comprehensive Guide.* London: SCM, 1998.

Wansbrough, H., ed. *Jesus and the Oral Gospel Tradition.* JSNTS 64. Sheffield: Sheffield Academic Press, 1991.

Paul

Becker, E.-M., and P. Pilhofer, eds. *Biographie und Persönlichkeit des Paulus.* WUNT 187. Tübingen: Mohr Siebeck, 2005.

Becker, J. *Paul: Apostle to the Gentiles.* Louisville: John Knox, 1993.

Ben-Chorin, S. *Paulus: Der Völkerapostel in jüdischer Sicht.* Munich: DTV, 1970.

Boyarin, D. *A Radical Jew: Paul and the Politics of Identity.* Berkeley: University of California Press, 1994.

Campbell, W. S. *Paul and the Creation of Christian Identity.* London: T. & T. Clark, 2008.

Das, A. A. *Paul and the Jews.* Peabody, MA: Hendrickson, 2003.

Davies, W. D. *Paul and Rabbinic Judaism.* 4th ed. London: SPCK, 1981.

————. 'Paul: From the Jewish Point of View.' Pages 678-730 in *Cambridge History of Judaism*, vol. 3, *The Early Roman Period.* Edited by W. Horbury et al. Cambridge: Cambridge University Press, 1999.

Donaldson, T. L. *Paul and the Gentiles: Remapping the Apostle's Convictional World.* Minneapolis: Fortress, 1997.

Dunn, J. D. G., ed. *The Cambridge Companion to St. Paul.* Cambridge: Cambridge University Press, 2003.

Engberg-Pedersen, T., ed. *Paul beyond the Judaism/Hellenism Divide.* Louisville: Westminster John Knox, 2001.

Haacker, K. *Der Werdegang eines Apostels.* SBS 171. Stuttgart: KBW, 1997.

Hengel, M., *The Pre-Christian Paul.* London: SCM, 1991.

Bibliography

Hengel, M., and A. M. Schwemer. *Paul between Damascus and Antioch*. London: SCM, 1997.

Holzbrecher, F. *Paulus und der historische Jesus: Darstellung und Analyse der bisherigen Forschungsgeschichte*. Tübingen: Francke, 2007.

Lohse, E. *Paulus: Eine Biographie*. Munich: C. H. Beck, 1996.

Longenecker, B. W. *Remember the Poor: Paul, Poverty, and the Greco-Roman World*. Grand Rapids: Eerdmans, 2010.

Longenecker, R. N., ed. *The Road from Damascus: The Impact of Paul's Conversion on His Life, Thought, and Ministry*. Grand Rapids: Eerdmans, 1997.

Murphy-O'Connor, J. *Paul: A Critical Life*. Oxford: Clarendon, 1996.

Niebuhr, K.-W. *Heidenapostel aus Israel*. WUNT 62. Tübingen: Mohr Siebeck, 1992.

Peerbolte, L. J. L. *Paul the Missionary*. Leuven: Peeters, 2003.

Riesner, R. *Paul's Early Period: Chronology, Mission Strategy, Theology*. Grand Rapids: Eerdmans, 1998.

Roetzel, C. *Paul: The Man and the Myth*. Edinburgh: T. & T. Clark, 1999.

Sanders, E. P. *Paul and Palestinian Judaism*. London: SCM, 1977.

Sandmel, S. *The Genius of Paul: A Study in History*. Philadelphia: Fortress, 1958.

Schnelle, U. *Paul: His Life and Theology*. 2003. Reprint, Grand Rapids: Baker Academic, 2005.

Segal, A. F. *Paul the Convert: The Apostolate and Apostasy of Saul the Pharisee*. New Haven: Yale University Press, 1990.

Stendahl, K. *Paul among Jews and Gentiles*. Philadelphia: Fortress, 1977.

Tomson, P. J. *Paul and the Jewish Law: Halakha in the Letters of the Apostle to the Gentiles*. Assen: Van Gorcum, 1990.

Westerholm, S. *Perspectives Old and New on Paul: The "Lutheran" Paul and His Critics*. Grand Rapids: Eerdmans, 2004.

Yinger, K. L. *The New Perspective on Paul: An Introduction*. Eugene, OR: Cascade, 2011.

Relevant publications of James D. G. Dunn

Unity and Diversity in the New Testament: An Inquiry into the Character of Earliest Christianity. London: SCM; Philadelphia: Westminster, 1977; 2nd/rev. ed. 1990; 3rd ed. 2006.

Christology in the Making: An Inquiry into the Origins of the Doctrine of the Incarnation. London: SCM, 1980; 2nd/rev. ed. 1989; Grand Rapids: Eerdmans, 1996.

Romans. 2 vols. WBC 38. Dallas: Word, 1988.

Jesus, Paul, and the Law: Studies in Mark and Galatians. London: SPCK; Louisville: Westminster, 1990.

The Partings of the Ways between Christianity and Judaism and Their Significance for the Character of Christianity. London: SCM; Philadelphia: TPI, 1991; 2nd ed. 2006.

Editor of *Jews and Christians: The Parting of the Ways, AD 70 to 135*. Tübingen: Mohr Siebeck, 1992; Grand Rapids: Eerdmans, 1999.

A Commentary on the Epistle to the Galatians. BNTC. London: A. & C. Black, 1993.

New Testament Guides: 1 Corinthians. Sheffield: Sheffield Academic Press, 1995.

Epistles to the Colossians and to Philemon. NIGTC. Grand Rapids: Eerdmans; Carlisle, UK: Paternoster, 1996.

The Acts of the Apostles. Epworth Commentaries. London: Epworth; Valley Forge, PA: TPI, 1996.

Editor of *Paul and the Mosaic Law: The Third Durham-Tübingen Research Symposium on Earliest Christianity and Judaism.* WUNT 89. Tübingen: J. C. B. Mohr, 1996; Grand Rapids: Eerdmans, 2001.

The Theology of Paul the Apostle. Grand Rapids: Eerdmans; Edinburgh: T. & T. Clark, 1998.

Christianity in the Making. Vol. 1, *Jesus Remembered.* Grand Rapids: Eerdmans, 2003.

Editor, *The Cambridge Companion to St. Paul.* Cambridge: Cambridge University Press, 2003.

General Editor, *Eerdmans Commentary on the Bible.* Grand Rapids: Eerdmans, 2003.

A New Perspective on Jesus: What the Quest for the Historical Jesus Missed. Grand Rapids: Baker Academic, 2005.

The New Perspective on Paul: Collected Essays. Tübingen: Mohr Siebeck, 2005; 2nd ed. Grand Rapids: Eerdmans, 2008.

Christianity in the Making. Vol. 2, *Beginning from Jerusalem.* Grand Rapids: Eerdmans, 2009.

New Testament Theology: An Introduction. Nashville: Abingdon, 2009.

Index of Bible and Other Ancient Writings

Index of Authors

Okpewho, I., 37n.18

Parker, D. C., 43n.32
Peerbolte, L. J. L., 140n.13
Pelikan, J., 155n.17
Perkins, P., 73n.9
Purcell, N., 169, 170

Rad, G. von, 150n.7
Reed, J. L., 6n.7
Reinbold, W., 136n.7, 139n.11
Renan, E., 5-6, 110n.56
Rengstorf, K. H., 105n.35
Reuter, E., 150n.7, 151n.9
Richardson, P., 168n.13
Riesner, R., 140n.13
Ritschl, A., 6
Robinson, J. M., 42n.29
Roetzel, C., 140n.12
Roloff, J., 166n.9
Rowland, C., 86n.53, 87nn.56,59

Saldarini, S. J., 101n.25, 149n.2
Sanders, E. P., xv, 36n.13, 96n.2
Sandnes, K. O., 141n.16
Schäfer, P., 86n.52
Schaper, J., 149n.2
Schiffman, L. H., 124n.12
Schilling, O., 46n.4
Schmidt, K. L., 166n.3
Schnabel, E. J., 140nn.12,13
Schnelle, U., 143n.25
Schrage, W., 144n.28
Schröter, J., 36n.12
Schürer, E., 101n.25, 123n.8, 149n.2, 166n.4, 1698n.13
Schwartz, D. R., 119n.1
Schwemer, A. M., 15n.22, 121n.6
Segal, A. F., 85n.47, 87n.54, 91n.65, 133, 149n.2

Segbroeck, F. Van, 52n.24
Smith, D. M., 77n.22
Söding, T., 143n.25
Stettler, H., 145n.32
Strauss, D. F., 71n.2
Strecker, G., 36n.12
Streeter, B. H., 28n.4, 35n.8
Strugnell, J., 85n.49
Stuhlmacher, P., 53n.28, 71n.1, 85n.45, 138n.10
Stumpff, A., 151n.9
Sumney, J. L., 146n.32

Tabor, J. D., 86n.52
Thatcher, T., 71n.1, 77n.21, 78n.27, 79nn.30,32, 80n.33, 83n.39
Thiselton, A. C., 144n.28
Toit, A. du, 130n.32
Tuckett, C. M., 77n.21

Urbach, E. E., 87n.60

Vansina, J., 37n.18
Verheyden, J., 71n.3
Vermes, G., 101n.25, 123n.8, 149n.2, 166n.4

Wagner, J. R., 46n.2
Wansbrough, H., 77n.21
Weeden, T. J., 57n.36
Wells, G. A., 5n.1
Wenham, G. J., 142n.21
White, L. M., 168n.13
Wisdom, J. R., 142n.22
Witherington, B., 145n.29
Wrede, W., 58n.38, 97n.13
Wright, N. T., 96n.2

Index of Subjects

Made in the USA
Middletown, DE
01 August 2023

36043704R00132